LANGUAGE WITHOUT SPEECH

LANGUAGE
WITHOUT SPEECH

by

Ruth F. Deich, Ph.D.
and
Patricia M. Hodges, Ph.D.

BRUNNER/MAZEL, *Publishers* • New York

Copyright © 1977 by Ruth F. Deich & Patricia M. Hodges

First American edition published in 1978 by
Brunner/Mazel, Inc., 19 Union Square, New York, N.Y. 10003

First published 1977 by Souvenir Press (Educational and
Academic) Ltd, 43 Great Russell Street, London WC1B 3PA

ISBN 87630-166-9

Illustrated by Frances Middlebrook

MANUFACTURED IN THE UNITED STATES OF AMERICA

Library of Congress Cataloging in Publication Data

Deich, Ruth F
        Language without speech.

        Bibliography: p.
        Includes index.
        1. Mentally handicapped children—Language.
2. Nonverbal communication. I. Hodges, Patricia M.,
joint author. II. Title.
RJ506.M4D37   1978   401'.9   77-27371

Contents

Authors' Note[*]

It is always hazardous to try to impart information to readers with diverse backgrounds, levels of expertise, and interests. This is especially true when one tries to provide information which is useful, yet neither too detailed for the lay reader, nor too simple for the reader versed in a particular field. The authors must tread the fine line between offering clear, crisp statements without distortion, and offering masses of information which are of little value to the nonprofessional reader.

The latter will rightly object if she/he sees reams of footnotes referring to Smith (1971), Pietro (1949), or Schlagheimer (1973). After all, it is not important to know who did what, if the reader is basically interested only in the practical aspects of teaching the handicapped to communicate. Yet, the specialist will rightly complain if she/he cannot find the sources short of writing to the authors.

We have compromised by offering a book with little jargon, and much information which is useful and undistorted. We have generally avoided referring to Smith, Pietro, and Schlagheimer (totally fictitious, by the way), but anyone who is interested can readily find the sources of our numbered references by checking the notes to each chapter grouped at the end of the book, plus the final author index.

Since our emphasis in this book has been on nonvocal communication techniques, we discuss these in some detail, but deliberately omit the so-called traditional techniques of teaching speech. We do, however, provide the interested reader with an overview of such techniques in the form of an annotated bibliography located in Appendix A. Our grateful thanks go to Roberta Savage, an expert in speech therapy, for having culled the literature and selected the most pertinent sources.

[*] Order of authors' names was determined by a flip of a coin.

Our thanks go also to the many people who have been involved in our project : research assistants and volunteers who spent many hours teaching the children, the children themselves, and the staff at Pacific State Hospital and at Claremont Methodist Nursery School who permitted us to go in day after day to work with the children.

Special mention should be made of such indefatigable and helpful assistants as : Richard Anderson, Richard Deets, Marjorie Gardner, Linda Halfon, Kerry John, Terry Magni, Bob Richardson, Nancy Squires, Carol Tormey, and Shelley Zavat.

Our secretaries, Michaeleen Crawford and Gloria Warner, have done a remarkable job deciphering our often indecipherable scripts.

Thanks go to our various colleagues who kindly consented to look at various chapters : Drs Valerie Ackerland and Jean Clayton, and Mr Ron Geckman for his editing on Chapters 4-6.

As always, any errors remain our own.

Special thanks also go to our husbands Herbert Deich and John Hodges who kindly read, and usefully criticised, the manuscript in its initial stages. (Even more special thanks go to my husband and to my children for their patience with an often preoccupied mother. —P.M.H.)

We have used throughout this book the American term 'mental retardation' where English readers will be more accustomed to the phrase 'mental handicap'. The President's Committee on Mental Retardation, PCMR, defines mental retardation as follows : 'Mental retardation refers to significantly subaverage general intellectual functioning (two standard deviations below the normal), existing concurrently with deficits in adaptive behavior, and manifested during the developmental period.' Certainly until recently, the criteria for admission to hospitals for the retarded in America included an IQ of 70, or less, on such standard intelligence tests as the Stanford-Binet.

Introduction

'The first duty of man is to speak; that is his chief business in the world.' R. L. Stevenson, *Talk and Talkers*.

This book was written with a specific goal in mind: to share the procedures we had developed for a non-vocal communication system which can be used to teach nonverbal retarded children to communicate. The book is directed to the teacher or parent of such a child and it contains step-by-step procedures for training. In addition the book may stimulate the interest of others who may wish to adapt these procedures to aphasic stroke patients, or to language delayed children. In these cases a simpler communication system may help to stimulate language development, or help in relearning speech.

The reader may wish to scan through the latter part of the book first to see how the symbol system can be applied. However, we feel it is important also to read the initial chapters in order to provide a meaningful framework for applying the system.

Both authors are psychologists with special training and interest in child development, learning and language. One of us, Patricia M. Hodges, is a professor in the department of psychology at California State University, Los Angeles. The other, Ruth F. Deich, had worked for several years at Pacific State Hospital, Pomona, which is an institution for the retarded of all ages.

Over the years the two of us have discussed various ideas, philosophical questions, and research suggestions. At a time when life seemed to be somewhat more leisurely, we used to meet for lunches and discuss psychological questions, which often became exciting debates, particularly in the areas of learning, language and perception. In the course of our luncheons we had been discussing the problems of nonverbal mental retardates. Such people are in a particularly frustrating position, since they are unable to make their needs and wants known, except in perhaps the most primitive way, such as by screams and gestures.

We had both read of David Premack's stimulating and thought-provoking work with chimpanzees. Premack had taught a number of chimpanzees to communicate by using a plastic symbol system in which each plastic shape represented a word. The chimpanzees were able to answer questions posed by their trainers, follow commands, and make up their own sentences—all by means of arranging these plastic shapes in a consistent order. They were able to write out sentences such as 'Sarah want apple', or 'Brown colour of chocolate'. Thus, the chimpanzees had a ready means of communicating needs, desires, and concepts to someone else, despite the obvious facts that the chimps were unable to speak. It seemed clear to us that these nonvocal, non-human-language primates had an effective, understandable, communicating system.

Pat Hodges had also recently read of a successful application of Premack's system to an adult aphasic population. The idea seemed quite exciting and she felt the Premack system would be of great value for other nonvocal populations. The topic of our next luncheon meeting then focussed on the simple question, 'If a chimp can learn to communicate meaningfully with symbols, why can't this technique be applied to teach those retarded children who are also unable to speak?'

It fascinated us that a system which had worked with a non-linguistic species might very well be the open door through which nonvocal humans could be freed to express themselves in a heretofore closed world. Once the question was asked, the applicability seemed obvious, and we decided to try this technique for retarded children.*

We therefore visited Dr David Premack who was then at the University of California at Santa Barbara. He had completed his initial work with Sarah, and was in the process of training other chimps. We spent an informative afternoon with him talking about language and language acquisition, and basically about

---

* At that time we were unaware that Joseph Carrier at Kansas University had also thought along these lines. He, too, later adapted Premack's system in somewhat different form.

how little we knew of what the lower limits of language were. We were shown around his laboratory and saw chimpanzees at work communicating with their trainers. Dr Premack kindly gave us his blessing for applying such a symbol system to the nonverbal retardate. He also realistically cautioned us not to expect instant learning.

Indeed, it might take thousands of trials for the retardate to learn to connect symbol with object, to learn that a symbol stands for a word, and, later on, to create meaningful sentences from this array of symbol shapes. However, we blithely assumed that any human could readily outdistance a chimpanzee in terms of learning rate. And in this assumption we were partially correct, as some of the retarded children did indeed learn much faster than the chimpanzees. Yet, other retardates seemed actually to be slower, partly because initially they were not very attentive to the learning situation.

When we first began to teach retardates to use the symbol system, we did not realise that we would be involved in a task of several years' duration. Nor did we realise that we would become more and more intrigued by the possibilities inherent in such a system. What started out as an interesting thought problem ended up as an exciting project of theoretical and practical interest.

At the end of our training programme with the initial group of retardates, various news media in the United States and in England reported our success. After this we were deluged with inquiries. We had no idea what a tremendous need there was for a viable system of communication which could be used where speech therapy was not possible. Hundreds of letters poured in from here and abroad, from developmental centres, from teachers of retardates and the autistic, and from parents. The parents were desperately looking for an alternative way of teaching their children to communicate meaningfully, even when these children were unable to speak, or to write in the conventional sense.

The need was so great that we have been invited to speak at various conferences and workshops, have received additional grants to teach this system elsewhere, and were also invited to write this book. Initially, we felt that it was premature to write a book on the use of this system, as we had barely completed one project. We did not know the limits of physical and mental handicaps within which this system might be applied fruitfully, although we had a very good idea regarding whom, and how much, we could teach. Upon reconsidering we decided that, after all, it would be eminently worthwhile to disseminate what information we now have, if only because of the simple fact that we were successful in teaching nonverbal retardates to communicate : that is, to write sentences and make some of their needs and desires known. We felt that a book might benefit the many people who had inquired about alternative modes of communication. And we decided to share the knowledge we had acquired and the procedures we had developed on how to teach a system which is readily applicable by others such as parents, teachers and paraprofessionals.

To enable the parent or teacher to use the system in a more meaningful manner, a portion of the book is also devoted to giving some background on language and communication : what language is; how it is acquired; and what the processes are in normal and abnormal development. In addition we compare nonverbal groups of varying ages and abilities, and take a look at handicaps such as autism, retardation, and brain damage. Later discussions of nonvocal communication will become more meaningful if we have some knowledge of what characteristics differentiate these diverse groups and what characteristics they might hold in common.

1: Language and Communication

'Words form the thread from which we string our experiences.'
Aldous Huxley, *The Olive Tree*, 1937.
'Language is not a mere cabinet curio or museum exhibit. It does definitely function in all human life.' Ezra Pound, *Literary Essays*, 1935.

This chapter is devoted to an overview of language and communication, its meaning, importance and effects, as well as a discussion of some controversies which may have implications for teaching both the normal and the handicapped.

MAN'S NEED TO COMMUNICATE

Thanks to archaeologists and palaeontologists, there is a good deal of evidence to show how and under what condition early man lived. We obtain a rich feeling for pre-historic events filtered through the evidence of prior climatic conditions, housing styles, potsherds, cave paintings etc. But, for more detailed and sophisticated evidence of social interaction and communication, we must go to a people's written language, such as hieroglyphs, ideograms or a language expressed by means of an alphabet. Each represents a permanent system whereby a person removed in time or in place has access to the ideas and thinking expressed by others. Although intimately tied to spoken language, the written one is a nonverbal mode of communication.

In addition to written forms of communication, there are unwritten ones of varying degrees of sophistication and permanence, like smoke signals, morse code, sign language and body language. The last often forms the major part of books devoted to nonvocal communication. The present book explicitly excludes body language because it is not sufficiently precise for the type of communication which we can teach the handicapped.

Expressions of body language are unclear except within proper context. This means that, without such context, specific cues can often be interpreted in a number of very different ways. If we see a person blush, we may interpret the blush as embarrassment, excitement, or overheating. If we see a person crossing his arms, we may think the man is hiding a feeling, showing withdrawal, or perhaps just needing a sweater. With the exception of such superb mimes as Marcel Marceau, there is a lack of precision in bodily expression, especially when context is lacking. Furthermore, there is an inherent limitation to the facts, opinions, and especially, abstract ideas which can be rendered with such 'language'.

Because of these limitations we concern ourselves with the much more flexible expression of ideas, concepts, needs, and desires which are possible with what we ordinarily call language, whether expressed verbally or in some written form. However it is expressed, the need to communicate is attested to by the thousands of languages which have been developed, and are in constant process of change. Despite the variety and change, there exists a basic list of words which is common to every known language.[1] This includes such words as 'I', 'we', 'one', 'two', 'all', 'many', 'man', 'woman', 'fish', 'bird', 'tree' etc. In addition to commonality, the myriads of languages also manage to express the cultures' needs, which range from naming real objects to naming abstract concepts.

THE IMPORTANCE OF LANGUAGE

We take it for granted that everyone, including the newborn, wants to communicate. One of the most meaningful and powerful ways to do so is by means of language.

Language is necessary for meaningful human interaction, and it is crucially important in many ways. It permits the transmission of cultural information so that an individual or a group can pass on information to others within his group, or across cultures, or across time. The power and flexibility of language allows humans to treat events as separate in time and in space, as well as to sort out fact from fiction.

Since communication across time is feasible with language, the person of today has at hand a vast storehouse of prior information which he can call upon at will. The storehouse eliminates the need for each person to generate findings anew on his own. In turn, previous findings can be used as the basis for solving increasingly sophisticated problems whether in medicine, physics, chemistry, or what-happened-in-history. The storehouse is thus the stepping stone for faster and more effective problem solving. Ordinary students of today have at their command more sophisticated knowledge of the physical world than did Aristotle. Indeed, one of our children, aged ten years, is as sophisticated about the function of rods and cones in the human eye, as we were when we were twenty.

Language lets us learn many simple and complex tasks, related to different processes and skills. Without language they could either not be learned at all, or not learned as well. For example, if a child can talk to himself and give himself verbal clues he can learn other skills more easily, such as finding hidden figures.[2] The child's increasing skills in perception, like finding hidden figures, is tied to his increasing ability to verbalise.

Language facilitates the development and formation of new concepts, permits an individual to think in abstract terms, and is the vehicle whereby one can communicate ideas to someone else. The ability to develop new concepts and to think abstractly also implies that the individual has developed a metalanguage, which means that he can communicate ideas about language.

The person with language has the flexibility to communicate a wide range of thought. He can communicate concrete ideas, and so can talk about a specific green apple with one short stem. He can also use metalanguage and discuss the greenness inherent in a certain class of fruit, including a certain type of apple. This flexibility has been nicely described by Alexander :[3]

He who possesses language can deal with abstractions, with concepts and ideas, with things that are not physically present.

He can describe past events or predict future events. The man who speaks one language can use it to learn another language. He can use language to discuss language itself, as in this sentence. It is this language-based ability to handle concepts and abstractions that supports man's great intellectual prowess.

In short, language lets us communicate in symbols which may stand for real objects, ideas, or abstract concepts. Symbols permit us to think about things which are not physically present, and even about things which we have never experienced in actuality.

Symbolic processes can also occur outside of language, such as in drawing, drama or games.[4] Yet language encompasses far more complex symbolic processes. One can use language for the opposite purpose. Instead of using it as an aid to further conceptual thinking, one can use it in semi-rote fashion to carry out behaviours where the rationale is not understood. Does the young child understand why 'If you follow the stream from the top of the mountain you will find your way down'? Does the uneducated person understand how interest rates are derived as he punches them out on miniature computers?

Language also helps us cope with, and have a measure of control over, our environment. This can involve something as simple as calling for a taxi when it rains, or as complex as acting the role of mediator to avert a strike. Language lets us relate in broader and more complex ways with others, beyond mere physical contact. We can talk to each other and discuss the weather, the colour of the sea, or whether Stonehenge represents an ancient astronomical centre.

Language can even be, and has been, used in negative ways in order to lie, or to cover truths with irrelevancies. Every day the various news media give ample evidence of obfuscation, lies couched in bureaucratic jargon, and propaganda spewed out by dictators and non-dictators alike. Mauthner[5] goes so far as to say that by means of language men have 'made it impossible to get to know each other'.

LANGUAGE, SOCIAL INTERACTION AND SOCIALISATION

Last, but not least, language is crucial for later normal interaction of the individual with society, and crucial to the initial socialisation process.

If a person feels he is at least minimally understood he is motivated to attempt further communication and interaction with others. If his language is, or becomes, too distorted and/or inadequate, he may revert to gestures or signals. If these also fail, he may give up entirely and withdraw into himself. Some cases of schizophrenia and autism seem to fit this pattern. There may also be other cases of abnormal development in which no real effort at communication and interaction is ever made, and contact is never established.

The socialisation process in effect starts at birth. By socialisation we mean the training by which a child becomes a member of the particular culture to which he/she belongs. Where language is not available, or not understandable, socialisation is delayed, sometimes in bizarre ways. Examples include the above-mentioned autistics who behave in peculiar, asocial ways. Autistic children generally have defective language, and have not followed the normal course of socialisation. Behaviour is strange, and this strangeness shows most particularly in their uninvolvement with others.

In earlier times there were many reports of so-called feral, or wolf, children who grew up supposedly alone, or in company of animals, in the woods of Europe and Asia. One of the most famous was the 'wild boy of Aveyron' who was laboriously trained by Dr Jacques Itard.[6]

At the end of the eighteenth century a naked and so-called wild boy was seen by some woodsmen in a small village in France. The boy was captured by them and put on display in the public square. He managed to escape, and roamed the woods until captured once more a year later. At this point Dr Itard took the boy in and began to educate him. The boy, whom Itard called Victor, was mute, although he sometimes made noises and laughed.

The great difficulty in teaching this boy was that he initially did not understand any words at all. He could therefore follow no commands, except those communicated by gestures. At the beginning, Victor was totally unsocialised. He initially responded only in the most primitive way to a female caretaker, and to his mentor, Dr Itard. The latter devised a series of ingenious techniques to teach discrimination, responsiveness, conceptualising, and simple reading and writing skills. These techniques were adapted and amplified at the turn of this century by Maria Montessori.[7] Among other things, she successfully taught reading and writing to Italian slum children, and to what were then called 'idiots'. These techniques were more recently incorporated into the behaviour modification approaches so widely in use today.

EFFECTS OF LACK OF LANGUAGE

The example of the 'wild boy' not only shows the effects of lack of socialisation, but also the accompanying terrible isolation this boy suffered because he was without language.

Inability to communicate one's ideas and needs can be merely temporarily frustrating, or it can be permanently crippling, to the extent of preventing, or impairing, normal development, normal communication and normal thinking processes.

The reader with normal language development can get some idea of what it is like not to be able to use language if he has ever been 'abroad'. If he has ever gone to a foreign country of which he had no inkling of the language, he will undoubtedly have found himself shut out from understanding any but the most basic things. If he was staying for a brief time, this may have been merely an inconvenience. If he was staying for a long time, this might be a genuine source of frustration. We might be perfectly capable of communicating in our own language in our own country. We can get our ideas across, and ask questions. We can, and do, expect others to respond to us, and to give us mundane answers to questions like 'What will the weather be like?', 'Where is the nearest grocery?', or 'Where is the local library?'. Yet if we are in a foreign country and do not know the language, we can neither ask questions nor receive answers. Were we to go to a restaurant, we could point to foods on display, but could not ask for them, nor could we specify how cold or how hot we would like them to be. If we wanted to go somewhere, we could not ask directions of a stranger nor could we understand directions, unless they were drawn on a map.

Altogether, if we, as travellers, know neither phrases nor alphabet, and have no other clue as to the unknown language, we will feel lost and tremendously frustrated. However, we have a choice. We can learn the language, or we can return home. The inconvenience is temporary and we know it. Others are not so fortunate. There is no return and there is no other language available.

Thus lack of communication can be experienced as a temporary, frustrating inconvenience or, in other circumstances, it can be perceived as a devastating and terrifying experience. In all cases there is frustration since we feel impotent to convey ideas and feelings.

Many of us, whether parents or not, have seen this frustration in the very young normal child with very few words at his or her command. The child tries so hard to talk to us and make himself understood. When he fails, he may cry, stutter, or pull the person over to where he wants some action taken. The child clearly shows both his frustration, and his desire to communicate. The traveller to a foreign land, and the very young, normally developing child with little speech, offer examples of temporary feelings of frustration and resulting isolation.

We assume that both frustration and isolation exist in many people with language defects, whether due to improper development or trauma, such as a stroke. We make this assumption because of the many maladaptive behaviours that we observe in persons who cannot communicate by word, deed, or writing. They include the many mentally retarded who are totally unable to speak and, because of their retardation, also never learn to write. They include the autistic, most of whom either lack language completely, or show inappropriate or much delayed language. They include those with cerebral palsy whose mental functioning may be adequate but who, because of much motor damage, are unable to make themselves understood. They include the large class of aphasics, i.e. those who cannot speak, and who may or may not fit into the aforementioned categories.

Those who cannot communicate cannot tell us directly of their frustration. But those of us who have worked with such handicapped know the positive changes that can be brought about when the ability to communicate is increased, whether by improved speech, sign language, or nonvocal symbol systems. Increased communication is often accompanied by decreased self-stimulatory, destructive, and self-abusive behaviours.

There are others who can tell us their feelings once they have learned or relearned to communicate. We have talked to a number of recovered stroke patients who told of their feelings of terror at being unable to find words to express their needs and ideas. In their case we assume that thinking remained more or less unimpaired even while they could not talk.

Perhaps the most vivid example of frustration, isolation and behaviour problems can be found in Helen Keller's[8] autobiography. When about two years old, Helen became both blind and deaf due to a childhood illness. She became an unmanageable child, a behaviour problem who was lost in her own silent and dark world. Before her illness she had learned some words, but all of those were lost except the word 'water' which she managed to enunciate as 'wah-wah'. She was able to communicate in a primitive way by gestures, and also understood some of her mother's gestures. Yet by and large, she was an isolated child until the age of seven when she acquired a teacher named Ann Sullivan. The latter taught Helen to communicate by tapping signals into Helen's hand. One day Helen made the momentous discovery that everything has a name.

> Somehow the mystery of language was revealed to me. I knew then that 'w-a-t-e-r' meant the wonderful cool something that was flowing over my hand. That living word awakened my soul, gave it light, hope, joy, set it free !

Before her great discovery that everything-has-a-name, she was often an unhappy and destructive child. After the door to communication was opened, she not only stopped her wanton destruction, but also claimed to have felt for the first time feelings of remorse at her destructiveness. In short, the beginnings of language triggered a whole series of other processes in this child.

IS LANGUAGE ACQUIRED SPONTANEOUSLY?

Many students of language emphasise that language develops spontaneously. Alexander says that 'in a normal environment an infant cannot be prevented from acquiring the ability to talk'.[9] This is not entirely true. Natural language development is hindered only if the environment is detrimental. Yet we cannot reasonably assume that the majority of those whose language is impaired—and this includes the autistic, retarded, asphasic, and cerebral palsied—were born into a detrimental environment, unless the uterine environment, or their own bodies, are included in the definition of 'environment'. However, we have found that an abnormal environment may develop with time, as parents and others react very differently to a child showing distinct lags and handicaps.

Alexander strengthens his case for spontaneity by stating that 'human beings apparently are born able to learn language, and what is more use it automatically and compulsively'.[10] Many others including Hebb emphasise that human language learning is spontaneous, and in fact occurs 'despite a complete lack of teaching by the mother'.[11]

If by spontaneity we mean the child wishes to, and does, learn, and also spends much time practising sounds, words and so forth, then spontaneity applies to the vast majority of infants. However, there is the small but significant group mentioned above which has enormous problems in learning language, and indeed shows little spontaneity. In these cases, the normal course of language acquisition does not apply. Instead, most of these handicapped children require long and arduous training to acquire comprehensible speech and some level of language understanding. They require a great deal of outside intervention to learn even the simplest of responses according to the smallest possible increments.

The handicapped child slowly learns to make sounds, then proper mouth movements, then to imitate sounds and words, and ultimately, hopefully, he acquires proper speech. It is with this small but significant group of non-spontaneous speakers that we are concerned. This group may benefit from alternate language intervention systems, such as the nonvocal symbol system described in the latter half of the book.

DEFINITIONS OF LANGUAGE

In the aforegoing we have been talking about language as if there were a common definition shared by reader and writer alike. Although there is a general notion of what is meant by language, there are, in fact, many different definitions. Hebb, Lambert, and Tucker[12a] talk about levels of language and communication. At the most primitive, there is reflexive communication, characteristic of communicative behaviour of the social insects and the emotional behaviour of other animals. Next in the hierarchy are purposive gestures, such as those found in primates. Lastly there is the highest level, 'true language', which they view as the exclusive province of man. Hebb *et al.* define 'true language' as

> distinctive in its combination of two or more symbolic acts (words or gestures) into one situation and in the ready recombination of the same parts in another situation or for another purpose. This ability to combine and recombine representative actions ('I thirsty,' 'Mommy thirsty', 'no thirsty', 'Mommy fix,' 'Daddy fix') occurs only in man and makes his communications qualitatively distinct from anything seen in the natural development of other animals.[12b]

Animals such as the chimpanzee may show purposive communication. But if communication does not include symbolic behaviour then true language is not present. Whether the kind of communication that chimpanzees have demonstrated[13-16] may be considered a 'true' language according to Hebb's definition, is something that we will discuss later in this chapter, and in greater detail in the chapter on animal communication.

Other definitions of language range from those emphasising

language as the exclusive province of human beings, to attempts to detail what minimal variables must be present in order to qualify for the label of language. The Planning Committee, 1964, defines language as

A system of communication among human beings of a certain group or community which comprehends and uses symbols possessing arbitrary conventional meanings according to the rules in that community.[17]

To Hartley and Scott[18] language includes both the ability to speak and the ability to understand speech. They consider language to be a 'technology', which is built up and acquired over a long time span. Therefore, by the time a person reaches adulthood his linguistic fluency reflects a skill which has been acquired after much practice.

A simple definition of language has been selected by Critchley[19] which he cheerfully labelled 'both comprehensive and crisp'. For his purposes language is

the expression and reception of ideas and feelings. Here is implied an alignment of language with the contemporary expression 'communication', whereby information is passed from here to there. Note that the foregoing definition of language does not specify the means whereby ideas and feelings are expressed or understood, coded or decoded. Verbal symbols stand out conspicuously among these channels, but they certainly are not the sole means of communication.

Broader and more ambiguous definitions include that by Lenneberg[20] who discusses the knowledge of language in terms of 'a family of processes, in other words, as cerebral activity states— states that are labile and easily affected or modulated by environmental conditions'.

The broadest definition we have found was given by the *Encyclopaedia Britannica*: 'Language in the widest sense of the word is . . . any means of communication by living beings.'[21] This definition encompasses too much and is therefore not sufficiently useful for our purposes. It would include the language of bees in telling each other where and how far to go for food sources; the language of ants whose chemical trails tell of food sources; the language of whales which can inform others that a companion is in need of help; and the language of dolphins who send signals of cooperation and distress to each other.

In contrast to inclusive definitions of language, others such as Carroll[22] define language

> as a structured system of arbitrary sounds and sequences of sounds which is used or can be used in interpersonal communication by an aggregation of human beings and which rather exhaustively catalogues things, events, and processes in the human environment.

In this case, the definition is too restrictive for our purposes. Since Carroll restricts language to vocal sounds he is defining only speech, and this context is too narrow for us because we are interested in communication, whether written or spoken, whether signed or signalled.

The problem of selecting an appropriate and workable definition of language has been recognised by O'Connor.[23] We agree with him that many definitions have arisen and the choice of a specific definition is difficult, because the definers look at language from different vantage points, ranging from ambiguous, all-encompassing statements to one which excludes nonvocal language such as writing.

For clarity and inclusiveness for purposes of this book, we will define language arbitrarily and operationally as : the ability to convey information from the most concrete to the most abstract, e.g. from 'chair', to 'the seat of justice', as well as the ability to develop and form new concepts, e.g. the development and comprehension of the Theory of Relativity. This definition includes the conveying of information about needs, ideas, and feelings. It also includes the possibility that a metalanguage can be developed, i.e. the ability of language to 'talk about' language. Language by this definition means that a person can ask or answer questions spontaneously, respond to commands, and think about things and ideas and, in general, show linguistic communication with others. According to this definition an echolalic person does not command language since he only echoes, or parrots, what he hears.

Our definition includes both primitive and sophisticated modes of communication. It includes symbolisation, and is not restricted to vocalising. Accordingly, a person who is unable to speak, but who can communicate in some other way, such as signing or writing, has language. By subsuming speech under language, we set the stage for later chapters showing how the nonvocal, non-verbal persons can be taught to express himself in other modes besides speech.

NAMING/LABELLING, CONCEPTS AND LANGUAGE

If we look at language we see that labelling or naming is implicit in language. Things, feelings, percepts and ideas tend to be labelled. Yet labelling does not define the limits of language, nor include all the implications of what language means, does and implies. Thus we would agree with Lenneberg[24] that it would be a gross oversimplification to consider words as mere labels for things.

Clearly the notion of a label implies something far beyond labelling in terms of a simple stimulus-response association of name with thing or idea. Names can be used by the child 'both as *labels* and *levers* which make things happen . . . they serve both the progressive socialisation and internalisation of behaviour-communication and inner discourse'.[25]

Perhaps the best example of the impact and importance of naming and its associated implications may be seen by referring again to Helen Keller's autobiography.[26a] She describes her terrible isolation until the day she learned that everything has a name. Once she had learned to make this connection,

> every object which I touched seemed to quiver with life. That was because I saw everything with the strange, new sight. On entering the door I remembered the doll I had broken. I felt my way to the hearth and picked up the pieces. I tried vainly to put them together. My eyes filled with tears : for I realized what I had done, and for the first time I felt repentance and sorrow.

Further on she says what we have quoted once before : 'Somehow the mystery of language was revealed to me . . . (the) living word awakened my soul, gave it light, hope, joy, set it free !'

The excitement and joy are contagious. Helen finds that names are not simply labels, but that in effect they set her free to communicate. Her teacher and mentor, Ann Sullivan, was of course aware of the momentous import of what Helen learned. Not only did she learn about naming but also that 'the manual alphabet is the key to everything she wants to know'.[26b] The crucial points for our discussion of language are that Helen learned to make the connection of name-to-thing, and that she quickly learned more words than she knew actual things. She was able to conceive that everything has, or could have, a name, whether this refers to an actual object with which one comes in contact, an object which is not presently there, or to an idea or a concept.

Helen described not only labels qua labels, but labels which represented concepts. In effect she described concept formation, the classification process which permitted her to cope with the world. Deese describes concept formation as

> This process of categorizing so that all the infinite variety of the external world can be dealt with by our mental processes and language, is one of the most essential elements in human thinking.[27]

The concept itself is a 'generalised class of meaning . . . (in which) most symbols stand not for a unique object or event but for a general class linked by some common element or relationship'.[28]

> The concept may be a butterfly. It may be a person he has known. It may be an animal, a city, a type of action, or a quality. Each concept calls for a name . . . Concepts of this type have been formed gradually over the years from childhood on. Each time a thing is seen or heard or experienced, the individual has a perception of it. A part of that perception comes from his own concomitant interpretation. Each successive perception forms and probably alters the permanent concept. And words are acquired gradually also . . . Words are often acquired simultaneously with the concept . . . A little boy may first see a butterfly fluttering from flower to flower in a meadow. Later he sees them on the wing or in pictures. Many times on each occasion he adds to his conception of butterfly. It becomes a generalization from many particulars.[29]

IS LANGUAGE UNIQUE TO HUMANS?

When we defined language we avoided the question of whether language is the specialised province of human beings.

Some researchers like D. Premack,[30] Scott,[31] and Rumbaugh[32] conclude that the difference between animal and human language is one of degree. Others such as Chomsky,[33] P. Adams,[34] and Hebb, et al.,[35] argue that the difference is a qualitative one and that true language exists only in man.

The reader may wonder why, in a book dealing with nonvocal human language, we should be concerned with the difference between animal and human language. The point is that the findings from language and communication studies in non-humans will have different theoretical and teaching applications and implications for human beings, depending on whether we find the difference between animal and human language qualitative, or quantitative.

If the difference between animal and human language and communication is qualitative, either we cannot apply the findings from animal behaviour at all, or we can apply them, but in a limited way. And we cannot expect to make predictions of what sort of learning to predict in humans if our experience is based on subhuman learning.

If the difference is seen as quantitative, on the other hand, we can take the findings from subhuman language learning and apply them to humans who are impaired or delayed in language. Application from animal findings may still be limited, but we can make predictions concerning the course of language acquisition. For example if, as has been found, chimps can learn to communicate nonvocally with humans, we may predict that retardates of roughly comparable mental age can also learn to communicate using the same technique.

If we assume a quantitative difference, we can make deductions concerning language acquisition by looking at organisms which are far slower at picking up language than is the normal human infant. When D. Premack[36] chose to train chimps, he did so in hopes of finding the limits of language, as well as the discrete steps by which language is acquired. The chimp learned faster and far more than was predicted, and so Premack found neither the limits nor the discrete steps. Yet analysis of chimp learning was, and still is, useful in generating clearer theories of human language acquisition.

The resolution of the debate between qualitative and quantitative differences between animal and human language cannot of course be conditioned by the convenience of those of us who are interested in its teaching applications. However, we shall shortly show some evidence that the quantitative model is the more likely one—with the qualification that, at more complex levels, human language remains unique to humans.

If language is unique to humans, then we assume that animals do not have language in our defined sense of the term. Yet, non-humans do communicate. Bees have a communication system which is apparently innate. This system permits them to convey information about sources of food, their distance from the hive, etc.[37] Other examples of animal communication of different types are readily available. [38, 39]

Until recently only passionate animal lovers and Dr Doolittle fans believed that nonhumans could communicate purposefully and symbolically. If the animal seemed to have language he was actually only 'reacting to symbols'.[40] Indeed some writers continue to see examples of animal communication as merely more instances of the talking horse, Clever Hans. This animal performed beautifully for an appreciative audience in nineteenth-century Europe. Unfortunately it was shown to be responding in fact to the minimal cues of its trainer, and not to have any real linguistic skills at all.

Borgese[41] reported that she had trained diverse species such as chimpanzee, dog and elephant, to discriminate between two words, and between two sets of numbers. The animals learned to associate a sound with its object and with the appropriate printed word. The dog was given a new picture book which he had not seen previously and reportedly pointed to the picture of a dog and the appropriate word that went with it. Although Borgese's writing was not altogether clear, we feel she showed evidence for simple forms of communication. Yet this is not anything like the level of symbolic activity shown by some chimpanzees.

Primates have been taught to communicate with humans by means of a variety of ingenious techniques ranging from sign language, to using plastic symbols representing words, to pressing appropriate buttons on a computer.[42-44] Some authorities, like Calder,[45] object that the chimp's facility in using plastic shapes to convey messages does not necessarily mean that its thinking process is the same as that of humans. This conclusion is reasonable and we have no proof. By implication, Calder suggests that chimp language may yet be qualitatively different from ours. We see the difference as quantitative, because we find clear evidence for symbolic thinking in chimpanzees. Chimps have shown purposive language use, plus the ability to conceptualise, generalise, make up new sentences spontaneously, and respond to a wide variety of untaught questions and commands. Some type of symbolic thinking is occurring, regardless of how the chimp actually conceptualises.

Teaching a chimp to communicate requires far more effort and time than teaching a normal child. Hebb[46] cites this difference as additional proof that chimps do not have 'true' language, i.e. theirs is qualitatively different. But it is not a fair test to compare the type of language learning imposed on the chimp with ordinary human language learning. The language learned by chimps, as reflected in their response to computers, sign language or plastic symbols, is basically not 'natural' to a chimpanzee, while human language is natural to humans.

Several years ago the Russells[47a] made a serious attempt to compare human and nonhuman language, to determine whether nonhumans could be considered to have language. If they could, then language would not after all be unique to humans. The Russells analysed animal call systems into basic sound signal units, or calls, and compared them with human sounds analysed into phonemes. (The latter are units of sound which combine consonants and vowels, and vary from human language to human language.) They found that human language and animal call systems are comparable in terms of the vocal signals which are emitted. However, these authors were unwilling to conclude that Japanese monkeys, with their grand total of thirty-seven call units, were therefore linguistically more sophisticated than Hawaiians who must 'make do' with only thirteen call units.

The Russells neatly resolved the debate as to whether language is the exclusive province of humans.

> The use of symbols or symbolization used to be regarded as unique to human language. This is now known to be nonsense . . . Symbolization simply means that a set of things or events can be translated into a set of signals, with one signal for each, and that the individual who receives the signals can translate them back into the things symbolized. There is no doubt at all animals can symbolize in this sense, both as signallers and receivers, as we shall see most clearly in the case of honeybees.[47b]

They then go on to differentiate between two kinds of symbols : representative and arbitrary. The former have something in common with the things that they symbolise, while arbitrary symbols have no formal resemblance at all to what they symbolise.

We think that the findings from animal communication studies show evidence that animal species are capable of, and do use, representative and arbitrary symbols to communicate food sources, danger warnings and emotional responses.[48-50] Among nonhumans, chimps seem most closely to approximate the young child's language learning, since they are able to perceive relationships, name things, and communicate purposefully and symbolically. Yet their 'language' is not as flexible, as inventive, as abstract, nor as wide ranging as that of a normally functioning human being. Human language makes use of a far greater number of arbitrary symbols, depending on the age, intelligence and inclination of the communicator. Furthermore, the availability of arbitrary symbols, as well as our ability to generate yet more arbitrary symbols, gives us the flexibility to represent, to conceptualise, and to clarify complex, or abstract, ideas and concepts. Thus, humans have words like *constitutionality, justice* and *abstraction,* and so far no one has claimed such abstractions to be within the subhuman province.

We have shown evidence for symbolic and purposeful language, particularly among chimps, and have suggested that the differences between chimp and human language are quantitative. Despite these statements we incline to the view that language is unique to humans, beyond a certain level of nonhuman facility, precisely because of the far more complex and abstract levels of thinking of which we seem capable.

Furthermore, for us, human language is largely independent of heredity, in contrast to that of other organisms such as birds and bees whose language is largely inbuilt and preprogrammed. As we have shown, even chimps seem to have limitations on how far they can go with a 'foreign', i.e. human, language. Yet any human can learn any language, provided development is normal and learning starts early enough. A number of years ago there was a Berlitz School advertisement in the *Los Angeles Times* which showed a small Chinese girl with a typical Chinese-style haircut. The caption was something like, 'She can learn perfect Chinese. Why can't you?'

ENVIRONMENT, HEREDITY AND LANGUAGE

One cannot study language acquisition and knowledge without sooner or later coming across the age-old but still vital heredity-environment controversy. This concerns whether factors and characteristics are innately set and determined, i.e. due to heredity, or whether they are externally determined, i.e. due to experience or learning.

The question of whether a variable is due partly or entirely to heredity or to environment has provoked heated controversy for centuries. On an everyday basis it is easy enough to observe the effects of each, either separately or in conjunction. The reader has probably seen some child who appears to be the 'spitting image' of his grandfather whom he has never seen (the reader deduces : heredity). This child may also have adopted some peculiar mannerisms of his unrelated bosom friend (the reader deduces : environment).

Our simple observations provide some apparent evidence. There are also known incontrovertible genetic effects. Both colour blindness and haemophilia are inherited. Interaction of heredity with environment complicates the issue. We know that the average Japanese is shorter, for genetic reasons, than the Swede. Yet the Japanese-American is taller than his mainland Japanese father because of differences in diet.

The controversy continues for academic, theoretical and practical reasons. Teaching procedures, and even how a person is treated by others, depend on how much we attribute to the effects of heredity and/or environment. These attitudes can be seen in such stereotyped statements as, 'She can't help it. It's in her nature,' or 'What can you expect with his background?'—which implies either 'dumb' parents or low socioeconomic status.

Thus our views on heredity/environment may influence our teaching procedures. On an *a priori* basis we may decide not to try to teach some types of language-impaired persons at all, or we may attempt different teaching approaches depending on the person, his environment, motivation, and what we estimate to be his innate capacities.

INNATE FACTORS AND LANGUAGE ACQUISITION

Some ethologists, earlier writers, and linguists assume that there is an innate, or hereditary, basis for language and communication behaviours. Marler[51] studied sparrow songs. He found, for example, that the White Crowns can mimic only their own species' songs, but they must first hear the song in order to reproduce it. But other birds such as the Song Sparrow can sing their species' song even if they have not previously heard it from an adult member. Marler deduced that animals, including humans, are equipped with genetic templates which provide models for communication behaviour. Hence an innate basis for communication exists.

Earlier theories of human language acquisition accepted innateness as given. It was merely a question of which language would appear spontaneously in an untutored child. The following amusing and interesting examples were gleaned from two widely different books, Christophersen's on second-language learning,[52] and Koestler's *The Act of Creation*.[53]

The first known recorded experiment on natural language acquisition was reported by Herodotus. He noted that in the seventeenth century B.C. a pharaoh conducted an experiment to find out which was the most ancient nation. He had two infants placed in isolation. The children were well cared for, but no one spoke a word in their presence. The plan was to note what language they would begin to speak spontaneously. After two years they were heard to utter the word 'bekos' which was identified as the Phrygian word for bread. And so, reluctantly perhaps, the Egyptian experimenters concluded that the Phrygian nation was of greater antiquity than any other.[52]

A number of later experiments, one conducted by Emperor Frederick II in the thirteenth century, and another conducted by James IV of Scotland in the fifteenth century, were no more conclusive. Frederick's babies died. James' babies reportedly started to speak a 'good' Hebrew after having been left in the care of a mute woman. However, the report was not considered conclusive insofar as few people in Scotland knew Hebrew and so were not adequate judges of the babes' fluency.

More recently, Chomsky[54, 55] has provided a sophisticated analysis and a lucid, if unproven, rationale for an innate basis to language acquisition. Chomsky postulates an innate 'deep structure', common to all human languages, upon which the infant builds as he/she develops language. Such a 'universal grammar' is a basic given which provides restraints and constraints within which language usage operates. This implies that there are unspoken rules common to different languages which prevent our getting words in the wrong order. In English, for example, it makes sense to say 'Peter ate the strawberry', but not 'The strawberry ate Peter.' The 'deep structure' provides the basis for logical relations, and governs and underlies the 'surface structure'. Chomsky does not deny the effects of learning and maturation, but he does propose that a genetic predisposition for language exists. Linguists who agree with Chomsky's position include Bellugi,[56] E. Lenneberg[57] and McNeill.[58]

The results of observations within and across cultures have been used as evidence that innateness may be a real factor in language acquisition. For example, early stages of acquisition show great regularity of appearance : sounds, babbling, emission of words, and later, complete sentences. Regardless of language or culture studied, the stages, and times of onset of stages, seem to be regular and universal. In addition, children acquire language not by strictly imitating the structures of adult language, but by generating and creating their own predictable, and apparently universal, system of rules. This universal grammar of the child has been cited as further evidence of innateness.

There are some arguments which can be raised against the Chomskian position on innate factors. In contrast to Chomsky, Hartley and Scott[59] state that 'creativity' in language use does not necessarily prove the existence of inbuilt structures. In their view, the speaker's ability to 'create' grammatically correct sentences, and the listener's ability to understand sentences he has not previously heard, are evidence of 'complexity and flexibility' rather than evidence for innateness of structures.

Our own view is that while it is true that there is flexibility and complexity in language, we do not think that this negates the possibility that such flexibility is built upon an innate propensity. After all, we assume that high intelligence and the ability to think complexly and abstractly has a genetic base.

However, we do criticise Chomsky on two other counts. We feel that he begs the question when he says that, since it is hard to conceptualise how a principle of universal grammar can be learned uniformly by all speakers, one must assume that such a principle is not learned at all, i.e. it is innate. Furthermore, in order to contrast the innate and the learning theory, Chomsky oversimplifies modern learning theory, by apparently and incorrectly limiting the latter to simple conditioning on a stimulus-response basis.

LEARNING FACTORS AND LANGUAGE ACQUISITION

What evidence is there that learning is the prime factor in language acquisition? If we consider acquisition from a simple learning point of view we say that the infant hears; the infant imitates; the infant gets rewarded; and so imitates again. There is indeed an enormous amount of learning that goes on for the child. In fact, where learning cannot take place, such as when a child is isolated and has no chance to hear speech and imitate it, language will not develop.

However, a less extreme learning model for language acquisition makes more sense. In such a view [60, 61] learning models are not limited to primitive, mechanical, stimulus-response associations. Instead, learning is conceived more complexly in terms of a series of connections between classes of events. Hebb and his co-workers criticise the proponents of innate structures for not accepting that learned behaviour may be more complex than that based solely on conditioning and reinforcement of overt responses. Thus they conclude that language acquisition need not be based on innate structures. Indeed Hebb contends that what linguists call innate actually reflects that which is easily learned.

There is some interesting experimental evidence which could be used equally by proponents of innate structures or by those who explain language solely in terms of learning (i.e. environment is all). Consider for example a study by Condon and Sander.[62] They studied sixteen newborns ranging in age from half a day to two weeks. They found that the infants responded to the rhythm of human speech by moving their bodies, regardless whether the language spoken was English or Chinese. Yet the same infants remained unresponsive when the sounds were disconnected vowels or tapping noises.

If language has an innate factor to it, then the selective response of these infants to speech seems to indicate an inborn predilection. Alternatively, we could say that, since these infants were already a number of hours old, they had already learned to respond positively to speech on a conditioned response basis. In other words, they had already learned to associate speech with a positive reward, but had no such association with non-speech sounds.

We shall resolve this dilemma to our own satisfaction by not being overly concerned with theories of language focussing at either extreme of the innate versus learned spectrum.

Innate capacities are known to exist for auditory analysis, perceptual learning, and so forth.[63-70] It is not too difficult for us to assume that there may also exist an innate capacity for generalisation and abstraction, which stands the child in good stead as he/she begins to learn language, or any other skill. We still do not know the relative influence of innate versus learned factors. But an active awareness and acceptance of the mutual interplay of the innate (heredity) and learning (environment) facets offers much greater flexibility in dealing with facts, and opinions, and in planning teaching strategies.

IS THINKING PRIOR TO LANGUAGE?

The field of psycho-linguistics abounds in controversy. Another ongoing debate is whether language can exist without thought or vice versa. Can language arise without some sort of conceptualising process? Alternatively, is it reasonable to assume that one can conceptualise without language?

James Adams[71] avoids such questions altogether by assuming that there are various and separate types of languages: these include verbal, quantitative, pictorial, auditory, and tactile language. We who are concerned with language and alternate language intervention systems cannot avoid these questions, for the reason mentioned above, namely that teaching approaches will differ depending on the answers.

In general, this is a difficult area to come to grips with, for several reasons. The evidence which exists is scattered. Much of the thinking is confused, since the topic is somewhat difficult to verbalise and formulate. Lastly, there are times when the conclusions, even when logical, do not seem to follow from the evidence.

Nonetheless we will present findings to show that thinking can occur prior to language. We shall also consider the weaker and reverse argument that language is prior to thought and, in process, indicate our own predilections regarding this issue.

Experimental evidence to show that thinking can occur prior to language includes studies by Furth, Piaget and Sinclair. Furth[72] looked at performances of deaf children and compared them with those of hearing children aged seven to twelve years. He tested these children on three tasks. In one task the child had to choose two simple figures which were the same, in order to get a reward. In another task he had to choose asymmetrical figures for a reward. On the third task, the child had to choose the opposite choice to the experimenter's. If the experimenter chose the largest object, the child had to choose the smallest object, and vice versa. The assumption was that both hearing and deaf children would have the concepts of 'same' and 'symmetry' equally available to them, and that these were not dependent on language. Furth also assumed that the concept of 'opposition' would not be equally available. This concept is normally only learned by the deaf child around the age of fourteen, in contrast to the hearing child who grasps this concept around the age of six.

Furth's findings confirmed his predictions. In those learning tasks where prior experience of language did not favour the hearing child : i.e. in the selection for symmetry or sameness, the deaf did as well as the non-deaf. In the 'opposition' task, on the other hand, the hearing child had the advantage because of his familiarity with language. In that case, the hearing child performed better than the deaf one. Furth therefore concluded that a case had been made for thinking occurring without language. 'Language experience may increase the efficiency of concept formation in a certain situation but is not a necessary prerequisite for the development of the basic capacity to abstract and generalise.'[73]

We agree with his quoted conclusion, yet his results do not provide conclusive evidence for his theory for two reasons. First, we cannot exclude the possibility that perhaps the deaf has generated his/her own 'language', even though words, qua words as we know them, may not be reflected in the untutored deaf. Second, a detailed analysis of the data shows some results which are explicable neither in terms of the priority of thinking to language, nor the reverse.

For example, in the 'sameness' task, the deaf children actually performed better at some age levels, namely at eight and ten years, than their hearing counterparts. According to Furth, both hearing and deaf should perform equally well. On the other hand, when one analyses the results for different ages with respect to the concept of 'opposition', the deaf performed significantly lower than the hearing child at the age of seven, but they were not significantly lower at ages eight to twelve. These results are peculiar, and do not fit in neatly with Furth's categorisation that language facilitates learning for the hearing child under some conditions, and makes no difference for the deaf child under other conditions. Nonetheless, one may see that thinking can occur outside a linguistic dimension, *provided* one accepts that these seven- to twelve-year-old deaf children did not have some kind of language. This seems unlikely for school children at these relatively advanced ages. It seems more likely that these children had either devised some sort of idiosyncratic language or, indeed, had picked up a fair amount of receptive language.

Piaget is another advocate of the theory that thinking occurs outside of language.[74] He argues cogently that, although language is important in thinking, the basis of logical thinking is not to be found in language alone. Much of the child's knowledge about reality derives from his actions, from what he finds out by experience, and from the knowledge which he abstracts from the objects upon which he acts, and that act upon him. He says that 'simple abstractions (are) drawn not from the object acted upon but from the action itself',[75] and that in fact such action requires neither thinking nor any use of expressive language. This behaviour is both pre-thought and pre-language. Piaget bolsters the argument that conceptualising, or thinking, can occur prior to language by noting that, in comparison to normal children, deaf and dumb children are delayed far less than those who have been blind from birth. Since the blind cannot move around in space in the same way that normal children do in the first two years of life, Piaget surmises that the coordination of actions are delayed. This results in the greater delays shown in the blind child's development. He concludes that, although the delay is ultimately eradicated, learning language per se does not initially make up for the deficiency the blind child experiences as he/she moves through space.

Piaget then refers to the experiment of Sinclair[76] who studied the relations between operational and linguistic levels in children aged five to eight years. One group already had attained the concept of conservation. That is, they recognised that when a liquid was poured from one glass to another, even though the glasses differed in shape, the quantity inside the glass did not change. A second group of children were non-conservers who, when they saw liquid being poured from one glass to a differently shaped one, deduced that the amount of liquid had also changed. Madame Sinclair noticed that non-conservers described objects in terms of one characteristic at a time, or described one object at a time. The conservers were able to keep more than one characteristic in mind at once, and more than one object in mind at once. Non-conservers would say, 'That pencil is fat.' Conservers would say, 'This pencil is longer than that one, but that pencil is fatter than this one.'[77] Sinclair then trained the non-conservers to describe the objects in the same way as the conservers did, but she found that there was no significant difference in non-conserver's responses even after receiving training in language. Piaget therefore concluded that, 'Intellectual operations appear to give rise to linguistic process not vice versa'.

Experimental evidence from studies with animals also seems to indicate that some kind of conceptualising process occurs in the absence of language. When D. Premack taught chimpanzees to communicate[78-80] he made the reasonable assumption that: in order for chimps to learn to use a symbol system as a language, they must already have the concepts available for which the symbols stand.

According to Webster's dictionary, a concept is 'a thought . . . an idea . . . (or, alternatively) . . . a mental image of an action or thing.'[81] According to this definition it appears that the chimps did have concepts. Premack's chimp, Sarah, could accurately label a previously untaught object in terms of its colour, such as red, or its shape, such as round. She could also 'say', via symbols, whether two objects were the same or different.

Animals further down the phylogenetic scale also seem to show some primitive kind of conceptualising ability. Rats can distinguish a cross from an ellipse, and will jump towards the picture of one or the other, depending on where they are reinforced.

In Maier's famous experiment[82] he placed rats on the Lashley jumping stand and set them a task. The standard technique involved teaching rats to jump from the stand to a platform displaying two visual stimuli, each of which was drawn on a card. If the rat jumped towards the correct card, the card would move, and the rat could go past the card to obtain a reward. If the stimuli were drawn so alike that they were indistinguishable, the problem became insoluble and the rat developed an abnormal fixation. In that case, it would respond consistently to the same stimulus, regardless of whether it was punished or rewarded for this response. If the situation was then switched so that the problem became soluble, the rat still remained fixated in its original abnormal response. And if after this sequence the rat was randomly rewarded, and neither stimulus consistently signified reward nor punishment, the rat refused to jump at all. Yet when the rat was later manually guided to break this 'neurotic' habit of either not jumping, or fixated jumping, it learned the original discrimination again very rapidly, indicating that even during the time of non-meaningful response the rat was actually learning something.

It is possible to explain this type of behaviour strictly in terms of stimulus response conditioning. However, it is equally possible and more plausible to explain the rat's behaviour in terms of some sort of cognition or simple primitive conceptualisation. If we accept the latter explanation, and we feel it *is* a reasonable one, then we have provided evidence of conceptualising which obviously occurs without benefit of language.

There is also anecdotal evidence of conceptualising, or thinking, occurring without language. Two particularly interesting examples of such thinking by adults were reported by Albert Einstein and Friedrich Kekule. Einstein[83] wrote a letter to Jacques Hadamard in which he described the process.

The words or the language, as they are written or spoken do not seem to play any role in my mechanism of thought. The psychical entities which seem to serve as elements in thought are certain signs and more or less clear images which can be 'voluntarily' reproduced and combined.

There is, of course, a certain connection between those elements and relevant logical concepts. It is also clear that the desire to arrive finally at logically connected concepts is the emotional basis of this rather vague play with the above mentioned elements. But taken from a psychological viewpoint, this combinatory play seems to be the essential feature in productive thought—before there is any connection with logical construction in words or other kinds of signs which can be communicated to others.

The above mentioned elements are, in my case, of visual and some of muscular type. Conventional words or other signs have to be sought for laboriously only in a secondary stage, when the mentioned associative play is sufficiently established and can be reproduced at will.

Koestler[84] describes Kekule's complex thought process, which was a visual one and clearly not dependent on language. Kekule, a professor of chemistry in Ghent, had an illuminating dream in 1865 which helped him to discover the structure of the benzene ring. He reported that

I turned my chair to the fire and dozed . . . Again the atoms were gamboling before my eyes. This time the smaller groups kept modestly in the background. My mental eye, rendered more acute by repeated visions of this kind, could now distinguish larger structures, of manifold conformation : long rows, sometimes more closely fitted together; all twining and twisting in snakelike motion. But look ! What was that? One of the snakes had seized hold of its own tail, and the form whirled mockingly before my eyes. As if by a flash of lightning I awoke . . . Let us learn to dream, gentlemen.

Ghiselin, who was also the source for the Einstein letter, quotes a charming statement by Stephen Spender, which again suggests to us that thinking may occur prior to language. Spender wrote of, 'A dim cloud of an idea which I feel must be condensed into a shower of words'.[85]

Further deductive evidence is given by E. H. Lenneberg,[86] O'Connor,[87] and McNamara.[88] The latter describes how the infant first finds out the meaning which the speaker intends to convey to the listener, and then deduces the connection between the meaning and the word he has just heard.

A teaching approach based on the notion that thinking is prior to language was described by Wepman.[89] He felt that it was more appropriate to teach aphasics by 'embellishing thought', in terms of understanding, rather than by teaching specific words to increase language per se. A former psychiatrist, who became aphasic after a stroke, was taught by this method of 'embellishment'. Speech came back to this man after his colleagues went over his cases with him. Wepman therefore concluded that thinking was prior to speech and that speech was superimposed on thinking. The data do not necessarily warrant this conclusion since we do not know whether the psychiatrist still had intact thinking processes, and/or intact receptive language. If he were merely unable to express himself verbally, this is not proof that he was without language to think with. Many a stroke victim retains receptive language, and can understand, but cannot speak. Nonetheless, we agree with Wepman's conclusion that thinking may be prior to speech.

A fair amount of evidence has been marshalled to show that thinking can occur prior to, and independent of, language. Another viewpoint would have it that we accept this philosophy because we think in terms of European languages, which generally have equivalent terms in English, French, German, and Latin. Gombrich therefore says that language 'articulates the word of our experience'.[90]

Other writers too are not quite so consistent in positing thought as prior to language. Vygotsky wrote at one point that, 'A pre-linguistic period in thought and a pre-intellectual period in speech undoubtedly exist also in the development of the child'.[91] Yet a few pages later he says that, 'Thought is not merely expressed in words; it comes into existence through them'. By page 212 he reaches the stage where, 'Words play a central part not only in the development of thought but in the historical growth of consciousness as a whole'. In a somewhat different vein, we see that Bruner[92] seems to view language as something which is to some extent innate and ready to have symbolic thought impressed upon it.

In this sense the hypothesis is reversed and thinking is conceived as depending on language. Yet few will commit themselves to this view entirely. Stephens and McLaughlin[93] examined the performance of normal and retarded children on cognitive and verbal tasks, and concluded that cognitive development is not completely dependent on the maturation of language. Sapir on the other hand felt that language and thought cannot be separated but are, 'in a sense, one and the same'.[94]

LANGUAGE AND COGNITION

Although we feel that the preponderance of evidence—deductive, empirical and anecdotal—points to thinking as prior to language, there is no doubt that language development becomes part of cognitive development.* Deductive evidence comes from writers such as Piaget,[95] who suggests that language follows concepts, and concepts follow motor activity. The latter is considered as the basic step in the development of the child. For Piaget, sensory-motor intelligence is prior to language. In other words, it is the act of exploration by the child of his environment which stimulates his intellectual development. From such acts 'schemes' develop, which later evolve into concepts, and which beyond that may form the basis of language development.

Language development in the retarded clearly shows the interrelatedness of language and cognition, or concept formation. Retardates acquire the basic structures of language, although much more slowly than normal children. At the same time retardates lack the organisational capacities to permit them to deal with complex sentences. Where normal cognitive development does not occur, language acquisition suffers. Yet where language is available, it can serve as the vehicle for expressing concepts and categories in a more efficient and flexible way than may be possible without language.

Language goes hand in hand with cognition, and there are levels of development in both. Vygotsky separates rudimentary

* Cognition means literally the act of knowing, or the process of or capacity for knowing.

concept formation, which occurs in the young child, from what he calls 'genuine concepts', which occur only at adolescence. At that point a word becomes 'a means of concept formation' and 'is the immediate psychological cause of the radical change in the intellectual process that occurs on the threshold of adolescence'.[96]

EFFECT OF LANGUAGE ON THOUGHT

We have shown clear instances of thinking taking place without language. Nonetheless, once language is established, it can influence thought in numerous ways, which were partly discussed at the beginning of the chapter. The fact that we can use language as a recording device means that we can convey information to someone else who need not generate the same information by himself. This means that he can build on the findings and conclusions of others. Language can be used to clarify thinking, to generate logical deductions, and also to create negative or positive effects with respect to people's behaviour.

We do not agree with Whorf[97] that language literally changes perceptions. Yet one's attitudes towards the world may differ depending on the language one ordinarily uses in thinking or communicating.

In a recent article in the *Los Angeles Times*, a minority group of Italians requested that their children be allowed to use Friulian as their second language. (Friulian is a form of Romansch common to Italy and Switzerland.) In asking for the restoration of this language, a professor of Friulian said that there were certain things which Friulians can express in their own language which they simply cannot in Italian. Anyone who is familiar with languages other than his or her native tongue, will agree that there are certain nuances and feeling tones which are different and which cannot be exactly translated into another language. In some cases this applies to words; in others to phrases. There is no equivalent word for the Yiddish *'Schlemiehl'*, for the French *'gamin'*, for the German *'Lausbub'*. Nor is there a real equivalent in English to the Spanish *'simpatico'*, and the German *'sympatisch'*. There is no good translation for the implications and feeling tones surrounding the Viennese expression '*gnädige Frau*', nor for the word '*Kitsch*'. Further examples of lack of equivalences can be seen by comparing the German phrase '*der Erich*' to its exact English translation, which is 'the Eric'. In German, the phrase has a distinct meaning and connotation. In English it sounds somewhat nonsensical. And how would one translate the German '*Mamachen*' or the Spanish '*mamacita*' into English? The exact translation of 'little Mama' sounds ponderous, and certainly does not convey the sense of intimacy and, perhaps, smallness which such a diminutive conveys elsewhere. It is because of the untranslatability of some words and phrases into their exact connotative equivalent that there has been so much borrowing from one language to another. There have also been direct adaptations even where an equivalent word could be found, such as the French adaptation of the English 'beefsteak' to '*biftek*', or 'weekend' to '*le weekend*'. The German word '*kindergarten*' has been taken over into English. Numerous other examples abound.

Christophersen[98] emphasises what surely cannot be disputed, namely that language is centrally important to a community's culture, as well as being the most important vehicle for individual expression. There is general concurrence with his thesis that a person is influenced by the linguistic culture in which he lives. However, the degree and quality of such influence is viewed differently by different writers, the most extreme being the previously mentioned Whorf who felt that language actually shapes perception.

Whorf found support for his thesis by taking a look at the way different languages describe the natural world. He concluded that the grammar of a particular language is not merely for the expression of ideas, but 'is itself the shaper of ideas . . . the program and guide for the individual's mental activity, for his analysis of impressions, for his synthesis of his mental stock in trade'.[99] He found that people are bound by their linguistic systems which in turn influence the way they perceive life, their culture, and nature.

As an example of the way different cultures' languages may influence the thinking process, Whorf notes that the Eskimo have many different words for different types of snow in contrast, for example, to English which has only one word to cover a snow which is slushy, or hard-packed, or powdery, and so on. He shows how other languages, not based on Indo-European, vary in how they organise nature. The Hopi assign words like lightning, wave, smoke, and meteor, to the category of verbs because they refer to events of brief duration. In Indo-European languages these words would be classified as nouns. What in Indo-European languages is defined as an event, i.e. a verb, may be something quite different from what the Hopi define as an event. It is on the basis of these different ways of classifying the world that Whorf felt language shaped perception.

We have shown that language is crucial to meaningful human interaction and development. We have also shown that language per se, and languages in particular, may influence thought, and concluded that thinking or cognition can exist independent of, and prior to, language.

This conclusion is important for us in determining what teaching methods might be feasible with certain types of nonverbal persons. Having shown that concepts can exist prior to language, we can use nonvocal language systems and build on language concepts already present, even if they are primitive. From this base we can go on to expand both receptive and expressive language, as well as teach additional and more complex concepts.

2: The Normal Course of Development

'I am a barbarian here because I am understood by no one. (Barbarus hic ego sum, equia non intelligor ulli.)' Ovid, *Tristia*, Bk v. eleg. 10.1.37.
'I've had nothing yet, Alice replied . . . So I can't take more.'
'You mean you can't take less,' said the Hatter. 'It's very easy to take more than nothing.' Lewis Carroll, *The Annotated Alice*, 1960.

We have said that language is assumed to develop spontaneously. This is a correct assumption when language development is normal, but not, as we have seen, when development is abnormal. The present chapter deals with normal linguistic, and physical, mental and cognitive development. Emphasis on the normal will put the later discussions of abnormal and delayed development into a more meaningful framework.

If one looks at development over a period of time, one can observe when certain capacities first appear, or reappear, how well capacities hold up over time; and how well one can predict later capacities and performances on the basis of tests given very early in life. The normal course of development tends to follow general sequences and patterns which are apparently universal. Although time of appearance of a particular ability varies over a considerable range, the appearances, per se, are largely predictable.

DEVELOPMENTAL SEQUENCES

The normal child tends to develop approximately according to the following timetable adapted from Lenneberg.[1a] Other studies on children's development agree with this sequencing, although

Gesell[1b] places the average age for 'cooing' and comprehension of 'no' a few months earlier.

Age four months: Infant holds up his head and responds to others by cooing.

Age six to nine months: Child sits up, pulls himself up into a standing position, and babbles.

Age twelve to eighteen months: Child learns to stand and to walk by himself. He starts to use a few words, follows simple commands, and understands the meaning of 'no'.

Age eighteen to twenty-one months: Walking has improved. Child now crawls down the stairs and throws a ball. He/she understands simple questions, and begins to use two- and three-word sentences.

Age twenty-four to twenty-seven months: Child runs well, can walk up and down the stairs, and has a vocabulary of about 300–400 words.

Age thirty to thirty-three months: Child has good hand-finger coordination and can manipulate objects adequately. Vocabulary has increased in size, and speech consists mainly of three- and four-word sentences. Language begins to sound more like that of an adult.

Age thirty-six to thirty-nine months: Running is smooth. In walking upstairs the child is able to alternate his feet. He now can jump, ride a tricycle, and stand on one foot. He speaks in well-formed sentences, follows specific grammatical rules, and is generally understandable.

Appearance and reappearance of competencies

If we as parents, teachers, or psychologists observe the child's capacities, we get the impression that development is cumulative. This concept however needs qualification. An interesting article by Bower[2] suggests that such progress is neither strictly cumulative, nor nearly as simple as we assume. Instead, there are stages at which certain capacities inevitably develop in the infant. They may also disappear briefly only to reappear later on. These capacities include for instance aspects of sensory-motor coordination, ear-hand coordination, and imitation of actions by an adult.

Bower shows that neither behavioural nor intellectual development is in actuality cumulative. For example, there are sensory-motor behaviours which are already present in the newborn. Thus, if a newborn is supported by someone, he can make walking movements on flat surfaces. This ability disappears by the age of six weeks and then reappears again by the end of the first year. The infant also has an early capacity, which exists within the first few weeks of life, to reach out to touch and sometimes to grasp seen objects. This eye-hand coordination disappears by the age of four weeks, and reappears again at the age of five months. Another example is the ear-hand coordination whereby, if an infant hears a sound coming from a particular direction, his hand will make movements towards the source of that sound. This ability disappears by the age of five or six months, and may not reappear if the infant is blind. Another remarkable early competence involving perceptual motor skills is the ability to imitate actions : an infant can imitate an adult who sticks out his tongue, opens his mouth, or widens his eyes.

These repetitive reappearances of specific competencies are not limited to infancy, since other abilities disappear at later stages of childhood and subsequently reappear. Such later competencies are related to cognitive abilities, for example the comprehension of conservation of weight (this means that an object is judged to be the same weight regardless of its shape, provided the same initial mass is used in creating the shape).

Bower reports that if one presents an eighteen-month-old child with a ball of clay, the child lifts it several times, learns to judge its weight, and is able to lift it in smooth stages. If, then, the ball of clay is deformed and rolled into the shape of a sausage under the very eyes of the child, he apparently judges the sausage to be the same weight as the former ball—Bower concludes that the child makes this judgement because it hefts the sausage with the same controlled movements previously shown with the ball. Present this same task to the same child two years later. First show him the ball and then deform it into the shape of a sausage. Then ask him to rate which is the heavier. At that age, the child will generally say that the sausage is heavier than the ball, because the sausage is longer. If he is asked to lift the clay, he will tend to lift the sausage faster than the ball in order to make up for what he perceives as a change-in-weight. At this age the behaviour reverts to that typical for the one year old who has not mastered the concept of conservation of weight. By the age of seven or eight, the child again seems to have reacquired the concept of conservation of weight. By the age of about eleven, when asked to judge whether the ball or the sausage is heavier, he will again revert to his four-year-old response, and tend to judge the sausage as heavier. The concept of conservation of weight becomes stable only much later, by the age of thirteen or fourteen.

Another concept which disappears and reappears again has to do with numbering. Bower gave children who were old enough to talk a primitive counting test. Each child was shown candies (sweets)

> in pairs of rows in which the length of the rows, the spacing between the candies and the number of candies varied. The child was then allowed to choose the row he wanted. If he always chose the row with more candies, it was concluded that he had a primitive ability to count. A high proportion of the children between the ages of two and two and a half can give correct verbal responses to the problem. Thereafter, they are unable to respond correctly until they are nearly five.[3]

In the long run, however, despite these seeming exceptions in which certain abilities are present in infancy, disappear within weeks or months, and reappear later, development is cumulative and progressive. Knowledge increases exponentially as the child acquires more and more bits of information. If learning is delayed, then the whole process of ever-increasing knowledge is delayed and in some cases, never takes place. Those of us who have observed both the normal and developmentally delayed child have been struck by the rapidity with which the normal child outstrips the developmentally delayed by ever-widening gaps.

Physical development

The development of visual, auditory, and motor competencies is often assumed 'just to happen'. But animal and human studies have shown that this is not so. For example, if vision is to develop normally, there must be active motor interaction with the environment, since actual movement provides visual feedback. The famous experiments by Held[4] with kittens make this point very clearly. After an initial period of darkness, all of an experimental group of kittens were given equal visual stimulation, but some were prevented from moving around in their environment, because they were strapped in a harness pulled by other kittens. The kittens who could not actively interact with their environment became functionally blind, for they showed no depth of perception and did not blink at approaching objects. Such findings have a counterpart in what happens to blind humans. Blind persons often permanently lose the ear-hand coordination which enables them to move their hands towards the source of a sound.[5] And we might guess that the blind lose this ability because they cannot actually move in the environment towards the source of the sound.

Despite the requirement that infants interact actively with their environment to permit proper development, infants already show some remarkable competencies at birth. Whereas some years ago it was fashionable to quote William James' view that the infant perceives the world as a 'blooming buzzing confusion,' Bower and others[6, 7] have shown that babies are not as confused as all that—they are in fact quite perceptive. They respond to the world about them; show certain levels of perceptual development; and are even willing to suck on a nipple at a faster rate, or for a longer time, in order to get a reward.

The real impetus for studying the very young infant in depth has come from the investigations of people such as Gesell,[8a] Fantz,[8b] and Bruner.[9] The latter founded and still heads the Harvard Institute of Cognitive Studies, which is the source of a variety of interesting infant research. In one series of experiments Bruner placed four- to six-week-old infants in a well-padded seat, gave them pacifiers and showed them movies. The movie changed in clarity, depending on the infant's response. In one experiment, the children had to suck in long bursts to produce a clear focus. This they accordingly learned to do. In another experiment, the conditions were reversed so that sucking blurred the picture. The clever infants responded to this trick by actually stopping their sucking on the pacifier. Bruner maintains that this learned behaviour, where the infants deliberately reverse their normal response in order to produce a clear focus, involves very complex strategies of coordinating sucking and looking.

He and his staff then tried to find out what a pacifier actually does for the newborn. They measured brain waves and checked whether, and when, the infant looked at the movie while sucking. Bruner found that during the first few days after birth the baby cannot handle more than one activity at a time : he copes neatly with the problem of too much stimulation by closing his eyes while sucking. We shall see later that retarded children at a far later age are unable to take in many stimuli at one time.

As the normal infant grows older, however, he can absorb more information at one time, so that by the age of three to five weeks he sucks with his eyes open, although if the child becomes interested enough in a particular stimulus, sucking stops. Later, by the age of two to four months, the infant shifts his sucking behaviour and does a sort of 'mouthing' which keeps the nipple active, though at a reduced rate.

The newborn's visual abilities have been nicely detailed by the Maurers.[10] They report that the infant has fairly good vision about one foot away. Peripheral vision is not quite as good, because it extends only to a 60° angle, in contrast to the adult's 180°. Eyes are in fixed focus for the distance of one foot, and this focus lasts for about one month after birth. By four months, focusing is normal and visual acuity is near normal. Actually, the initial fixed focus is not a detriment. It helps the infant see depth, despite his lack of stereoscopic vision, lack of experience, and inability to understand perspective.

Eyes usually converge by three months. If they do not do so by six months, some form of intervention is normally advised, because lack of convergence means that one eye tends to take over the function of the other eye. If this happens, the other eye may become functionally blind. Here again is another example of normal development being dependent on active interaction with the environment: if the eye does not actively interact, it ceases to function.

Although newborns can and do respond to human faces, their discrimination is not particularly good. Thus, they will follow visually pictures of faces, regardless of whether the face is ordinary or distorted. In effect, the newborn essentially ignores the features that are inside the circle representing the face. With greater age comes greater selectivity and discrimination, so that at the respectable age of two months the infant will follow a regular face in preference to one which is distorted.

The Maurers' results contradict those reported by Goren, Sarty, and Wu,[11] who found that infants were more responsive to forms which looked more like a face than those which looked less like a face. And this at the tender ages of three minutes to twenty-seven minutes after birth!

Although newborns apparently do not respond to the figure as a whole, they do orient toward preferred elements in their visual fields.[12] Furthermore, children, in contrast to adults, show more short eye movements, and concentrate on the less informative details of what is shown to them.[13] Even though this type of concentration is not terribly effective, it does show that children pay more attention to detail than had previously been supposed.

The very young child depends heavily on near receptors, i.e. on such senses as the tactile and kinesthetic.[14-16] As the child grows older he comes to depend more heavily on far receptors such as sight and hearing. But this development is another that does not necessarily take place in the abnormal child. We have observed many autistic and seriously retarded children who seemingly ignore many visual stimuli around them, even when they are specifically asked to complete a task which requires perceptual-motor coordination. They grope without looking until their hand contacts the object which they need for the task. The observer gets the impression that the response is haphazard and certainly not visually directed. This type of response can make it difficult to teach even very simple tasks to the developmentally delayed.

Mental development

Many investigators have intensively studied mental development. One important question studied is whether one can predict later intelligence on the basis of tests given very early in life. This is a key question in relation to teaching approaches and emphases. So far, however, predictability of later IQ has been disappointingly low and variable. Part of the problem no doubt is the fact that the tests available for testing at the lower levels are primarily ones measuring motor development, and though the latter may interact with intellectual development, it is not predictive of intellectual capacities.

Predictive value of childhood IQ varies in range from poor predictability for the normal child, to more adequate predictability for the subnormal, i.e. retarded child. Greater predictability for the subnormal is not surprising, since such children are generally retarded in other areas as well as the intellectual. In these cases infant tests of intelligence also tend to pick up delays in sensory-motor coordination, and response to simple commands. If such neuromotor problems are present at an early age, they tend to remain permanent problems for the child.

The most thorough studies on intelligence have been longitudinal.[17, 18] Bayley reported on a study spanning thirty-six years and involving both personality variables and mental abilities. Despite low predictability from early childhood IQ to later IQ, there is one sub-item which emerges as predicting fairly well, but only for girls' scores : vocalisation made by the (girl) infant seems to be a good predictor of spontaneous vocalisation at the age of two and a half. But this too is not a predictor of general IQ, and overall findings remain that performance at a very young age is generally not a good indicator of what can be expected later.

Some interesting results have come from studies which ostensibly ignore the child's capacities and look at other factors instead. For example, socio-economic status is a better predictor of later intelligence than IQ tests given to average, or above average, infants tested at eight months.[19] Mother's education also predicts to some extent her child's IQ, even when the child is reared apart from its mother.[20] This finding appears more mysterious than it need be. We might conjecture that reports of older studies were based on an adult population that grew up before the availability of universal education, when maybe only the more intelligent women sought and received a good education. If so, the correlation between the mother's IQ and the IQ of her child reared apart from her could be dependent on a genetic factor.

Predictability of childhood intelligence tests for later IQ does increase by the time the child reaches school age. By the age of about six, one can predict with a fair degree of accuracy what the child's later IQ will be, since the correlation of earlier and later tests is about ·70.[21]

Cognitive development

Development of motor centres and sensory-motor aspects is relatively fast in the first year and a half. After that age, language development becomes increasingly important. Up to the age of five or six, language is part of total development. After that, it provides the medium for developing higher intellectual functioning. Language also simplifies information storage by providing labels to categorise or pigeonhole knowledge.

Nonetheless, information is not always stored linguistically. Haber[22] presented a series of pictures and words to his subjects and concluded that there is one kind of memory for pictorial material and a separate one for linguistic material. What was remarkable was that recognition for unlabelled pictures was extremely high, despite the large number initially presented. Subjects saw about 2,500 pictures, which were presented at the rate of one every ten seconds, for a total of eight hours of viewing time, over a span of two days. When the subjects were later given a recognition task of pairs of pictures, they were able to correctly identify which member of the pair had previously been seen with about 90 per cent success.

The study showed that there can be memory storage without language or labels. This is not surprising in view of the large amount of evidence regarding differences in functioning between one side of the brain and the other. One side, in most people the left, is mainly involved with language and analytical functions, while the other, the right, is more involved with such functions as spatial visualisation and imagery.

In a stimulating analysis of age comparisons across a variety of learning experiments, White [23a] suggests that the child starts with an associative type of learning. Here learning is of the stimulus-response type, involving, if we interpret him correctly, little or no cognition. By the age of about five to seven years, the child comes to use a more cognitive approach, in which verbal mediation assumes prime importance in problem solving and learning. This means that the child now begins to make use of language and verbalisation to organise and cohere his thinking processes, which in turn facilitate problem solving.

Cognitive learning is

> guided by concepts and not stimuli, and one significant aspect of a concept is the fact that a part of the presenting elements of a cue must be selectively filtered out from consideration if the cue is to stand for a concept. To see a cue as an instance of a concept, one might say, we must selectively ignore it. [23b]

Associative learning can be of two types. In the first type the stimuli remain the same from trial to trial, and the person learns to respond to one stimulus and not to respond to the other. In the second type of associative learning the cues vary from trial to trial, and White calls this 'quasicognitive' associative learning.

We agree with White that there are aspects of learning which can be most simply explained in terms of such associative learning. Yet, we feel that many, if not most, responses can be more convincingly interpreted as the product of hypothesis formation. This process involves making decisions and responding on the basis of information (whether pictorial, linguistic, or whatever), and so involves some kind of cognition.

The concept of hypothesis formation can be fruitfully applied even to the very young infant and to most levels of response complexity. The concept can be applied to visual perception, which often involves purposive behaviour. Hochberg[24] notes that when someone looks at a scene, his eye makes more fixations in one inspection than he can possibly hold in his short-term memory. Therefore, parts of the actual perception of the scene depend on recall of his previous fixations, which suggests that perception has some basis in generated hypotheses about the visual world.

The idea that development is based on hypotheses and decisions makes a wide variety of responses, both human and non-human, understandable and predictable. Though a strict stimulus-response type of learning theory is simple and can be usefully applied in some cases, it has neither the flexibility nor the power of a theory which invokes hypothesis formation, that is, in which responses are the outcome of hypotheses.

Although the latter provides a convenient explanatory framework, we must not ignore other variables which may affect the formation of hypotheses.

> Generation of hypotheses is so much at the heart of mental functioning that a variety of forces can influence it directly. Anxiety can lead to distraction and interfering hypothesis; motivation affects persistence of search; strength of particular beliefs might prevent proliferation of associations dissonant to the belief.[25]

Age is also a factor in hypothesis formation. The young child is capable of forming hypotheses. Yet when he must depend on his limited capabilities, and if further hampered by having little information at his command, his performance is far inferior to that of the older child. An interesting example of this age difference is given by Potter who showed photographs of familiar objects which were initially out of focus and gradually came into focus. Preschoolers took much longer to recognise the correct picture, and they repeated the same hypotheses often. In contrast, school age children were less likely to repeat hypotheses, and were more cautious and less ready to guess. In other words,

> the youngest children offered an unrelated series of hypotheses as to the nature of the viewed picture. Older children were better able to integrate the stimulus features and their memory store in a cyclical, hypothesis-testing manner.[26]

Many investigators, including ourselves, have also found that younger children seem to be stuck in position hypotheses—that is, they tend to respond to the position where the stimulus appears, rather than to respond to the stimulus itself. Older children who have more effective ways of problem-solving tend to attend more to relevant cues and thus do not get stuck in a rote response to position cues.

Another factor affecting hypothesis formation is intelligence. Bright children differ from average children in concept learning, and this is related to their differential abilities in hypothesis formation. Stevenson[27] compared a number of studies and concluded that bright children are more capable of analysing and defining problems, and also produce more hypotheses than average children. Differences between the two groups may or may not show up in their performance. When it is advantageous to formulate many hypotheses in order to obtain a correct response, and when there is feedback that a specific hypothesis is appropriate, then bright children perform better than average children. However, when the stimuli result in few hypotheses, and when the problem is clearly spelled out, then there are no differences between the two groups.

Language learning in effect involves problem-solving and can be viewed in terms of hypothesis formation. Even the very young infant is already learning and hypothesising about what goes with what, what sound consistently applies to which object, and what meaning is assigned to which sound. From these beginnings specific speech patterns emerge and levels of understanding develop.

It seems reasonable to assume that the child develops general rules or hyptheses by which he can learn to understand sentences and generate more of his own. Hypotheses help explain the child's ability to understand and speak sentences which he has never heard. McNeill[28] specifically views the process of language learning as a series of hypotheses which are constantly modified as the child obtains new data. When we later describe our nonvocal symbol system, we shall see that here too the child, regardless of level of functioning, appears to make hypotheses about which symbol stands for what word, and which arrangement of symbols will provide him with a specific reward.

The concept of hypothesis formation provides a useful tool to understand large aspects of learning, including problem solving, perception and language acquisition. Various constraints may shape hypothesis formation. They include constraints imposed by the child's innate capacity to acquire language, by his past experience, and by those stimuli present in his environment to which he responds and pays selective attention.

In short, we feel that the concept of hypothesis formation is useful because it can be applied regardless of age, ability, or learning rate. It even can be usefully applied to nonhuman learning, particularly if one looks at comparative animal learning data.

NORMAL LANGUAGE DEVELOPMENT

To professional and nonprofessional alike, the small child appears remarkable, and in fact somehow divorced from what we all were once. How, we ask, does the child ever manage to learn a language? The process of acquisition has intrigued many experts, and much effort has gone into observation and theorising.

Most of us have picked up one or more languages during the course of our lives. Yet we look back at the child's first language as a mysterious accomplishment. And rightfully so, for we no longer remember how we first associated sound with meaning, nor how we first conceptualised and memorised all that which now permits us to communicate so meaningfully. We might perhaps recall when and under what conditions we first learned to read, or learned a strange new word, or a strange new language. But we cannot recall how we originally picked up our native tongue. We must therefore go back like explorers in a strange land to find out how such learning takes place.

In detailing the course of normal language development, we have found it convenient to distinguish separate categories. They include : receptive and expressive language, competence and performance, stages of language acquisition, and internal and external factors which might influence acquisition, including attention, impulsivity, and culture. The distinctions are arbitrary, but help simplify discussion provided one is aware that the categories may overlap.

RECEPTIVE AND EXPRESSIVE LANGUAGE

Expressive language literally refers to expression, i.e. to speech, although for our purposes writing may also be considered expressive. Receptive language refers to what is taken in, i.e. how much is understood. Throughout all stages of language development there is a distinct difference between how much the child can express and how very much more he can actually understand. Being aware of the difference between expressive and receptive language is not necessarily critical when dealing with the normally developing child, since he will 'spontaneously' learn language. But it *is* crucial when dealing with, and teaching, the language-impaired child.

People tend to be impatient with the handicapped who cannot speak, and tend to dismiss them as stupid. True, some are stupid. Others, however, have an impressive amount of receptive language which may remain undiscovered for a discouragingly long time.

Fourcin[29] reports an interesting example of a man who was so badly handicapped by cerebral palsy that he could not communicate for years. At the advanced age of twenty-eight he was given a specially designed foot-activated typewriter which he learned to use within a few days. As he typed out his thoughts and desires, he astonished others by his remarkable command of syntax and semantics. Up to that point none but his parents believed that he understood much of anything, let alone was able to express himself at such a high level of sophistication.

James Renuk is another man who has cerebral palsy. At the age of twenty-three he too cannot speak, but he has learned to point to letters and to write laboriously. He wrote an article for the *Los Angeles Times*[30] in which he said wistfully that others thought him stupid, and so for years they did not bother to teach him. However, once he could express himself by writing, others came to understand that Renuk could think, had knowledge, and indeed could communicate by means of language.

Like these cerebral palsied adults, the young child understands much more than he/she can express. By the time he is about a year old, the child can understand and follow simple commands, such as 'come here', and 'sit down', but he may not yet be able to say them. The child begins to express himself as an infant by making all the variety of sounds one hears in the thousands of different languages. Initial babblings and cooings are followed by sound patterns which seem to imitate nearby adults. Somewhere around this beginning imitation stage, the sounds peculiar to the child's native language remain, while those foreign to his language drop out. Because initial sounds cover a wider range than is present in the child's native language, we assume that language imitation per se does not totally explain the development of linguistic competence in normal children. In any case, the final speech product reflects the sounds and speech which the child imitates from hearing others, plus the sounds which he initiates or self-generates.

Receptive language is acquired as the child attends to various sound stimuli and then learns to assign meanings to them. It follows that the child must discriminate one sound from the next, and this discrimination involves varying levels of complexity. At its simplest, the child must differentiate vowel from consonant sounds. As we noted in the first chapter, this ability seems to be innate. After the child has made selective responses to specific sounds and speech patterns within his/her environment, he can then make further discriminations and deduce which sound pattern accompanies which specific meaning. When, for example, the sound of *apple* is associated with a round food of a certain colour, texture, and taste, then meaning has been established and a receptive vocabulary exists.

As the child acquires language he also learns to make more complex distinctions, such as those between the same sounds with different meanings, as in the homonyms *bear* and *bare*; and between different sounds with the same meaning, as in *tomāto* and *tomato*. The latter is merely one example of the many, large differences in pronunciation which exists in different parts of a country, across various dialects, and within different sub-cultures. The child learns to recognise the same meaning despite the differences in pronunciation and sound.

LINGUISTIC COMPETENCE AND PERFORMANCE

We need to distinguish between linguistic competence and performance in much the same way we distinguished between receptive and expressive language.

It is commonly agreed that linguistic competence refers to knowledge of the language, its words, sound (phonology), grammar (syntax), and underlying meaning (semantics). By contrast, performance refers to language usage which may or may not be on a par with competence. If we understand Fowler, McNeill, and Wood,[31-33] it appears that their view of competence and performance largely overlaps with the distinctions previously made between receptive and expressive language. The overlap becomes even clearer if one assumes, as we do, that there are levels of competence, and that performance can be influenced by factors outside of linguistic competence.

Competence may exist at different levels. The child who knows the rules of grammar, but does not know the labels for many objects, is less competent linguistically than the child who not only discriminates the difference among objects, but also has appropriate labels for them. He in turn is less competent than the child who can also classify objects into categories or think about ideas.

Performance can be affected not only by the child's linguistic competence, but also by such nonlinguistic factors as distractibility (where the child constantly jumps from one task to another); impulsivity (where the child rashly guesses at an answer, or carries on an activity without weighing the information or consequences); and physical handicaps (where the child is slow in writing, not because of slowness in thinking, but because of motor impairment).

STAGES OF LANGUAGE ACQUISITION

We noted previously that normal language development follows predictable stages occurring within predictable age ranges. In the normal infant, speech sounds start at birth.

It is nearly trite to say that the first common sound is crying, and that this is used to signal hunger, fatigue and general distress. As we know, and sometimes to our despair, this is the only way in which the newborn can communicate with us. By the age of six weeks the infant adds cooing to his repertoire. Cooing universally indicates pleasure, and is accomplished by modulation via the tongue. These sounds are innate and apparently cannot be modified. Lenneberg[34] has reported that cooing is present in deaf infants until they are about two months old. Since these children cannot hear they are not reinforced for these sounds, and consequently sound production eventually stops.

Babbling appears around six months, and differs from crying and cooing in the number and types of sounds, as well as in the fact that pauses are produced. Deaf children also babble but the sound they make is more monotonous due to lack of auditory feedback.[35] One can increase babbling by rewarding the infant with external reinforcement. However many infants seem to be self-reinforced since they apparently babble for sheer fun, or perhaps for practice. Babbling seems to be related to maturational factors, and occurs when the infant begins to sit up, and when the fat pads on the cheeks have disappeared.

Ervin and Miller[36] analysed the types of sounds children make when they start babbling prior to learning English. Their data came from a number of studies which showed that at the beginning most of the vocalisations are vowels, of which the most common is a as in at. Three other common sounds are i as in it, e as in let, and u as in cup. The variety of vowel sounds increases from about four at the age of one month, to about eleven at the age of thirty months. At this young age the child already reproduces nearly all of the fourteen vowel sounds common to an adult. Consonant variety does not develop as rapidly. The infant produces about two consonants at the age of one month. This increases to about fifteen by the age of thirty months, in contrast to the adult's twenty-five.

We mentioned before that infants are capable of producing all sounds at birth (although not all are initially expressed), but that by the age of six months they stop using sounds not present in their mother tongue. The facility for other sounds is lost to such an extent that, unless the child is exposed early on to another language, he will find it hard correctly to mimic its sounds. Hence, the many 'foreign accents' of people who immigrate after the age of twelve.*

The infant begins to produce morphemes at about twelve months. A morpheme represents the smallest unit of sound which has meaning, (a letter, a syllable, or a word, like *ma*). First words tend to be composed of repetitive syllables like *bye-bye*, *ma-ma*, *be-be*, and *da-da*. By eighteen months the child has picked up a surprising number of words, with a vocabulary of about 200–300 words.

The child must attain a certain level of linguistic competence if he is to speak meaningfully. He must be able to generate words and imitate the sounds he hears. But this level won't be reached unless he also manages the nonlinguistic feat of distinguishing his own developing self from other selves and other objects. In process, he must learn the meaning of representation, i.e. that sounds can be symbols which represent, or stand for, objects.

By the age of four months the child already begins to understand that there is an object out there separate from himself. However, this concept is not fully attained until *roughly* the age of one and a half years.[37] Once he grasps this concept, he can begin to make other connections, including that a sound can have a meaning and/or stand for a specific object which is not present.

Heinz Werner[38, 39] is among those who emphasise the importance of learning to distinguish between object and self. Once the infant can make this distinction, he starts to refer to objects. He first does so by pointing to or touching them, and this is something that the reader has undoubtedly observed many times. For Werner this behaviour means that the infant has proto-symbols, or models of symbols. From this stage the infant progresses to the formation of other symbols, or nonlinguistic representation. Call sounds are some of the first such symbols which represent vocal counterparts

* Deich has found that after this age most immigrants tend to retain an 'accent'. The finding was based on pilot work with emigrants to the United States from countries including Germany, France, Israel, and Sweden.

to pointing. Such sounds tend to be short, repetitive and barely modulated. They include sounds like *mmmm . . . mmmm*, which are sometimes accompanied by pointing.

Like other theorists who make a strong case for the existence of thinking prior to language, Werner refers to mental images which are at first nonverbal. He then distinguishes a final step in language acquisition in which the child deduces that language can be used to convey information. We assume that this step of Werner's represents the point at which language becomes a vehicle for thinking.

Perhaps the most widely known proponent of the idea that the infant must develop a concept of self separate from objects before he/she can use mental symbols is Piaget.[40, 41] As noted above, the child fully attains this concept at about eighteen months.* Somewhat later the child begins to

> represent an object which is absent or an event which is not perceived, by means of symbols or signs, that is of signifiers separated from their significants.[42b]

We see here that the development of language is intimately interrelated with overall development, and particularly cognitive development.

Limitations of space prevent discussing Piaget's theory in great detail. However, it is appropriate to our purposes to look briefly at his exposition of cognitive organisation and 'schemes'. Organisation refers to the tendency to order processes into regular systems, and cognitive organisation is viewed within the framework of assimilation and accommodation. Assimilation for Piaget means that new events can be fitted into already existing cognitive structures. Thus new elements can be absorbed without any changes taking place within the overall structure. This means that assimilation produces neither new cognitive elements, nor new cognitive structures, regardless how inappropriately or how erroneously the new elements are absorbed. Accommodation is the opposite process in which cognitive structures must change to take in new elements.

---

* Piaget has elsewhere set the age at twenty-four months, and Lewis[42a] has given some interesting examples of self-concept occurring roughly at fifteen months.

Let us say that a small boy has a specific cognitive structure for the concept, girl. To him the concept of girl represents someone with long curls and a dress. He meets another little girl who also has long curls and also wears a dress. He assimilates her into his cognitive structure for girls without any difficulties. However, the next girl he meets has short hair and is wearing blue jeans. He may assimilate this little girl into his cognitive structure of boy, until someone explains to him that this is an incorrect classification. In order to incorporate the new element, into his cognitive structure for girl, he must accommodate his 'scheme' to include this new concept for girl.

The word 'scheme' is used in the broadest sense by Piaget. At its simplest, it is a reliable response to a stimulus, similar to a reflex. In other words, at this level a scheme is innate. Piaget refers to two important schemes which are independent of experience: sucking and looking. The infant organises these two schemes, and initially all cognitive elements are fitted into them. But 'scheme' can mean more than that. For example, it can represent a cognitive structure, or a class of similar thoughts. Schemes of this type develop through experience.

If we use other words instead of Piaget's initial schemes (which are independent of experience), and later schemes (which are dependent on experience), we get back to our previous discussion. Initial schemes can be viewed in terms of innate responses and reflexes and, possibly, primitive systems for hypothesis formation. Later schemes can be viewed in terms of hypothesis formation.

Much of the work on stages of language acquisition is based on detailed longitudinal analyses of very few children. Specialists such as Bloom, Brown, and Bellugi[43-47] studied language development based on samples of only two and three children. They then systematised the findings to detail when and under what conditions the child's grammar and overall expression first develop.

Brown divides language learning into five stages. So far, it is only the first stage for which he claims validity across many different unrelated languages. Stage I is defined as the one in which the average length of the child's speech first rises above one morpheme. In other words, this is a time when morphemes begin to be combined. Although we know that the rate of language learning varies greatly for different children, the rate of acquiring constructions and semantic knowledge is fairly uniform at a given level of expression.

Stage I children, regardless of which language they speak, produce sentences which vary in length from one to seven morphemes. These sentences are simple, and limited to a small set of relations. A brief list of eleven relations accounts for about 75 per cent of Stage I utterances in almost all language samples reported by Brown.[44] A longer list of about eighteen accounts for nearly 100 per cent of the child's speech. This includes expressions of reference (that ball), expressions of recurrence (more ball), expressions of nonexistence (all gone ball), possessives (Daddy chair), and two-term relations (Daddy hit). At this level, speech seems largely restricted to such two-term relations.

If one looks at overall language development rather than individual stages, it appears that language, like other aspects of development, changes from a global and undifferentiated process to increasingly greater specificity and differentiation. The reader no doubt has observed such changes in very young children. At first they make noises and produce speech patterns which sound very meaningful, but are in fact incomprehensible. In time, the language becomes more and more clearly understandable.

Semantic word usage is also global to start with, and becomes ever more specialised and differentiated. At first single words seem to be used to express complex ideas and to serve several functions. If the child says 'shoe', he may mean, 'Where is the shoe?', 'There is the shoe!', or 'Give me the shoe'. Similarly, 'apple' may mean not only a round object of a specific size and colour, but also that the child wants that particular object, or that he would like someone else to look for it for him.

This type of speech, where one word does the work of many, and/or expresses more complex ideas than it represents, has been called holophrastic speech. Indeed a number of earlier researchers on children's language suggested that holophrastic speech is equivalent to the full sentences of adult grammar.[48-50] However, it seems more probable that the child is limited in the number and types of words he can express, rather than that he/she is ingeniously using one word to take the place of many.

Despite his limitations, the child can comment on the world surrounding him. DeLaguna put it neatly when he said that,

> it is precisely because the words of the child are so indefinite in meaning, that they can serve such a variety of uses.[51]

When one of our nephews was first beginning to talk he was given a soft, furry jacket. He promptly labelled the jacket 'doggie', generalising cleverly, functionally and incorrectly from the soft, furry animals he loved, to the soft, furry jacket which entranced him.

Undifferentiated speech reflects the child's lack of development. With increasing development there is an increase in organising capacity in all aspects, including language. By the beginning of the second year, the child starts to use relational terms such as *more, same, before* and there. Interestingly enough, semantically 'positive' terms such as *more, same* and *before* are learned before semantically 'negative' terms like *less, different*, and *after*. Relational terms predominate until the end of the second year, when noun forms and references to classes of objects appear.[52-54]

DIFFERENCES IN CHILD VERSUS ADULT SPEECH: QUALITATIVE OR QUANTITATIVE?

Although he/she tends to imitate the speech patterns of teachers, peers and parents, the young child nonetheless seems to express himself differently from the adult. During the 1960s Brown and his coworkers[55, 56] described the young child's speech as 'telegraphic'. Like a telegram, the child's initial sentences are extremely brief, with apparently all so-called inessential words and information left out. What is left is similar to an adult telegram, which is largely composed of nouns and verbs, few adjectives and adverbs, and generally no prepositions, conjunctions or articles.

The similarity of the child's speech to telegrams seems to have been more apparent than real. McNeill[57] correctly pointed out that the child has no way of knowing whether a word is essential or informative, unless he knows in advance the syntactic role of each word. Furthermore, the kind of information which is dropped in the 'telegram' depends on the language. Children learning Russian drop inflections from their speech, despite the fact that in this language a great deal of information is given through inflections.[58] Thus the Russian child drops information which the American child retains. Indeed, Brown himself no longer considers telegraphic speech an apt, consistent or universal description for Stage I speech, although such speech does occur often.

The child's errors in grammar and sentence structure were formerly considered to be haphazard, but more recent evidence shows that errors are consistent, predictable and universal. Furthermore, correct speech develops without specific teaching or attention in the normal child.[59, 60]

Children's speech, then differs from adult speech, and follows certain unspoken rules. When children begin to talk they express themselves in roughly similar ways, even if their languages differ in grammatical structure, as do English and Russian. Expression seems to be based on logical guesses about the structure of language. By virtue of these guesses, and/or predispositional factors, grammar is consistent, even if incorrect by adult standards. The kinds of consistent errors which children make, and which in fact reflect their own grammatical styles, include such typical childhood sentences as, 'She holded the baby', 'He singed the song', and 'They runded fast'. These sentences are charmingly incorrect according to present-day adult grammar, yet reflect consistent deductions about how to generate a past tense from a present tense.

Increasing ability in speech is accompanied by application of rules, even though these are not consciously formulated. The child starts to use articles, such as 'a' and 'the', and pronouns such as 'he', 'me', and 'it'. He also learns to differentiate classes of nouns.

Ultimately, he learns 'tag' questions. The tag refers to the end part of a sentence which changes the statement into a question. In, 'Mary is coming home, isn't she?', the tag 'isn't she?' creates the question. There are numerous tags like, 'She is pretty, isn't she?', 'He can't write, can he?', 'I did that, didn't I?', 'They are eating, aren't they?'. Tags vary in complexity, so that simple tags like 'Right?' appear as early as Brown's Stage I, while more complex tags such as 'Can't I?', don't appear until well after Stage V, which occurs around four or five years.

By this age a specific stage of development has been reached. As we have seen, at this point the child is able to put sentences together, and can learn to do so in other languages, provided he is exposed to them. Also, by the fourth year most young children have a good command of semantics, as well as syntactic structure, i.e. grammar. Bowerman, Bloom, and others[61, 62] have emphasised that semantics and syntax are learned simultaneously. However, Bowerman disagrees with Bloom's thesis that correct sentence order is the equivalent to knowing syntax. The former shows that this is not so, by comparing the meaning of 'John is easy to please', with the very different 'John is eager to please'. In the first case, *John* is the object. In the second case, he is the subject. Clearly the structure is the same, but the functional relationship is distinctly different.

At this young age, the child knows word meanings and word order, correctly uses parts of speech, and has some knowledge of the functional relations between the elements of speech. His language approximates to that of an adult, but complete syntactic and semantic competence appears only later, in adolescence.

Is it possible to accelerate language development at an early age? A study by Cazden[63] seems to indicate that it is, provided that the technique is appropriate. Two groups of two-and-a-half-year-olds were seen each day for three months. In the Expanded Group, whatever a child said was expanded by Cazden. If the child said 'Baby hungry', Cazden would add the grammatically missing piece by expanding the sentence to 'Baby is hungry'. In the Enlarged Group, the sentence would be enlarged upon, but no part of the sentence would be repeated. Thus, in response to, 'Baby hungry', Cazden might respond 'Yes, he wants to eat'. At the end of training, both the expanded and enlarged groups had improved, although interestingly enough, the enlarged group did better than the expanded one. Perhaps enlarging the context and range of meaning is more important at this stage than grammatically correct structures.

A CHILD'S UNDERSTANDING OF LANGUAGE

As we discussed previously, the normal child's language development includes not only speech, but understanding, i.e. expression and reception. Although understanding is more advanced than speech in early development, it is not as sophisticated as it is later on, since complex word meanings are still being learned through adolescence. Knowledge and understanding take a long time to develop because many words require abstract reasoning ability, as well as much past experience with the meanings of simple and familiar words.

The young child interprets a sentence according to his own system of rules, which changes as he gets older. In the English language, the child considers order rather than meaning when a sentence is composed of a noun followed by a verb. Lenneberg[64] showed a sentence and its variants to a group, and found consistent and different responses depending on age. A two-year-old understands the sentence, 'The cow kissed the horse'. If, however, the order is reversed to 'The horse is kissed by the cow', the child's reaction is random and he may totally misinterpret the meaning. Rephrasing the sentence to 'It is the horse that the cow kissed', again results in correct interpretation, because the child looks at the noun and verb in their order of actor/action, i.e. the cow kisses. Therefore, the child understands this correctly. Interestingly enough, by the age of four, sentence analysis, although somewhat different, is not always correct. Whereas the two-year-old child responded randomly to the sentence, 'The horse is kissed by the cow', the four-year-old consistently misunderstood the meaning.

Understanding individual words, particularly relational ones, increases with increasing age. Thus two-year-olds can understand reference to the immediate future, and three-year-olds understand the meaning of 'yesterday' better than 'tomorrow'. Both 'before' and 'after' are understood better in the context of future time and action than in that of past time or action, but they are not initially understood as relationally ordering two events with respect to each other.[65]

Adults can generally put a word like 'old' within its proper context. Yet, if we listen to the young child, we may hear him call a person old whether he is twenty-two, forty-two, or seventy-two. Recent analyses[66, 67] have shown that preschoolers label a figure as older if it is larger than comparable figures, regardless of what the content might imply. Larger is older even if dress and body proportions suggest the reverse.

It seems to us that the child's mislabelling the larger figure may be due to an imprecise definition of what older really means. If the child equates older with bigger, then labelling the larger comparison figure as older is correct by that definition. Mislabelling and misinterpretation imply that he is using a different classification system. For example, we have often heard the young confidently assign names like mommy, daddy, and *baby* to abstract figures such as triangles. Inevitably, the largest triangle is labelled *daddy*, the medium-sized one, *mommy*, and the smallest one, *baby*. Here is an example not of lack of thinking, but of the reverse, since the child classifies his universe into meaningful components he can understand.

We have noticed that parents, especially those with high intelligence and much education, tend to give complex instructions and complex explanations to their young offspring. The child often seems to comprehend and follow the instructions remarkably well. Some of these children do understand fairly well. However, others understand only a fraction of the parents' meaning. The child is often a past master at giving the impression that he understands completely, when he actually understands only some aspect, although that aspect may be sufficient to let him understand the idea in context.

Occasionally however one is forced to become aware of these gaps in meaning, as for example in the following tragi-comic case of a three-year-old who had recently come to the United States from Israel. The child's American aunt gave her some ice cream. The child said, 'Too much, too much'. The aunt took half away. The child became very excited and said, 'No, too much, too much'. The aunt took away yet more, and the child burst into tears. The puzzled aunt finally realised that the child somehow had the wrong word for 'more'. She then gave her a heaping amount of ice cream and the child started to beam. So 'too much' can mean 'more' and not 'less'.

This is the age when the child begins to sort out the difference between 'more' and 'less' in its mother tongue. Apparently, 'more' is understood earlier than 'less', and there is a period when the child seems to think that 'less' is 'more'.[68] So it may be that the little girl who confused 'too much' with 'more' was not only confusing one language with another, but also following the predictable pattern of trying to sort 'more' from 'less'.

In short, the young may understand, and/or listen to, only part of what the adult has meant to convey, or has clearly said. This partial response is not of course limited to the child: both young and old may respond to a total context, or respond on the basis of what they think is expected of them, or guess successfully, because there is nearly always redundancy in language and in the surrounding context.

In this way, because of such guessing, the child may succeed in following verbal directions even if understanding is incomplete. For example, if one gives a child of about two years a small toy and asks him to put that toy in the box on the table, he can do this correctly because he sees the toy; he sees the box on the table; and he puts two and two together. We have found that when we test young children, and also the retarded, they can often carry out commands such as, 'Give me the kitten', 'Put the dog in the box', 'Put the scissors on the table', because their chance of guessing correctly is high. On the other hand, if one asks them to place the scissors next to the box, they often fail because they cannot guess, and they do not really know 'next to'.

If the child knows roughly what is expected of him, he tends to act on the basis of past experience rather than follow precisely the verbal instructions given to him. The less he knows, the more he is likely to guess. This fact has implications for teaching both the normal and the retarded.

In teaching the young child we want to know whether he understands what we are saying. At the same time, we need be aware of the conditions under which redundant, i.e. extra or repetitive, information is useful, so that he can guess the answer from the context. We also need be aware of when redundant information may be distracting. This is particularly true for the retarded child who may not be able to sort out relevant from irrelevant stimuli, which may or may not be redundant. Teachers or parents who know the child's comprehension level can simplify their speech so that the child understands easily. Alternatively, the adult can make speech somewhat more difficult, in order to challenge the child and expand his understanding.

Teaching in the schools leans heavily on language, and language-knowledge training. Such teaching is based on the assumption that the ability to use language is a necessity for logical thinking. We discussed previously whether thinking occurs prior to language, and concluded that it can. On the other hand, we also noted the great advantage that language offers in facilitating the thinking process. When the focus is on teaching, a strong case can be made for emphasising language, as well as conceptualising and classifying abilities. For example, if a child knows the names of things, he can categorise them more readily. He can group dogs, cats, human beings, and so on. Furthermore, as he determines what fits under which classification, he perceives similarities as well as differences among things.

Much of early school teaching emphasises learning words which can be applied in a larger context later on. These words involve relationships such as number, space, time and size. The child learns colours, and the meaning of *more/less*, *bigger/smaller*, *between*, *behind*, *before*, and so on. Such words have been labelled 'cognitive code' words. They are difficult to learn since they require that the child learn relational aspects within a context. This means that the child learns that a range of colours can be labelled 'blue', whether tinged with white, red, or yellow. He learns that a spider is bigger than a fly, but smaller than a horse. Because relational words require different contexts, teaching cannot be restricted to one example repeated many times. Instead, one must offer many different examples under different situations so that the child truly understands the abstract meaning of more, or bigger, or red.

TRANSITION STAGES AND AGE EFFECTS

We have talked about language acquisition and the stages at which the child first learns single words, and then combines them into two- and three-word sentences. These transition stages are not unique to language development. The child's behaviour, achievement and abilities show distinct changes which stand out for different age groups. We shall briefly review some of these changes since they are intimately related to language development, and can also affect teaching approaches.

The character of learning seems to change at the age of five. White[69] suggests that before this age, the pattern of learning seems to be akin to that of animals when taught with similar procedures. After this age, learning patterns seem to approximate more to those of human adults, so that learning changes from animal-like to human-like learning. The changes may be related to important reorganisations of brain chemistry which occur concurrently during this period.[70]

At the same time, there are changes in the means by which the child contacts and explores the environment. Within the first four years he tends to explore objects tactually. By the age of six, he explores largely by visual means.[71-74]

Schopfler[75] showed these changes in children, aged three to nine years. They were given a variety of objects to play with, including putty, a kaleidoscope, coloured blocks, and fur-covered blocks. The greater the age, the more children played with items involving visual choices. Interestingly enough, the absolute time spent on tactual items remained constant regardless of age, while the absolute time spent on visual materials increased.

As the child grows older, he also becomes better at solving problems involving spatial relations. Emerson[76] asked two- to five-year-olds to place wooden rings in nine positions of varying difficulty. All were able to do this task if they remained in the same position with respect to the rings. However, if they changed position they made more errors. The greater the change in position, the less accurate the placement, although the older children made far fewer errors than the younger. Experiments with other children up to the age of ten confirm these findings, and suggest that the older ones' greater ability is related to their 'encoding the ring location in conceptual-verbal terms'.[77]

Despite increasing refinement in recognition, which is partly dependent on increasing ability to use language for labelling and conceptualising, younger children may do better than older ones if forms are shown in a disoriented position in space. Deich[78] tested a hypothesis of Piaget[79] that the younger child ignores the coordinates of space. She compared the relative difficulty of reading inverted versus upright words in children aged seven to 13 years, who ranged in intelligence from average to above average. Reading inversions became relatively more difficult for the older child, despite general improvement in reading speed as developmental levels increased. Deich concluded that form is largely independent of orientation in the younger child, and that this is the case for higher chronological ages than those reported by Piaget, Whorf[80] or Vernon.[81]. The results suggest that the young child responds equally well to a different orientation because he ignores it, and not because he is superior in responding to disorientation.

If we come back to White's analysis of the five- to seven-year-group, we see further evidence of important changes occurring at this time. The correlation of IQ tests given at these ages reaches its maximum predictability (·70s) with later IQ tests.[82] This suggests that development approximates to later functioning more significantly at this stage. It is also at this stage that the child learns to plan, becomes increasingly capable of abstract behaviour, and makes increasing use of verbal mediation for learning and problem-solving. Even the types of word associations change. Younger children tend to give associations which are phrase completions, while older children can associate freely according to parts of speech, that is noun to noun, adjective to adjective and so forth. White concludes that the period from five to seven seems to be modal for most of these transitions.[83] However, the age range at which these changes take place encompasses three to eight years, depending on other variables including sex, socio-economic class, intelligence and differences in test procedures.

UNIVERSALITY OF LANGUAGE DEVELOPMENT

Language development seems to follow the same pattern regardless of nationality, socio-economic background, and even physical handicaps such as blindness or deafness.[84-88]

Slobin[89] has studied linguistic development in a variety of cultures and social settings. In all of them the child has acquired basic grammatical operations by the age of four. In all of them the sequencing, which we previously described, is the same: namely, the process of saying simple words, then two- and three-word sentences, and so on to more complex speech. In all of them it seems that the child has difficulty at the two-word stage in using his word-knowledge to create three-word sentences. Slobin and his coworkers feel reasonably certain about the generality of their conclusions since their data comes from at least eighteen different languages, some of which, like Finnish, belong to a different language group altogether from the Indo-European languages such as English, German and Russian.

Although the basic pattern is universal, there are some differences in the rate at which children acquire language in different countries, because the grammatical structures differ. For example, it takes a German child longer than a Russian to learn correct endings to his words, because that part of German grammar is more complex than the Russian counterpart. Furthermore, those who learn a Indo-European language generally take longer to learn prepositions showing locations, such as *on*, *in* and *under*, than those who learn Hungarian and Turkish where the location is attached to the end of the noun, and case endings express locations.

Despite such minor differences, basic rules recur in varying degrees in all languages. This means that different languages can be learned with the same ease by all children. In many cultures it is the child's peers and not the mother from whom the child learns language, yet this does not seem to affect development negatively since the sequences and speed of learning seem similar.

Besides, even in those cultures where mothers actively speak to their children, such as middle-class America, the mother does not spend a great deal of time correcting the child's grammar. Most of her corrections are aimed at the truth of the child's speech rather than at its grammatical correctness.[89] (As we shall see later, there are interesting exceptions to this finding: parents react differently to their autistic child's speech than to the speech of their normal offspring.[90]) Thus it makes no difference whether the child comes from a home where the emphasis is on learning and the parents have a broad educational background, or from a poverty-stricken environment where the parents lack formal education: the course of development in a normally functioning child remains the same.

Although the normal course of language development is the same for different languages and cultures, however, the end product of linguistic ability and facility is significantly influenced by factors external and internal to the child. External factors include socio-economic status, cultural values, and parental attitudes. Internal factors include attention, impulsivity and memory, and all are complexly interrelated.

Sex could be included under external as well as internal factors, since sex differencies have their source in culture, heredity, or a combination of both. The complex interrelationships need not concern us here, except for one important sex difference directly related to language, namely verbal competence. At all stages of the developmental period females generally exceed males in verbal competence, except for verbal abstract thinking.[91]

EXTERNAL FACTORS INFLUENCING LANGUAGE DEVELOPMENT

Lesser[92] studied children from four cultural groups at two social class levels in New York City, and found some interesting differences. Chinese performed better in tasks of spatial competence, while Jewish children performed better on tasks of verbal abilities. Both were generally superior to Blacks and Puerto Ricans on other tasks. In all cases, the middle class from each of the four cultural groups did far better than their working class 'cultural' peers.

Possibly differences in attitudes towards book learning affected the differential competencies of these groups.

Many investigators[93, 94] report cognitive and linguistic deficits among the socially disadvantaged, and in some cases attribute the deficit to lack of stimulation. Bernstein[94] found that lower and working-class children in the United States and in England showed 'impoverished' verbal expression in comparison with the standard English used by the middle-class child. He argues that the 'impoverished' speech child has access to the same words, but does not make use of them in the same way. Others have shown that regardless of class, complexity of speech increases as the child gets older. Nonetheless, middle-class children remain consistently ahead of the lower and working-class ones.[95]

Much of the so-called impoverished verbal expression and/or cognitive deficit of the disadvantaged and/or lower-class child may reflect different competencies which this child has in contrast to the middle-class child. The disadvantaged and/or lower-class child is generally not measured on competencies peculiar to his group, but peculiar to the middle-class. If he is verbally facile in his dialect but not in standard English, then his test results may suffer if the tests emphasise standard English.

An interesting cross-cultural study reported by Kagan and Klein[96] emphasises that children in different cultures may show cognitive competencies at different ages. They contrasted the development of children in a small Guatemalan village with children in an American city. The Guatemalan children lagged significantly behind their North American peers when very young, but caught up with them by the age of eleven.

INTERNAL FACTORS INFLUENCING LANGUAGE DEVELOPMENT

In normal children one is not overly concerned about language development since it seems to occur predictably, sequentially, and naturally, unless the child is in some way prevented from learning. However, children who have problems in learning language and who do not develop normally, need special training.

In those cases, we are particularly concerned with aspects of responsiveness within the child which may help or hinder language development. Factors within the child include 'egocentrism', attention, impulsivity, response to irrelevant stimuli, verbal control of behaviour, memory capacity, intelligence and age. We will not discuss age separately because it is interwoven with the other factors and so will be considered with them.

'Egocentrism'

The child's ability to communicate with others is hampered not only by his incomplete command of the language, but also by what Piaget calls egocentrism. Egocentrism in this case means that the child expresses himself and describes things from his point of view without considering the point of view of the listener. Therefore, much of what appears perfectly clear to the child, may be totally obscure to his listener.

A study illustrating this type of response was done by Krauss and Glucksberg.[97] Two children were seated at a table with a screen between them. Each had an identical set of blocks with abstract drawings on them. Child A was asked to describe a drawing so that child B could pick it out on the basis of the verbal description. Young children did not do well on this task. For example, a little boy labelled one drawing 'the sheet'. This description was perfectly clear to him from an egocentric point of view, for it reminded him of his wrinkled bedsheet when he got out of bed in the morning. The description made no sense to his partner who had no clue as to which drawing represented 'the sheet'. It is only when the child reaches the age of about thirteen, that he can describe with sufficient accuracy for the other person to understand what he means. At this point descriptions are no longer egocentric, but instead consider the level of understanding of the listener.[98]

Most recently Krauss and Glucksberg[99] concluded that the concept of egocentrism is insufficient to explain the child's behaviour. Instead of the child's inability to consider the other's point of view, it may be that he cannot do a task which is too complex. Regardless of what explanatory labels are used, we can see that the child has trouble in explaining things to others.

Despite such egocentric or idiosyncratic descriptions, and despite gaps in understanding and communication ability, the child does express himself fairly well by the age of four to five and, as noted before, has learned most of the underlying grammatical rules of his language.

Attention, irrelevant stimuli and impulsivity

The motivation, and ability, to sustain attention are crucial to learning, problem-solving and cognition. Attention involves orientation, selection, and maintenance of attention. An infant can gaze fixedly at objects for up to several minutes. Provided the stimuli are sufficiently interesting, most two-year-olds show some measure of sustained attention and inhibition of inappropriate responses on a variety of tasks. They can find a hidden object, inhibit false starts, and maintain interest in the task at hand.

Nonetheless younger children, like retardates and most autistic, have difficulty in paying sufficiently long attention and in tuning out irrelevant stimuli.[100-104] They tend to be undiscriminating and to respond unselectively to many different stimuli, whether they are relevant or not. Therefore young children, autistics and retardates, are often labelled 'distractible'. We, and probably the reader, have seen this sort of distractibility many a time where a totally unconnected and irrelevant stimulus takes the child's attention away from the task at hand. If we ask the child to follow a command, or respond to a question, we may get only a fitful reply as he busily turns towards a different sound source such as a voice, a train dashing by, or the rustle of leaves against a window pane.

Gollin[104] compared eight-year-olds with adults on tasks requiring them to choose whether two forms were the same or different. When the forms were composed of a regular arrangement of tacks, the children did as well as adults. However, if larger tacks were interspersed among the others, the adults readily ignored the irrelevant, distracting information, while the children did not. Additional studies by Gollin[105] and others show that the younger child is consistently more distracted by irrelevant stimuli than is the older child.

Despite distractibility, the young normal child can block out monotonous and unattractive irrelevant stimuli, like the noise of a typewriter.[106] Autistic children also often block out noises but in an erratic and peculiar manner. At times they appear extremely sensitive to slight noises and cower at the drop of a pin. At other times they appear completely unresponsive even to very loud sounds, such as a gun fired close to their head.[107]

As the normal child gets older, he learns to be quite selective in tuning out irrelevant stimuli and paying attention to relevant ones. Alternatively, if he is younger he can learn to pay better attention, provided he is given specific task instructions,[108] or the task cues are designed to stand out very clearly.

In addition to being distracted by irrelevant stimuli, the young child finds it difficult to attend if many different stimuli are shown at the same time. Consequently he may ignore important cues which could be helpful in problem solving, and he may make hasty judgements. Thus instead of considering a number of hypotheses and choosing the most reasonable, he may impulsively choose the first one that comes to mind, or he may respond to the stimulus which stands out most clearly in a particular situation. As a result the young child often comes up with the wrong answer.

Kagan and his coworkers[109-113] looked at impulsivity/reflectivity within and across age groups. As the child's age increases from six to about nine years, he responds more slowly on certain tasks. The slower response does not mean lesser competence. On the contrary, it shows greater reflectivity, i.e. the child is less impulsive in giving answers. Consequently, he makes fewer errors as he gets older. Nonetheless, individual differences in responsiveness remain, so that one can separate the impulsive from the reflective child even when he is older.

Characteristics of the impulsive child include a tendency to respond faster, scan the environment less carefully, come from the lower class, and have less motivation to inhibit responses. By contrast, the reflective child responds fairly consistently all the time, tends to play with toys longer, and seeks less physical contact.

Verbal control over behaviour

Adults regulate their own and others' behaviour by means of language. They can give themselves a series of instructions such as setting a daily schedule, or 'if-then' statements of the order : 'If it rains, I'll stay home and read. If not, I'll play tennis.' Adults can also ask others to follow their instructions.

Children learn to do the same as they get older. When very young they can use speech to initiate behaviour, but cannot use speech to regulate behaviour until they are around four years old. At that age speech is only one of a number of stimuli having such regulatory power. The school-age child has advanced significantly further, for he is beginning to develop inner speech, meaning that he can 'think words' and can separate 'meaning from explicit pronunciation'.[114] In other words, once inner speech develops, the child can give himself verbal instructions and regulate his own behaviour.

Luria's[115] analyses show that around twenty months the child has an orienting response to language, i.e. he attends to spoken words. When he is somewhat older, verbal instructions seem to make him continue to do what he had originally intended to do. At the next stage, he responds by obeying simple commands. At the most advanced level he can give himself verbal instruction. A two-and-a-half-year-old can obey a simple command such as, 'Press the bulb when the red light comes on', but he does not wait for the light. A three-year-old can wait for the light, but cannot handle the complex instruction : 'Press the bulb when the red light comes on, but do not press if a green light comes on.' The six-year-old is advanced enough to handle this instruction. He can solve both parts of the problem; which means that he can both give appropriate responses and inhibit inappropriate ones, if necessary.

Memory

Part of the child's difficulty in using language to control his and others' behaviour lies not only in incomplete linguistic and cognitive development, but also in limitations on memory.[116-118] Memory is generally conceived in terms of two storage systems : long-term and short-term. Long-term memory, LTM, refers to an enduring system of filing information which may be coded verbally, pictorially, symbolically etc. The limits of how long and how much can be filed is presently unknown, although factors such as filing strategies, intelligence, age and trauma have their effects.

The phenomenal capacity and enduringness of LTM becomes evident under hypnosis in which a person recalls vast amounts of material from long ago. Reminiscences without hypnosis may also be impressive, especially if they come from the very old, who hark back to their early childhoods.

In short-term memory, STM, information can be held only for a few seconds. If it is not transferred to long-term memory storage within that time, the information is lost. Furthermore, STM storage is limited in the amount of information it can hold at one time.

Limitations in capacity, organisational abilities, and strategies of learning and retrieval from memory, affect memory processes.

Adults can hold seven (plus or minus two) chunks of information at a time in STM,[119] where the chunks can be unrelated one-digit numbers, randomly selected words, or meaningful groups. The young child's STM capacity is significantly lower, with one study placing it in the range of two to three chunks of information for a preschooler, to about five chunks for a seven-year-old.[120] Others report that by five and a half, the child's capacity is already close to the adult's.[121]

Adults tend to organise information for both STM and LTM storage, for the simple reason that one can hold far more information if it is organised according to some system. Mnemonic devices are good examples of such organisation. Thus, it is far easier to remember one's licence plates if they are composed of one's initials, age, or weight, than if one has to memorise a random series.

Initially, the child does not have adequate organisational strategies, and does not remember any better regardless of whether he is encouraged to do so or not.[122]

By contrast the adult imposes his own strategies. If he wants to hold information longer in STM, he repeats and rehearses until the information is used, or is transferred to long-term memory.

When labelling, or rehearsing aloud, is externally imposed by the teacher, the younger child does improve on recall.[123] Furthermore, the young as well as the retarded can perform at higher levels provided that the teacher shows them how to use meaningful categories and how to organise their responses.[124]

By the age of five or six, the child begins to devise his own learning and recall strategies which are then generally more effective than those externally imposed. On the other hand, he still has difficulties in integrating a large number of items. Thus the five-year-old can do well if he needs to take only one conceptual step between the stimulus he is given and the response he must make, or if he has only to make a simple object identification.[125]

Short-term memory seems to increase with age, education and intelligence. This can be seen on tests measuring digit span, i.e. the number of digits a person can repeat immediately after hearing them.[126] However, experiments which don't depend on retrieval and retention suggest that STM superiority for the older or more intelligent person may be due to superior learning and/or retrieval strategies, rather than problems with memory per se.[127] Such superiority also seems to hold for long-term memory.

Intelligence

The factor of intelligence has played an integral part in our discussions of other (internal) factors influencing language development. A favourite and reliable test is the vocabulary test which is part of many standardised and well-known tests of intelligence, such as the Stanford-Binet and Wechsler tests for adults and children (WAIS and WISC). A test of vocabulary is often used to obtain a quick, rough index of intelligence, other factors being equal. Certainly we could list nonlanguage tests, or parts of tests, which could also give a measure of intelligence. However, the point is that, for years, a standard accepted measure of intelligence has been derived by measuring facility in language.

In this chapter we briefly discussed normal developmental

sequences, stages of language acquisition, competencies, and factors which may indirectly affect language functioning. The more we know what to expect from the child (normal and handicapped) the more readily we can gear our teaching to his level of competence.

3: Brain and Language Impairment

'Marr swelled with speech unuttered.' B. A. Williams, *Coconuts*, 1962.
'Silence after silence strangled my voice . . .' Carlos Pellicer, *Sketches for a Tropical Ode*, 1967.

We discussed previously how language develops exponentially for normal children, and how they pick up language 'naturally' without requiring any special efforts to teach them. We also emphasised that this is not the case for such as the retarded, autistic, aphasic, cerebral palsied, and others showing developmental delays in which language impairment is an obvious handicap. What characterises these groups and what can we say about their developmental processes?

In the present chapter we shall look at the linguistic and cognitive deficits of such handicapped groups. In the process, we shall also consider normal and abnormal brain functioning. Some background in these areas will help us clarify causes and effects in relation to language impairment, and suggest appropriate rehabilitative teaching approaches.

NORMAL BRAIN FUNCTIONING:

Much of what we know regarding normal brain functioning is actually based on injuries to the brain,[1-6] although recently findings have also been deduced from the non-injured brain and include special techniques involving listening, vision, and injecting drugs into the brain.[7-9]

What happens when specific parts of the brain are destroyed? If destruction leads to loss of specific functions, this suggests that such functions are localised. If, instead, destruction leads to equal functional loss regardless of where injury occurs, this type of functioning is labelled equipotential.[10]* A third possibility is that destruction does not seem to affect functioning. This may be so if testing is inadequate, or if there is holographic representation in the brain. Just as only one small part of a holographic picture can evoke the whole scene, holographic brain representation means that even if some areas of the brain are destroyed, other areas still faithfully represent the whole function or behaviour. Pribram suggests that this type of representation occurs for perceived images.[11]

The issue is not totally resolved, and this is partly because our knowledge of brain functioning comes not only from humans, but also from animals at lower levels of the evolutionary scale. Nonetheless, there is firm evidence for both localisation and overall representation. The recent conclusions of John[12] are relevant. He suggests that a good part of the brain is involved in all processes, although some parts may be more specifically involved than others in a particular process. Indeed, Gazzaniga talks of cerebral functions as being in

> dynamic relation with other cerebral sites . . . a variety of spheres . . . influence . . . the brain, some overlapping with functions of others . . . all interacting in a dynamic way to produce a final integrated behavioural response.[13]

These views seem reasonable, for they can explain both localisation and equipotentiality. They can also explain why some people with brain injuries seem to recover all, or nearly all, of their functions, while others do not.

What evidence do we have of the effects of specific injuries? Although aphasia (speech disorder due to brain damage) has been the object of study since ancient times, it was only about a hundred years ago that its connection with brain injury to one half of the brain was conclusively shown by Paul Broca.[14] He found that injury to specific areas (generally in the left half), resulted in aphasia, while injury to corresponding areas in the opposite half (generally the right), did not disturb language ability.

---

* Although this theory has been criticised, Lashley showed evidence for equipotential functioning in rat vision in the 1920s.

Damage to Broca's area leads to specific type(s) of speech impairment. The person shows great difficulty in articulating, and his speech is slow and expressed like a telegram. Geschwind reports that when a patient with this type of damage is asked to describe a trip, the best he can manage is 'Go . . . New York'.[15] However, language comprehension remains intact. By contrast, damage to Wernicke's area (named after another important nineteenth century investigator) leaves fluency, articulation and grammar intact, but speech content and comprehension are impaired. Here the person may use circumlocutions like 'what you use to cut with' when he cannot remember the word for 'knife', or he may use substitutions like 'knife' or 'fork'.

Development of specialisation

To get a clearer view of the brain in relation to the rest of the body, we shall remind the reader that we are bilaterally symmetrical in many ways. Arms, legs, eyes, ears and cerebral hemispheres come in sets of twos, and are arranged symmetrically across a central axis. Even our single appendages are generally symmetrically distributed.

Each half of the brain largely controls sensation and movement on the opposite side of the body. Thus, a massive stroke to the left hemisphere generally paralyses the right side. The case for vision is somewhat more complex since information from the left half of the retina of each eye goes to the left hemisphere, while that for the right half of each retina goes to the right hemisphere.

The two hemispheres are largely symmetrical, undifferentiated and unspecialised in young children but, with time, brain functions diverge and one brain half generally assumes dominance over the other. It naturally follows that, as dominance increases, there is also an increase in differentiation and lateralisation, i.e. one side of the body dominates over the other.

The process of dominance and lateralisation is associated with the development of language and hand preference. Handedness begins around the age of two and is thought to be completed by three to six years of age.[16, 17] As differentiation proceeds further, speech functions become localised, and usually in the left hemisphere. We say usually because there are exceptions in which there is either no dominance or reverse dominance (see later discussion).

According to Vogel and Broverman,[18] relative lack of differentiation and dominance is the case not only in young children, but also in the retarded, the brain damaged, and in impaired geriatric patients. Brain wave readings from the visual cortex of these groups have been most successfully correlated with intelligence in those subjects whose cognitive and, presumably, brain functions are relatively undifferentiated.

Relative lack of differentiation is evident in the young child's lack of hand preference, and this has probably been observed by most parents. Further evidence comes from the fact that if the left hemisphere is damaged before the child starts to speak, the right takes over the language function.[19]

Nonetheless, some differentiation between hemispheres does exist shortly after birth. Molfese[20] found that the left hemisphere in forty-eight-hour old infants responded more strongly to speech sounds, while their right hemisphere responded more strongly to non-speech sounds.

The ultimately dominant hemisphere becomes generally the more differentiated and specialised one. This is deduced from a variety of findings, including that brain injuries to specific areas of the left hemisphere seem to impair specific tasks, while injuries to the right hemisphere do not have this specific effect.[21]

We agree with most other investigators that hemispheric specialisation is a uniquely human attribute, although there have been some reports of some degree of specialisation in lower animals.[22, 23]

How do the two halves interact? The case of the split brain

Instead of taking the accepted view that one hemisphere is dominant over the other, some like Bakan[24] and Zangwill[25a, b] suggest that a double dominance model makes more sense. This means that each hemisphere could play a different role depending on the functions involved, such as musical intonation, comprehension of written language, or speech production. Such a view makes good sense, since there are functions which are unique to each hemisphere as well as others which are held in common by both hemispheres.

Within the last two decades Sperry, Gazzaniga[26-34] and their coworkers have added enormously to our knowledge of brain functioning in relation to language and thinking. Much of their original findings were based on work with 'split-brain' patients, first with cats and monkeys, later with humans.

In Myers and Sperry's classic experiment on the cat, they showed what happens when a brain is, quite literally, split. They cut most of the connections which serve to transmit messages between the two hemispheres: the corpus callosum, the optic chiasm, and the anterior commissure. The operated cat was then taught a visual discrimination task with one eye covered. When the cat was retested on this well-learned task by means of the untrained eye, it could not perform the task. The latter had been learned by one half of the brain but, because the connections had been cut, the other half had no idea at all of what had been learned. Yet if the connections had not been cut, the untrained eye would have responded just as accurately, because the information would have been transmitted from one half of the brain to the other.

The findings from the split-brain humans were even more interesting and complex. Patients with intractable epileptic seizures had their brains sectioned in a similar manner to the cat, in order to prevent the spread of abnormal brain waves. The operation was a success. Patients had fewer seizures and they appeared normal to their friends and relations. However, specific tests revealed peculiar responses which have helped enormously to clarify the roles of the two halves.

By their disability these patients showed that messages cross from one side of the brain to the other. Furthermore the messages, which travel via the corpus callosum, integrate the functioning of the two brain halves so that a normal person knows what is happening with a unified sense of consciousness.

Simple but ingenious experiments were designed to obtain information from one hemisphere at a time. Sperry took advantage of the previously noted fact that the nerves from the outer half

of the retina of each eye go to the same side of the brain where
the eye is located, while of the nerves from the inner, nasal, half
cross over to the opposite side of the brain. The patients were
shown pictures which were visible only to one half of each eye.
This meant that only one hemisphere would receive all the information coming from one half of an eye. The other half of the
brain remained in the dark and received no information, since the
split brain has no way of transmitting messages from one half to
the other.

The patients' responses clearly showed that there was no information crossing between the two halves. Their responses also
helped to clarify what the specialised functions of each half were.
If a picture of a woman was flashed to the left hemisphere, the
patient said : 'That is a woman.' If the picture was flashed only
to the right hemisphere, the patient said he saw nothing, because
the right hemisphere cannot communicate in the same way that
the left can, i.e. it can 'recognise' but cannot 'talk'.

The right understands simple instructions. If a picture of a
toothbrush is shown to the right hemisphere, and the patient is
asked to identify which object matches the picture, the patient's
left hand (which is controlled by the right hemisphere) correctly
finds the toothbrush from among a number of other objects. If
he holds a pencil in his right hand, he can describe it, but he cannot do so if it is in his left hand. Ornstein also reported[35, 36] that,
if the patient is right-handed, he can write with his right hand
but has difficulty with spatial tasks like drawing. This situation is
reversed if the patient uses his left hand. Interestingly enough,
because of the 'split', the patient can process more information
simultaneously than can a normal person.

These and numerous other examples show that the right hand
literally no longer knows what the left hand is doing, when information is no longer relayed across the corpus callosum. (There
are some exceptions, as we shall see later, since a small amount of
information does go through the lower brain stem.)

A further example showing how the two halves of the split
brain work in clearly separate ways comes from another of Sperry's
visual presentations, in which he flashed the word *heart* on a

screen. *Heart* can be broken up into two distinct words : *he* and *art*. If the *he* is flashed to the right hemisphere, and *art* to the left hemisphere, the patient can read the word *art* aloud, but not *he*. On the other hand, he can copy these words, one with each hand, with the information conveyed from the opposite hemisphere. At the same time, the split-brain patient cannot put the two words together to produce the single word which is so obvious to the rest of us.

The responses of split-brain patients have shown that the two hemispheres seem to have two separate systems and, in fact, two separate 'minds'. In the split brain, one side is unaware of the other, because the corpus callosum is not there to integrate the two sides. Gazzaniga thinks that the young child functions like a split brain patient because he does not have a functional callosum until the age of two. By that age, myelenisation (the development of the fatty sheath around the nerves) has become more or less complete here as well as elsewhere in the brain.

Other tests of hemispheric functioning
Further confirmation of obvious and more subtle hemispheric functioning comes from a variety of surgical as well as nonsurgical intervention techniques.

FINDINGS FROM SURGICAL INTERVENTION
A case reported by Zangwill[87] involved a patient whose dominant left hemisphere had been removed entirely. This man lost most of his ability to speak, but could still say 'yes' and 'no' correctly, and occasionally such phrases as 'Dammit, I can't'. At the same time, the man had fairly good receptive language and could follow simple instructions. He could read individual words, write his name with his left hand, and copy some letters and words. Zangwill deduced that all these abilities apparently resided in his still intact right hemisphere.

FINDINGS BY DRUG INTERVENTION
Brenda Milner and her coworkers[88-40] injected sodium amytal into the carotid artery which resulted in temporary loss of func-

tioning of the hemisphere located on the side of the injection. They confirmed that localisation of speech was in the dominant hemisphere and that dominance was related to handedness, but that nonetheless most right handers and the majority of left handers have the left as their dominant hemisphere.

DEDUCTIVE EXPERIMENTS
Z-lens, dichotic listening, eye movements, alpha waves, vision : *Z-lens* : Other experiments have included a variety of ingenious techniques. A recent one makes use of the Z-lens devised by Zaidel[41] which can be placed over the eye. The lens can relay information selectively to only one half of the brain by stimulating only half of one eye. This avoids the previously noted problem that each eye has nerve connections to both halves of the brain.

Dichotic listening : This technique presents sounds to each ear and takes advantage of the fact that auditory connections cross to opposite halves of the brain. Kimura[42] found that both normal and brain damaged people are more accurate in reporting digits heard from the right ear. Others[43, 44] have also shown a slight right ear advantage (in normal right handers) when stimuli are verbal. This is so because sounds directed to the right ear go directly to the verbal left hemisphere. Therefore, if the sounds are verbal, processing can take place as soon as they reach this (verbal) hemisphere. Alternatively, if a sentence is heard by the left ear, there is a slight delay of 20–50 milliseconds, since it must go from the right hemisphere to the left for processing. When other sounds are presented, such as a car starting, there is an advantage to the left ear since the opposite (right) hemisphere does the processing.

Eye movements : Interestingly enough, even eye movements give clues as to which hemisphere is actively involved in which functions.[45-48] Generally speaking, if a person is solving logical problems or problems involving language, the eyes move to the right, meaning that the left verbal hemisphere is being used. If a person is solving problems involving spatial perceptions, or if emotional and/or creative aspects are involved, the eyes move to the left, suggesting that the right hemisphere is being used.

Alpha waves: The particular brain wave called the alpha wave has added further useful information regarding brain functioning. Alpha suggests idling or a relative state of rest. Therefore differences in alpha between the two brain halves could tell us which half is more active for particular tasks. If a person is writing, alpha increases in the right half, since that half is idling and not involved in the task. If a person is arranging forms in space, alpha increases in the left half since it is not involved in the task. However, in general, the left is associated with a higher state of arousal and this has less alpha than the right.[49-50]

Vision: Even temporary or permanent loss of vision offers clues on functioning. If right-handed children are asked to draw geometric forms with both hands, they seem to perform better with the left when they are blindfolded. Apparently the latter lets the right hemisphere function without interference. The left hand is also superior in reading Braille, which again shows the dominance of the right hemisphere.[51]

Brain functioning and handedness

We have already given ample evidence that the major difference between the two hemispheres is that language and speech are generally associated with the left. We say generally because there are exceptions.[52, 53] Nearly all right handers and the majority of left handers have speech located in the left hemisphere. However, some lefties have speech located in the right, while others show diffuse organisation across both hemispheres.

Let us briefly summarise the function of each half.[54-60] The left hemisphere is dominant for : verbal and skilled tasks, integrating similar units, manual skills, the language skills of writing and speech, symbolism, and fine discrimination. In general, it is seen as the logical, sequential-processing, verbal, analysing half of the brain.

The right hemisphere is dominant for nonverbal tasks, for spatial perception and ability, and for perceptual motor activities. This includes recognition of melodies and visual/verbal material, body image, imagery and artistic talent. In general it is seen as the creative, intuitive, nonanalytical, nonsequential-processing half of the brain.

In addition, the right has some limited capacities for spoken and written language. It is better at copying geometric designs, i.e. the left hand does a better job at this than the right. In contrast, the right hand, i.e. the left hemisphere, copies cursive writing better. The right hemisphere also processes faces faster than the left. Because of specialisation, the hemisphere which is called into play sometimes depends on the person's interpretation of incoming information. For example, if he hears a sound he may respond with the right or left hemisphere depending on whether he is set to interpret the sound as linguistic or as non-linguistic.[61]

Formerly, handedness was simply seen as the reflection of brain dominance. Since the left side of the brain usually controls the muscles on the right side of the body and vice versa, it is easy to conclude that the right hander has a dominant left hemisphere, while the reverse is true for the left hander. This same division has also been assumed for language. More recent evidence[62, 63] shows that these deductions are nearly always correct for the right hander, but not nearly so predictable for the left- and mixed-hand preference individual. Indeed, as was mentioned previously, the majority of lefties also have speech in the left hemisphere.

In contrast to righties, more lefties and ambidextrous seem to have bilateral representation of speech. This is based on a number of findings:

Left-handed people with left temporal lobe lesions seem to have less difficulty with language after this damage than right-handed people, and furthermore, left handers recover more quickly.[64]

If one compares right- and left-handed college students on tests of intelligence, one finds that they have equal verbal IQs but that lefties have lower visual-spatial IQs. This finding led Levy and Miller to conclude that linguistic abilities are spread over both hemispheres in the left hander.[65] The implication then followed that in lefties language partly displaced spatial ability in the right hemisphere and accounted for the lower score.

Right-handed relatives of lefties will regain language faster after trauma.[66] We might guess that either these individuals show a brain organisation closer to that of their left-handed relatives, or that the righties were originally lefties who were forced into right handedness when they started school.

If a child is brain damaged, and the functions shift to the opposite side, this results in more lefties who were genetically programmed to be righties. Only about 12 per cent of the population is left handed. Interestingly enough, 16 per cent of epileptics are lefties, suggesting perhaps that they might have become right handed had they not sustained brain damage. The data on speech disorders is somewhat inconclusive. It is not yet known whether there are more lefties who are speech disordered than the general population of lefties would warrant. Aside from the relationship between handedness and brain dominance, other correlations, such as between handedness and IQ, have not been found.

Language, sex and dominance

Although sex differences in language and spatial ability have long been observed,[67, 68] it has not been clear whether these differences were cultural or constitutional.

The developing female is ahead of her male counterpart in verbal competence, except in verbal abstract thinking, but she is worse on tasks of spatial ability.[68] It has been conjectured that localisation for language is more diffuse in females,[69] which factor, like the example of the lefties given above, might lead to lower spatial ability. Yet the evidence is neither clear nor consistent.[70]

An elegant study by Waber[71] suggests why some of the confusion exists. She looked at females aged ten to thirteen years and males aged thirteen to sixteen years, and found that, regardless of sex, early maturing adolescents perform better on tests of verbal than spatial abilities. Late maturing subjects show opposing patterns and show more lateralisation for speech than those maturing earlier. Thus the sex differences in these behaviours are probably there because of differences in the distribution of sexes along the physiological continuum.

On the basis of her findings she concluded that sex differences in verbal and spatial abilities have different aetiologies and cannot be explained by a common set of causes, whether these are cultural or constitutional. Instead the rate of maturation seems to play an important role in the organisation of higher cortical functions. Thus sex has only a small influence in comparison with the maturation rate.

Although we, and others, have generally emphasised differences between right- and left-dominant and non-dominant hemispheres, in actuality this is probably a matter of degree. Despite different capabilities and localisations in the two hemispheres, we find that interdependence must be considered as an important aspect of brain functioning. This will become even more evident as we discuss brain impairment.

BRAIN IMPAIRMENT

Birch and Diller[72] carefully separate brain damage, which refers to anatomical destruction, from organicity, which is the observed functional impairment which may attend such destruction. They note the difficulty of determining brain damage from observing behaviour, because damage may result in two different kinds of behavioural change. In one case the change is subtractive and the deficiency does not lead to active interference, such as convulsions, perseverations (repetition of acts), or perceptual distortions. In the other case the change is additive, and the damage produces disturbances over and above the subtractive effects.

The effects of brain damage are quite different depending on the extent and locus of damage, as well as the age of onset. Behavioural effects can include poor speech, stereotyped and perserverative behaviour, difficulties in dealing with abstract concepts, as well as impaired learning, memory, comprehension and motor performance.

Locus of injury

Specific injuries to the brain result in specific disfunctions. These can involve the ability to: control eye movements; coordinate eye with hand movements; understand meanings of words or letters; and integrate actions into appropriate or meaningful sequences.[73] We mentioned previously the effects of lesions in Broca's and Wernicke's areas. Many other disabilities can arise in various combinations, depending on the type of lesions.

The effect of lesions on an adult can be more or less devastating, depending not only on locus and extent, but also on the person's profession. A lesion to the right hemisphere affects the artist (painter) in a peculiar way. The lesion does not stop artistic creativity, but there is a loss of contours and placement of details. Gardner[74] cites the interesting case of a well known German artist who had such a lesion. For months thereafter he painted faces with the left part missing. On the other hand, lesions to the verbal, left hemisphere would affect a writer or speaker more severely.

Age of onset of brain damage

If there is left hemispheric brain damage or loss before the onset of speech, the right can take over speech, as well as reading and writing functions. At this level the prognosis is good, because the hemispheres have not yet differentiated, and damage does not create the catastrophic effects which occur at a later age. If lesions occur after the onset of speech, but before the age of ten, there may be some aphasia. If a child has temporal lobe damage, he rarely has difficulties with speech and comprehension, in contrast to the adult.[75] If brain injury is early enough, the child does not show the differential pattern of impairment seen in adult brain damage, nor does he show the hyperactivity, impulsivity, and distractability which are often distinguishing characteristics of brain damage.

Nonetheless, damage does result in generalised perceptual and cognitive defects.[76] and left-sided lesions before the age of two have 'worse consequences for language development' than right-sided lesions.[77] Indeed, Boll[78] found few if any areas of functioning in which a child with brain damage equalled the performance of a normal child. He compared normals with children damaged at birth, between the ages of two and four years, and between the ages of four and seven years and found, strangely enough, that the longer the child has to develop normally prior to brain damage, the less damaging is the trauma. This is in complete contrast to the general finding that, where the brain is undeveloped, damage has a less negative effect than later. In another study[79] Boll found that these children were impaired on tests of concept formation, perception and motor speed.

Despite the effects of damage, one can also marvel at the enormous plasticity of the body. Gazzaniga reported how split-brain patients got cues as to what was happening in the other half of the brain, despite loss of the corpus callosum. They cleverly adapted to their loss by getting cues from head movements.

Another interesting case was reported by Goleman.[80] A girl had paralysis and poor vision when she was five. At the age of nine she developed epilepsy, and at the age of twenty her right hemisphere was removed. Remarkably enough she recovered from her paralysis and showed no loss of vision in the left visual field, which would ordinarily be associated with the right hemisphere. Evidently the other half of the brain was able to carry out the functions of both halves.

ABNORMAL COURSE OF LANGUAGE DEVELOPMENT

In trying to teach alternate modes of language communication, we need to consider the types of population with which we are dealing. If one suspects that there may be differences in the ability to profit from experience, in learning rates and abilities, in comprehension, perception and so on, one needs to know how these children or adults differ from the normal population. Knowing the differences among various diagnostic and/or behavioural groups is important because it enables one to tailor teaching techniques to fit the individual. In this way one can maximise the learning process, even though handicaps exist.

Language impairment and other problems may have a variety of causes, and appear in different diagnostic categories. When a child shows deficits in language and cognition we in effect have the learning disabled child, who pops up in a variety of diagnostic categories. Impaired language is a characteristic of sub-groups within specific diagnostic categories. It can include those with early or later brain damage, and those who show no provable signs of such damage. The latter include psychotics, people with environmental deprivation, the deaf who may be mute, the autistic, the retarded, the cerebral palsied with language difficulties, and other developmentally disabled, such as the retardates.

Deficits found within these categories sometimes appear the same, and often appear to overlap. Nonetheless, one can distinguish different types of deficits associated with the linguistic and cognitive problems of the various groups and sub-groups.

Some individuals show an overall developmental lag : linguistically, cognitively, motorically etc. This is generally more true of retardates. Others show more lag in language than would be predicted from their mental age. This may be true of any of the handicapped.

There are some who instead of developmental delays, show deviant language and/or cognition in acquisition, reception, and expression. Hermelin and O'Connor[81] have shown evidence for deviant language development in the autistic child, while Tallal[82, 83] has shown such deviance in aphasics, with the cause in the latter seemingly linked to auditory sequencing problems.

Lastly some cases of defective language are due to an interaction of factors mentioned in the previous chapter. Language and cognitive development do not occur in a void. Other factors which may help or hinder—depending on whether development is appropriate, or delayed and/or impaired—include strategies of acquisition (i.e. learning) and retrieval (from memory storage), attention, distractability and perceptual problems. Perhaps a delay in acquisition means impairment, not only because the child lags behind his contemporaries and becomes progressively more so, but also because he has lower motivation, practices less or has less adequate learning techniques. Perhaps, too, the time is no longer ripe for full language learning, i.e. he has passed the critical phase for facile language acquisition. In our experience with retardates, particularly lower-functioning ones, we have seen how consistently low motivation, distractability and inefficient learning strategies operate detrimentally.

There are cases where bright children develop language far later than is considered the norm, like Virginia Woolf and Albert Einstein. Generally however, when language develops significantly late, this is a cause for concern because it is tied in with other developmental abnormalities.

A child with language impairment has difficulty organising materials.[84] The defect has a cumulative effect, so that, like the Queen in *Alice in Wonderland*, the faster he runs the behinder he will be in comparison with his normal peers. The latter will forge progressively further ahead since they can handle competently more information at one time.

Language impairment and individual diagnostic categories

Many of the observed behaviours overlap across different diagnostic groups, partly because some of the same behaviours have different causes, partly because the categories themselves are not precisely delineated nor necessarily exclusive. For example a retarded child may also show autistic behaviours, and be brain damaged as well, and an aphasic person would, by definition, also be brain damaged.

We will describe briefly some of the categories of handicap which could benefit most from learning a symbol system, either as an alternate language, or as a stimulus to language development. These categories include: brain damage, cerebral palsy, aphasia, deafness, autism and mental retardation.

The reader will notice that more space has been devoted to the autistic and retarded, for whom we feel the symbol system can be most fruitfully applied. Greater detail will help the teacher know what responses to expect, as well as suggest teaching approaches which consider strengths and weaknesses.

BRAIN DAMAGE

As we have seen, this term encompasses much. The behaviours

observed as associated with brain damage can vary radically, depending on extent and locus of damage, age of onset of damage, and so forth. Nonetheless, there are certain characteristics which generally describe this population.

According to Mittler[85] the primary behaviour syndrome of the brain damaged is their distractibility. Other behaviours may also be observed to a greater or lesser extent.

First, and this is part of their distractibility, all stimuli excite them equally. Instead of paying selective attention, they respond with equal attention to events of unequal importance, for instance to the voice of a person, the sound of a distant train, or the scratching of a pen.

Second, there is perseveration, in which the person continues a behaviour even after it is no longer meaningful. For example, if he is asked to copy a brief series of dots, he will keep on and on copying dots unless told to stop. We have often seen this type of behaviour. Sometimes asking the child to stop is sufficient, while at other times we literally have to take the pencil away to have them stop.

Other characteristics may include low frustration tolerance, poor motor control, hypo- or hyperactivity, emotional and social ineptness, overresponse to stimuli, and inability to combine elements meaningfully.

Last, language may be impaired. This may include poor to no speech, inability to understand or use language for thinking, automatic speech, or communication by singing rather than speech.

APHASIA

The aphasic has a speech disorder due to brain damage rather than to defective hearing or speech mechanisms. Aphasics seem to be impaired in their ability to understand word order.[86] Yet this is not an exclusive problem with them. More importantly they have very specific impairment with respect to auditory stimuli.

Tallal and Piercy[87, 88] compared twelve childhood developmental aphasics with normal children on auditory perception. The aphasics had no hearing problem, but they had great difficulties in discriminating sound quality, as well as in perceiving the order of rapidly presented auditory stimuli, such as vowels and consonants.

The impairment in perceiving order showed up consistently. Aphasics did worse when stimulus exposure time was shorter and there was a smaller time interval between stimuli. They could process two- and three-element sequences at slow presentation rates of 200 milliseconds, but they could not do this when presentation rates were faster. By contrast, normal speech is 80 milliseconds per phoneme, and normal people can readily process this information when it is given at that speed.

The impairment in discrimination of sound quality did not show up when vowels were presented, since they by their nature last longer, i.e. 250 milliseconds, but it showed up with stop consonants which lasted only 43 milliseconds. However, it was possible to get the aphasics to discriminate correctly, if there was an artificial stretching of consonant transition from 43 to 95 milliseconds. Tallal therefore concluded that these deficits underlie the aphasics' impaired development of speech. This is an extremely important finding, since it suggests that ordinary speech therapy and language training would be useless with such children.

CEREBRAL PALSY

The cerebral palsied are brain damaged in the areas which control and coordinate muscles. Consequently there is characteristic nerve and muscle malfunctioning. Sometimes this disability is visible only in the person's somewhat awkward gait. But usually there are other accompanying handicaps, such as epileptic seizures, and varying degrees of impairment in hearing, seeing, learning and speech.

Because the disabilities are extremely frustrating even in the mundane aspects of everyday living, the cerebral palsied often show psychological and behavioural problems as well.

Estimates of the incidence of cerebral palsy in the United States range from 0·6 to 3·5 per 1,000 in the population.* Of these about

* In UK the estimate for cerebral palsied children is between 2·0 and 3·0 per 1,000, according to Mr. James Loring, Director of The Spastics Society, speaking to the International Cerebral Palsy Society Conference, University College, Oxford, on 31 March 1977.

25 per cent have problems in vision, and a somewhat larger percentage have impaired hearing. Most importantly for our discussion, about 80 per cent have speech impairment, of which 20 per cent are unable to speak at all. Furthermore, a far higher percentage of cerebral palsied are retarded than is true of the general population. In the latter, 3·5 per cent are retarded, in contrast to 60 per cent retardation among the cerebral palsied.[89]

DEAFNESS

By definition, the deaf are always language impaired in terms of speech, although they may have good receptive and written language. In addition, many learn to communicate by means of sign language.

The deaf develop concepts at a slower rate than hearing subjects.[90] This information is neither new nor surprising. Many others, such as Furth[91], have found this delayed acquisition of concepts. However, we must remain aware of the problem since delay in conceptual development is accompanied by delay in language development. This was confirmed in a study by Jarvella and Lubinsky[92] who found that the language of eight to eleven year-olds was like that of a much younger nondeaf normal child. The deaf tended to respond to most multiple clause sentences as though the events were to be understood in the order in which they were mentioned. Language delay in the deaf occurs for a variety of reasons, including lack of auditory feedback (since the child cannot hear), and lag in conceptual development.

AUTISM

Many kinds of behaviours and characteristics have been associated with autism.[93-96] The child generally looks normal and physically healthy, has good motor coordination, memory and spatial ability, and responds well to nonverbal tasks. However, he shows bizarre behaviours, as well as language impairment. Formerly parents were told that faulty upbringing, or genetic predisposition, caused the child's autism. The present trend is to avoid the problem of causation, and instead look at how maladaptive behaviours can be appropriately managed and how learning can be facilitated.

Bizarre behaviours may include the presence of one or more of the following in a particular child : detachment from others in the sense of appearing physically and emotionally uninvolved; insistence on sameness; inappropriate response to sensory stimuli; head banging; bizarre play; staring at lights; spinning; rocking; stereotyped behaviour; obsession with mechanical objects; and repetitive purposeless behaviour, including hand movements.

Again some of these behaviours are not exclusive to the autistic. For example, repetitive behaviour has also been found with blind and deaf children.[97-99] Furthermore, self-stimulatory behaviour such as rocking and head banging may be seen in young normal children, but only if they have nothing better to do. In contrast, the autistic will self-stimulate themselves even when there are toys available.

About 75 per cent are self-destructive and of these 25 per cent require restraints to prevent injuries. Half of the autistic are mute; others are echolalic, i.e. they have only mimicking or echoing speech; and all show language problems. Although autism has been shown to be present with any level of intelligence, most of the children have an IQ below 60, and one third seem to have some central nervous system damage.[100] The disability strikes more boys than girls, and decreases with increasing age. If the IQ is at least 60 and the child develops language before the age of five, then there is a fair prognosis, even though only 15 per cent actually make good social adjustment later on.[101, 102]

Most investigators report that the autistic respond more to objects than to people, but Hermelin and O'Connor disagree.[103] Instead they found that autistics generally have a lower level of responsiveness, in comparison with other groups such as retardates and normals. Hence the autistic are seemingly less responsive to people, not because they have a peculiar aversion to people, but because their overall level of responsiveness is less. In short, in contrast to others who assume that these children suffer from over-arousal, Hermelin and O'Connor guess that the children suffer from under-arousal.

Possibly because of this under-arousal they show defects in both visual and auditory processing. The reader may recall our previous statement that such children may ignore the sound of a gun shot, or alternatively cover their ears at the drop of a pin.

They tend to prefer proximal receptors (tactual and kinaesthetic), and rely more on perceptual activities than on perceptual analysis. Although there are similar tendencies for younger children, the autistic are less able to use alternate strategies when visual information must be used, and they show shorter visual inspection time. These findings are interesting since vision precedes tactual discrimination in development. Thus the autistic's response may actually be a deviant one rather than representing a lag in development.

In visual motor discrimination the autistic rely primarily on distinctiveness of motor stimuli, and in fact cannot solve problems without such motor cues. This disability indicates a real defect in classifying and integrating visually presented information, and shows up in their inability to arrange squares of different sizes in sequential order. In turn, sequential ordering problems show up in their language problems.

Many autistics are mute. Others show varying degrees of speech facility. Where speech is developed, it is generally impaired and tends to be concrete, literal, metaphoric and echolalic. Errors in speech are distinctly different from those of retardates and normals, and language is often distorted so that the order of object and subject is reversed. Even more typical is the reversal of the pronouns *I* and *you*, so that the question, 'Do you want candy?', or the statement, 'You want milk,' may also stand for, 'I want candy' and, 'I want milk.' This strange behaviour has been explained by assuming that the autistic are unaware of their identity. Our experience and that of Park[104] and Schreibman[105] suggest that the reversals more likely represent echolalic responses.

Park carefully observed and reported the first eight years of her autistic daughter. Elly could originally neither understand nor speak. Her family taught her by touch, since she was selectively 'blind' to vision as well as to sound. Elly was anxious only about things which were present, presumably because she could not conceptualise what was not actually there. The child's need for order showed up in much meaningless ritual. In addition, she showed little motivation, purpose or curiosity, which is something we have also found typical of the autistic children seen by us.

It was easy for Elly to learn relatively abstract words such as 'equals,' and hard for her to learn words relating to people and to relationships, although she did become more responsive to people over the years. At age seven and a half years, although distinctly language-delayed, she functioned above her mental age on a nonverbal test requiring analytical and synthesising ability,— this was the Block Design test on the WISC test of intelligence for children.

Rimland suggested[106] it might be useful to present language tasks spatially rather than by means of sound, because of the child's difficulty in analysing and synthesising what he hears. However, this approach will not be successful unless memory ability is also taken into account. Hermelin and O'Connor found that where autistics have difficulty in discrimination, this is not due to poor discriminatory ability, but rather due to inability to remember, from one presentation to the next, the 'spatial properties which define the shape associated with reinforcement'.[107]

Like young children and the retarded, the autistic have difficulty with short-term memory. We have resolved this problem, for teaching purposes, in later chapters describing our alternate language system. By using symbols which always remain in view, problems associated with remembering from trial to trial are bypassed.

The autistic tend to respond only to one small aspect of a complex stimulus, or to a wrong aspect in the environment. For example, such a child may not recognise an experimenter if her hair is cut to a different length, or if the experimenter has added or subtracted glasses. However, we may say that this disability is not exclusive to the autistic. A very young normal child will also appear greatly puzzled when a person takes off a pair of glasses or changes his/her hairstyle.

Response to only one aspect of a complex stimulus has been reported by Schreibman[108] and by Reynolds, Newsom and Lovaas.[109] Normal, autistic, and retarded children were given three types of cues which were part of a complex stimulus. The cues (visual, tactual and auditory) were to be used to solve a discrimination task. Normal children responded to, and tended to make use of all three cues, retardates responded to two, while autistics responded only to one cue. Such selective responding creates a learning problem since other aspects of a situation are ignored. However, since a few of the normals also responded selectively to only one part of the complex stimulus, Reynolds *et al.* concluded that this response represents a developmental lag, rather than a deviant response.

Such children are impaired in understanding the meaning of word order and impaired in the use of meaningful and syntactic aspects of language. Therefore, although their memory is adequate, their recall, in contrast to other groups, does not improve when they are given meaningful, rather than non-meaningful, material to remember.

The autistic treat both meaningful and ordered sequences in the same way as they do random ones. Although they impose a pattern on what is presented to them, this imposition has no relation to whether the original information was meaningful or not. In addition, their patterns are on a simpler level than those of the normal child. Both ignoring the meaning, and responding at a simple level, may explain the autistics' peculiar behaviour in play, social interaction and speech. The limited responses of the autistic appear even more peculiar when they are given in situations requiring complex responses which are beyond the capacities of these children.[111, 112]

Hermelin and O'Connor[112] conclude that a major characteristic of the autistic is language impairment, and that the accompanying basic cognitive defect reflects an inability to perceive order and meaning in the stimuli which are presented to them. This inability may also explain their stereotyped response patterns. However, Hermelin and O'Connor rightly emphasise that there are distinct differences in degree of impairment, depending on the level of intelligence. We shall also keep these real differences in mind for the next category, namely the retarded.

MENTAL RETARDATION

Mental retardation has been defined as manifesting itself 'in poor learning, inadequate social adjustment, and delayed achievement. The condition is present at birth or starts during childhood'.[113] To this definition we would also add the retardates' impaired cognitive and language skills, their deviant and/or delayed behaviours, abilities and achievements, as well as attendant problems regarding motivation, attention, perception and, often, motor control. In most if not all abilities, retardates function at a lower level than their chronological-age peers and sometimes, in some language skills, they also function below their mental-age peers.

When we talk about retardates and compare their level of functioning with that of other diagnostic categories, we must realise that a very broad group is included within this group. It includes many sub-categories such as microcephalics, Down's Syndrome, and so-called environmental deprivation. Each of these diagnostic categories may show differences in the types and degrees of learning and language deficits. The range of retardation is large, going from the borderline who are near-normal, to the profoundly retarded. The borderline and mildly retarded are not grossly different from normals. But lower functioning retardates show gross quantitative and qualitative differences.

There are also overlaps with other categories, so that some retardates show autistic-like behaviours, deafness, blindness, aphasia, and/or are brain damaged. The latter is the case for a large proportion of retardates, but has not been proven for all. We think of the higher functioning retardates as merely being at the lower end of the normal curve, while the lower functioning ones seem to represent a different group qualitatively as well as quantitatively. As with the other groups mentioned above, knowledge of specific areas of impairment and strength will help in planning individualised teaching strategies.

One of us, Deich,[114] looked into the question whether retardates have perceptual and/or motor deficits when they perform more poorly on tasks of reproduction, such as copying geometric figures. Deich found that the retardates she tested were perceptually as well as motorically impaired. They had greater difficulty than matched-mental-age normal kindergarten children, not only in copying the figures, but also in matching them to their identical mates.

Retardates also show difficulty in attending to relevant, or important stimuli unless the situation is simple and familiar. O'Connor and Hermelin[115] suggest that this represents an inability to focus attention rather than an inability to attend to the stimulus, although we feel that this may be a matter of which particular retardates are being studied.

Learning deficits show up consistantly. They appear directly in slower learning rates and difficulties with abstraction and stimulus generalisations. They appear indirectly in how learning is affected by attentional deficits, distractibility, impulsivity and, often, lower motivation.

The evidence is conflicting regarding the distracting effect of extraneous stimuli,[116, 117] possibly because retardates, as a group, have been labelled distractible. However, certain researchers have found that some are hypo- and others are hyper-distractible,[118-122] and that their degree of distractibility may actually change during the course of a learning task.[122]

The concept of under- and over-distractibility may partly account for the greater variability in learning found among retardates in comparison with normals. Level of functioning may also be a factor, since we have found huge differences in learning and distractibility during our 1976 Symbol System Programme, depending on whether the mental age was above or below two years.

The retarded require many more learning trials than normal children, plus many repetitions of previously learned materials.[123] On some tasks the problems are compounded because the child tends to respond to the position in which the stimulus is shown, rather than to the stimulus itself. Thus he may consistently and wrongly respond always to the left position, rather than to the right. This position preference becomes more pronounced the lower the functioning of the child, and creates problems for those teaching the retarded. One way to reduce position preference is to force the child to choose from among three stimuli. This reduces his chance of guessing, and increases the chance of his paying attention and discriminating.

Like normals, and in contrast to autistics, retardates perform better if the material is meaningful.[124] Furthermore, if they are moderately retarded and labelled 'educable', they show improved recall the better the material has been organised by the experimenter. The normal child on the other hand does better with less externally imposed organisation.[125] We may venture to guess that the more competent normal child functions more effectively if he can impose his own organisation on the material.

In the previous chapter we noted that difficulties in intentional learning have been attributed to defective acquisition strategies.[126, 127] Retardates also have difficulties with incidental learning. For example, if a normal child is asked to sort items according to their shape he tends, incidentally also to learn the colours of each shape. Denny[128] hypothesised, and Deich[129] confirmed, that retardates are inferior to their normal (kindergarten) peers in such learning ability. This would suggest yet one more reason why the normal child's achievement becomes progressively greater than the retardate's. The former learns faster and more of everything, including both those things he manages to learn incidentally and those he is taught directly.

Clinical and experimental observation have shown that retardates are not only less efficient in learning but are apparently impaired in short-term, immediate memory storage. O'Connor suggests that retardates may be handicapped both in 'structural grasp' and short-term memory.[130] This makes sense, since overall level of functioning is not only at a lower level but is deviant in many respects in comparison with normals. O'Connor and Hermelin[131] concluded that the difference between retardates' and average adults' short-term memory functioning may be partly due to the retardates' less active acquisition strategies.

The latter found that if three digits were shown all at once to retardates, their immediate memory decreased as exposure time became shorter. No such effect was seen in normals matched on the basis of mental age.

Despite many contradictory experiments, the consensus is that there is an overall memory deficit. Belmont and Butterfield[132] think that the deficit may be due both to impaired acquisition and/or retrieval deficiency, since both retardates and normals forget at the same rate. Furthermore, part of the acquisition deficit may be related to the retardates' failure to rehearse the material after storage in short-term memory. (See previous chapter's discussion.)

When something new is introduced into the learning task, the retarded have a more difficult time than do normals. If functioning is sufficiently low, then even the smallest change means that the child must be taught this change, since he cannot make the small conceptual leaps involved, because he is impaired in generalising and deductive abilities. Our ongoing teaching programme involves teaching a large group of institutionalised nonverbal retardates to communicate by using the plastic symbol system. The children may range in actual age from six to sixteen, yet if their mental age is below two years, as is the case with most in this programme, they have difficulties when even slight changes are introduced into the learning procedures.

If for instance they have previously learned the names for differently shaped concrete nouns, all coloured red, then they have difficulty when the more abstract, but still simple, verb *give* is introduced, not only because of the change from noun to verb, but also because of the change from red nouns to blue verbs. Furthermore, if they learn to make the initial association between the symbol and the actual object by tapping the symbol to the object and placing the symbol on the learning board, they later have difficulty if they are asked to place the object on the board instead of, or in addition to, the symbol.

Such difficulties are probably related to impaired conceptualising ability. The lower the level of functioning among retardates, the more difficulty they have not only with language, but with cognitive and conceptualising tasks.

The low-functioning children from our 1976 programme have IQs of 30 and below. But if one looks at older and higher functioning retardates one obtains a somewhat different picture.

Deich[133] compared retardates with diagnoses of brain damage with those without such diagnoses. They were asked to sort sets of cards according to colour, then according to shape, and last according to number. Retardates with average IQs in the 50s learned to sort correctly according to the appropriate concept, and were able to shift from one sorting principle to another, although the brain-damaged took more trials to learn the task. However, in comparison with normals, retardates have greater difficulty in shifting the dimensions by which they classify stimuli.[134]

The differences between retardates and normals can be seen in other tasks. For example, Stephens et al.[135] showed that when retardates were still grouping pictures and printed matter on the basis of similar visual characteristics, their matched-mental-age peers among normals were already grouping on the basis of what the object actually could do. In other words, normal children were ahead of retardates in terms of conceptualising and abstracting ability. This advantage for the normal child means that he also benefits from verbal as well as nonverbal instructions on a transfer-of-learning task. The poor retarded does not seem to benefit from either type of instruction.[136]

Fowler[137] made a detailed comparison of two-year-old children with average IQs of 150, with four-year-old retardates with average IQs of 60. He found that the bright younger child was ahead of the retarded one on most functions, including conceptualising, generalising, knowledge of the environment, learning strategy and language.

The various examples above, plus direct comparative observations of others, show that language development becomes progressively slower as IQ becomes progressively lower.[138-140] Nonetheless one can identify different types of language disabilities and errors in speech among different diagnostic sub-categories of retardates. For example, we and others[141] have observed that Down's syndrome children have greater articulatory problems than do some of the other retardates.

Many studies of retardates,[142-144] as well as brain damaged children,[145, 146] have shown language impairment which is quantitative, i.e. the impairment represents delayed development. In other cases, language impairment, whether among retarded, aphasic, autistic, or other handicapped children, is qualitatively different from that of normals.

We have seen examples of qualitative differences in the autistic, such as when they say 'Do you want milk?', instead of 'I want milk.' Among the lower functioning retardates we have seen qualitative differences in which vocalisation may be restricted to noises or grunts, or to a few unclear words or phrases. On the other hand retardates generally try to communicate verbally despite defective speech, in contrast to the autistic who generally do not use speech to communicate.

A number of investigators,[147, 148] including ourselves, have found that sometimes retardates have language deficits which do not reflect their mental age scores, so that they may have a mental age of five, but a language level of only two years. In short, retardates are at a disadvantage linguistically, conceptually, and in learning ability, since these and other impairments interrelate to restrict and distort normal functioning.

Effects of handicaps

Impaired language affects all other functioning within the person, as well as how other people act towards and relate to him. Impaired language means that the person cannot adequately communicate either his needs or his interests. If the person is a child, he is at an ever increasing disadvantage with respect to the normal peer who begins to outstrip him at an exponential rate.

The retarded or language impaired person suffers socially. Others either do not understand at all, or they misunderstand. Often they have neither the patience nor the time to listen to what the handicapped person is trying to say.

We can get some inkling of the difficulties the language impaired encounter by listening to those who were formerly unable to communicate and now, somehow, are able to do so. A particularly poignant example comes from a recent article published in the *Los Angeles Times*. A cerebral palsied man, now aged 23, reminisced that when he was young he liked to go outside and play with other children. They would start by asking him why he moved so peculiarly, or what was his name, but

> Nothing but sounds came out of my mouth. They started to laugh and ape me. And sometimes they would throw stones at me. So I was stoned because I could not speak the language of my society. So I was forced to play alone.[149]

It is also clear from his report how adults responded to him.

> I know why the teachers never really tried to teach me any reading or spelling. They looked at my IQ tests and said it would not do any good to teach me anything. This was all because I could not speak the language to communicate to them that I understood what they were saying. The real problem was that they could not understand what I was saying.

Even when a mode of communication is available, this is no guarantee that it will be accepted by others. Dalgleish[150] found that deaf children prefer sign language to speech, but neither parents nor the people of the community actually know the signs. Thus, the deaf suffer doubly, first because they do not know other people's language, and second because others do not understand their particular language.

Parental responses to their handicapped children are complex. Often there is a large element of guilt, compounded by the frustration that they cannot understand what their child is trying to say. Yet despite difficulties in understanding, parents generally do catch on to much of the obscure communication of their handicapped child.

Gray and Ryan[151] compared the interactions of verbal and nonverbal three- to six-year-old children and their parents. Parents of nonverbal children tended to reinforce anything verbal, regardless of its appropriateness, while parents of normal-language children tended to correct their children's errors. Thus parents of the nonverbal indiscriminately reinforced all responses, in contrast to parents of normals who were selective in reinforcing. Of course, it is impossible to determine cause and effect from this study. But one might conjecture that the parents of the nonverbal child, perhaps frantic at not getting any kind of response, reinforced anything that was even remotely labelled speech. Unfortunately, although the results are interesting, the samples used were so small that one cannot come to any firm conclusions based on these findings.

Teaching the language impaired

Language deficits often go hand in hand with other deficits. In teaching the language impaired and the learning disabled, we must know their present level of receptive and expressive language, as well as their other deficiencies which may have hindered language development.

If the person is impaired in conceptualising, then he will be linguistically deficient in areas which depend on such conceptualising. If there are problems relating to attention span, sensory motor deficits, and learning rate, we will want to know them. Lastly, we need to know whether a child can respond to pictured objects. If functioning is too low, he cannot do this, and so real objects must be used for initial teaching sessions.

Knowledge will guide us in our search for more appropriate teaching techniques, and offer clues as to whether one should bypass or strengthen the child's weaknesses. The autistic have difficulty in perceiving order and meaning in the stimuli which are presented to them, the aphasic show impaired auditory processing, and the retarded show short-term memory defects. All have difficulties with ordinary, normal language acquisition. Bypassing or eliminating areas of impairment could mean successful communication by alternate means, or possibly even stimulate actual language acquisition.

It is possible to design a more effective individualised teaching approach, provided one has knowledge of behaviours and problems unique to the individual and/or his diagnostic category, as well as knowledge of behaviours and problems common to all categories. Different approaches will be needed for the nonverbal child who has no concepts even of simple abstractions such as 'like', and 'give', in contrast to the nonverbal child who has such concepts.

Regardless of level, the goal in teaching the language impaired is communication, but communication which is meaningful, generalisable to other situations, and useful in other contexts.

Optimising conditions for learning language

Besides gearing teaching to an individual's specific impairments, one can also make use of two factors which, if consistently applied, can help optimise learning. Most of the learning disabled will benefit by learning under nondistracting and well structured situations.[152, 153] It therefore makes sense to structure and organise both task and surroundings to reduce distractibility and focus attention.

In addition, cues should be distinct and stand out clearly. If the child cannot isolate and pay attention to the relevant stimuli in his perceptual field, he cannot learn simple classification tasks, nor can he learn language. If the cues do not stand out, the child does not pay attention to which word, spoken or written, goes with what object or thought. Failure to attend to relevant stimuli is a crucial factor with respect to the poorer performances of groups such as the autistic, retarded, and brain damaged.

Who benefits from nonvocal language systems?

When we attempt to teach the language impaired an alternate, nonvocal language system, we assume that at least some sort of basic and primitive conceptualising system is present, in the same sense that lower primates can discriminate between, for example, a circle and an ellipse.

We recommend using an alternate, nonvocal language system with the primary aim of encouraging meaningful communication. This communication could be accomplished by using the alternate system directly, or as a stimulus towards more adequate language expression. In no case would we want to substitute an alternate system, if speech itself were possible.

There are a variety of handicapped nonverbal or low-verbal persons who could benefit from our symbol system. They include : the person who has an easier time with receptive rather than with expressive language; the autistic child who cannot make proper use of structuring and sequencing verbal, meaningful material, but who has some conceptual ability; the child who, past the age of five, has difficulties encoding in the presence of irrelevant stimuli; the aphasic who has no difficulties with vision, but does have problems in comprehending speech and perceiving the order of auditory stimuli presented at normal speeds; the aphasic whose brain damage prevents him from expressing himself by means of speech, and who also can no longer write; those with impaired short-term memory (no memory is required in our system because all the symbols are visible on the learning board); and, lastly, those who have visual and tactile abilities available in their repertoire (since the emphasis with symbols is on the visual and tactual rather than on the verbal).

4: From Monkey to Man

Communication is the binding force in every human culture and the dominant influence in the personal life of every one of us. *The American Speech and Hearing Association, 1977.*

Some readers may wonder why we find it necessary to review the research conducted on primate communication in a book about teaching retarded children. Others may erroneously assume that we are drawing a parallel between the chimpanzee and the non-verbal retarded child; however, no comparison is intended. The major reason for examining language systems developed for animal use is that we are looking for new techniques, and systems designed for non-linguistic organisms are forced to develop such techniques.

Language training programmes for the language impaired child have traditionally emphasised the same skills and patterns that seem to occur in the natural acquisition of vocal language. In the past, the area of speech therapy has been conceptualised within that framework, and specific exercises have been aimed at developing good oral and aural habits. Where the child has the perceptual mechanisms and there is no brain dysfunction, these techniques have worked quite well. When the child has organic brain damage these techniques have in many cases failed, and it is therefore reasonable to conclude that we must start looking for those conceptualisations of language that will lead to new techniques.

In developing language systems for the chimpanzee no assumptions about the processing of language could be made, for as far as we know there are no areas in the chimp's brain corresponding to the language processing areas in the human brain (see Chapter III). Therefore, in teaching the chimp a language no reliance could be placed on any inherent language acquisition structures. The debate as to whether language is preprogrammed or learned was ignored by the chimpanzee teacher, who was thus free to concentrate on developing simple training techniques. The goal of this training thus became teaching language skills first by examining the function of language, and second by breaking the teaching process into the smallest possible sequential units. In this chapter we shall cover the work of three psychologists currently developing communication systems for chimpanzees, and see how their work has influenced intervention programmes for the non-verbal retarded populations.

SIGNING

In the late 1960s, Beatrice and Allen Gardner[1] taught a female chimpanzee named Washoe to use the American Sign Language. This language differs from some of the other sign languages in its use of specific signs to represent words as well as having signs for the alphabet. For example, to sign **open**, the hands are placed flat, side-by-side with the palms down, and the hands are then drawn apart while the palms are rotated to an upward position. **Drink** is represented by showing the thumb extended from a fisted hand and touching the mouth. (See page 122).

Washoe has her own adaptations for many of these signs. For example, in signing **sorry**, which in the American Sign Language is a fisted hand rubbed over the heart in a circular

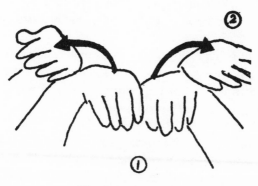

Signing 'Open'.

Signing 'Drink'.

motion, Washoe signs with a fisted hand clasping and unclasping her shoulder.

The Gardners' work with Washoe is interesting because it demonstrates the large number of words and concepts that chimps can learn. It is easy for the chimpanzee to master this system because of the animal's natural manual dexterity, and Washoe mastered a very large vocabulary and spontaneously used signs in novel situations. She also created some adaptations of her own, and has shown a great deal of ability to generalise and transfer signs from situation to situation. The Gardners did not teach Washoe to combine signs in order to build sentences. Yet after only ten months of training Washoe spontaneously signed word combinations.

In spite of being exposed only to grammatically correct models of signing, however, Washoe has apparently not been able to deduce grammatical order, and thus she signs **give apple** or **apple give** with the same meaning. In order to understand her signing, the observer must be aware of the situation context. One of Washoe's favourite phrases is **tickle** and when signing **tickle Roger** she is asking Roger to tickle her.[2] Washoe has not created any new signs but has used signs to produce novel combinations.

An interesting sidelight on Washoe's actions is that she attempted to sign to her offspring. (Unfortunately the chimp infant died shortly after birth from a congenital heart defect.[3]) The image of this chimpanzee mother signing **love** and **hug** to her nonresponding infant evokes a poignant picture.

When first announced, Washoe's considerable skills in signing were ascribed to her possibly being a 'mutant intellectual genius'. Further studies by Dr Roger Fouts[4] at the Institute for Primate Studies in Norman, Oklahoma, demonstrated not only could other chimps acquire sign language, but also that there were individual differences in their language acquisition rates.

Fouts cites many interesting novel combinations of signs by another chimp, named Lucy.* For example, when presented with a radish, Lucy first signed **fruit food** or **drink**. However, on the next day when she first bit into the radish and spat it out, she immediately signed **cry hurt food** and has continued to sign either **cry food** or **hurt food** for the radish. Fouts has also demonstrated that the chimp could transfer a sign taught for a vocal English word to the object the word represented, without any direct teaching of sign to object.

Fouts[5] recently reported an ongoing study with nonspeaking autistic and cerebral palsied children. He reported a rapid acquisition rate for signing and, for some children, spontaneous generation of vocal words and phrases. Fouts utilised a technique called Total Communication, in which the teacher simultaneously signs and vocalises. The child is required to sign the response and, at first, the child's hand may be 'moulded' into the desired response. This passive moulding is gradually faded into a more active imitation. Fouts had found moulding more effective when teaching signs to chimps, and this was also the case for the autistic and cerebral palsied children. Fouts emphasised that some of the children respond better in groups of two than alone. He also emphasised the necessity to demonstrate that a particular sign represents not one particular object but a generic class of objects,

* For an account of Lucy's language development see *Lucy Growing Up Human*, by Maurice Temerlin, Souvenir Press 1976.

i.e. the sign for car, applied first to a particular toy car, should be demonstrated with other cars, both toy and real.

In summarising his work, Fouts stresses the effect of 'learned helplessness,' a term coined by Seligman.[6] Seligman states that when a person is faced with an outcome that is independent of his or her response, that person learns helplessness. As a result the motivation to respond is lessened, the ability to anticipate success is undermined, and the person becomes disturbed. The child who lacks language skills has certainly lost a great amount of control over his or her environment. The passivity, lower motivation and greater emotionality observed in these children matches the effects of this 'learned helplessness'. When these children have been taught to communicate and thus control their environment, the behaviours associated with this helplessness will change.

In a somewhat different system of teaching signed speech to autistic and mentally retarded children, Dr Benson Schaeffer[7, 8] has reported dramatic success. His system differs from Total Communication in that signing and verbal imitations were first taught as independent skills during different lesson periods. When the three children in the study initiated integrating the two skills on their own, Schaeffer switched to signed speech, that is, having the children sign and speak at the same time. Schaeffer suggests four propositions : (1) instruction in signing facilitates spontaneous communication for children with severe language problems; (2) signing facilitates speech initiation for these children; (3) signing and speech can be integrated; and (4) the relationship between sign language and goal behaviour suggests a function-based developmental structure for these children. In this last proposition, Schaeffer is suggesting that language systems which build upon the functional relationship that communication has to goal behaviour are probably more successful for the language-impaired child. If the child has a word for 'desire' and a person concept, the child can enlist the aid of another person in satisfying his/her goal.

Schaeffer is particularly excited by the spontaneousness of the language used by the children. The three boys in his study signed to themselves and to one another, and also used signs to control their behaviour. They created new linguistic structures and generalised to untaught situations. As an example, one child, named Jimmy, had been taught to sign **help** for aid in opening food jars and in buttoning his pants. When he experienced a coughing fit he spontaneously signed **Jimmy want help.**

As the children began to speak, their speech patterns followed the same trend as did the signing patterns, that is they were more spontaneous and they were used to initiate conversations with others and to control their own behaviour. This spontaneity is remarkable in view of the many studies which have successfully taught autistic children to use words correctly, only to find that though the children respond with prodding they generally fail to use the words in any spontaneous manner.[9]

Konstantareas[10] and his colleagues have also reported considerable success in an intensive five-week training programme utilising simultaneous signing and speech for a group of eighteen autistic children. Most were able to acquire a number of signs and communicated both when prompted and spontaneously. One of their later studies[11] is of particular importance since it investigates the 'iconicity' of signing—a feature usually lacking in vocal language. Iconicity refers to signs whose physical appearance has some resemblance to the object or action the sign represents. The resemblance may take any of four forms: (1) performing an abbreviated imitation of a part of the word (eat); (2) outlining in the air the object referred to (house); (3) evoking a property (fat); or (4) mimicking in a fragmentary fashion (sleep). Ratings on iconicity were obtained for 126 signs from first grade and college students, and the ten signs within each grammatical class (noun, verb, adjective) judged as most and least iconic were taught to a group of three children. Iconic signs were learned better than non-iconic signs in both receptive and expressive modes. There were also significant differences in learning grammatical classes, with verbs and adjectives being learned better than nouns. Konstantareas suggests that this difference in learning may have occurred because the signs for these words were more iconic than were the signs for the nouns. (In general, both the college students and first-graders had perceived the verbs and adjective signs as more iconic). He also suggests that verbs have been conceptualised as being semantically and conceptually the least complex for the child to acquire, since the child is operating within an action-oriented sensori-motor framework.[12]

A brief report by Ronald Kotkin and Steve Simpson[13] summarises the new trend in sign language programmes for non-deaf children. The majority of such programmes use signing to enhance verbal behaviour, though a few have dealt with increased receptive language, and a few have used signing itself as the communication goal. These programmes have been used with considerable success with the autistic as well as with the moderately to severely retarded child. For the child who has some language but who has difficulty in learning the labels or names applied to objects, and has not responded to speech therapy, a programme might have the following steps :

(1) the child is taught the sign for an object;
(2) the child is taught the verbal response;
(3) after mastering steps one and two, the child is presented with the object (or picture of the object), the teacher asks simultaneously what the object is, makes the correct sign, and says the correct name;
(4) when the child can do step three correctly, the teacher stops the verbal modelling and uses only the sign;
(5) when the child learns to say the label on presentation of the sign and object, the sign is faded.

The signing seems to act as a cue for enhancing the labelling process. For children with delayed speech patterns a programme using speech therapy with simultaneous signing should be used. Signing programmes have also been used to increase sentence length for the child who uses only short sentences, or who makes syntactical errors. These programmes are similar to the one described above.

The Alabama State Department of Mental Health recently published a catalogue[14] of original programmes for language intervention systems for the retarded. Dr Lloyd, co-author of the catalogue, reports twenty-three successful studies on signing or manual communication programmes in his new book, *Communication Assessment and Intervention Strategies.*[15]

Fouts[16] emphasises several advantages for signing : (1) its great flexibility as compared with computer communication boards or plastic symbols; (2) the ease of use and portability of equipment (hands versus bulky devices); (3) the spontaneity allowed the child; (4) the creativity which may be curtailed in artificial, rigid programmes; and (5) the ease of teaching by moulding the child's hands into the desired sign.

COMPUTER LANGUAGE

Dr Duane Rumbaugh[17] has developed a new language, called 'Yerkish,' to teach Lana, a chimpanzee, to communicate. Rumbaugh's alphabet consists of nine design elements, which can be combined in a variety of ways to produce 'lexigrams', which are the word symbols of the system. The lexigrams are colour-coded, for example, red is used to indicate items which are edible or drinkable, while green is used to represent the various parts of the body.

Rumbaugh's system has an advantage over the previously cited work in that the computer language, Yerkish, is not ambiguous in form or syntax. By controlling the signs and symbols, Gardner and Premack avoided ambiguities that occur in spoken English words, such as 'dear' and 'deer'. However, there was no attempt to control for syntactical ambiguities. Rumbaugh cites as an example of syntactical ambiguity the sentence, 'Visiting professors may be boring'.[18] The ambiguity in this sentence exists not because of the lack of specificity of any individual word, but because one does not know if it is the professors who are doing the visiting or if it is the professors who are being visited. Therefore, the ambiguity comes from the syntactical structure of the sentence.

Yerkish grammar has been designed to avoid this type of ambiguity, as it is derived from a correlational grammar developed for computer use. In Yerkish the connectives represent specific relations between two conceptual classes, rather than between grammatical classes as syntactical systems do. The words 'visiting professors' implies a correlator. In English you cannot tell which correlation is intended. This ambiguity would not occur in Yerkish, since the grammar is not subject-object based but actor-activity based.

In a computer-controlled environment Lana has learned to use a keyboard to build sentences such as, **Please machine give candy**, and **Please machine tickle** etc. She is also able to respond to lexigrams produced by the experimenter. Lana is apparently sensitive to the order of the lexigrams for, if they are presented in an order which in her experience is not correct (that is non-rewarded), she rejects the sentences by using the erase key. Rumbaugh's work is particularly helpful in pointing out that the chimp can be taught hierarchical structures and if-then connections (discussed below), and it substantiates Premack's[19] work which also demonstrated this sensitivity to syntactical features that are not directly taught.

The results of another study of four young chimps, carried out by Dr Rumbaugh and his wife Dr Susan Savage-Rumbaugh, helps to clarify the conceptual processes used by Lana.[20-21] The method used in the second study differed from that of the first in that, instead of being taught a stock sentence (**Please machine give candy**, or **Please machine give banana**), the chimps were required to label an object held up by the experimenter. The response required was depression of the correct (backlighted) key, after which the animal was rewarded. The animals did not learn a single label in a four-month period, whereas Lana had learned three stock sentences in the same period. The major difference seems to be one of the amount of control the animal has over its environment. Lana controlled the use of the keyboard by turning the major switch on/off, all food items were within her view, and she was always given what she requested (whether she had intentionally requested the item she received is a moot point). In contrast, the young chimps played a more passive role. They did not initiate exchanges and were required to respond only when the experimenter held up an object for them. Conse-

1. Cecily being taught symbol for **give**.

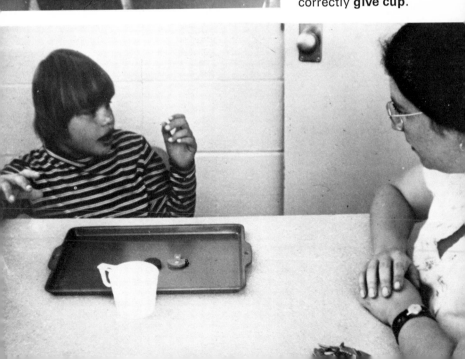

2. Here Cecily is learning verbs **give** and **clean**. At this point she must correctly **give cup**.

3. Vivienne is asked to **give apple**. She 'reads' by pointing to symbols and then carries out command.

4. 'You want me to give you something? Here's a cup', i.e. Vivienne 'reads' the symbol for **give** and carries out an act.

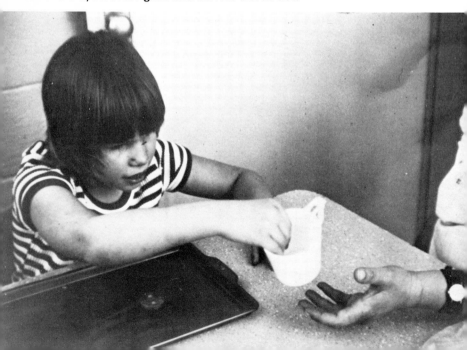

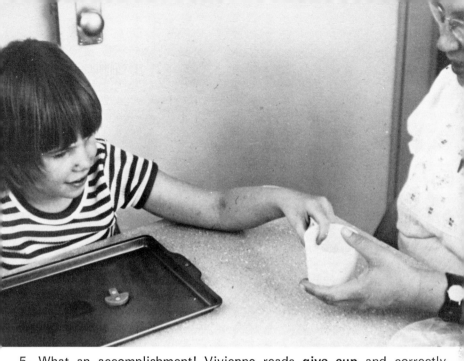

5. What an accomplishment! Vivienne reads **give cup** and correctly does so.

6. She chooses an apple for the teacher after correctly reading **give apple**.

7. She learns to **give cup** and not to clean it.

8. Jane emphasizes her choice and will **give cup** to her teacher.

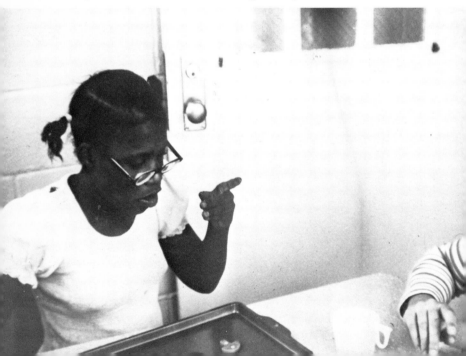

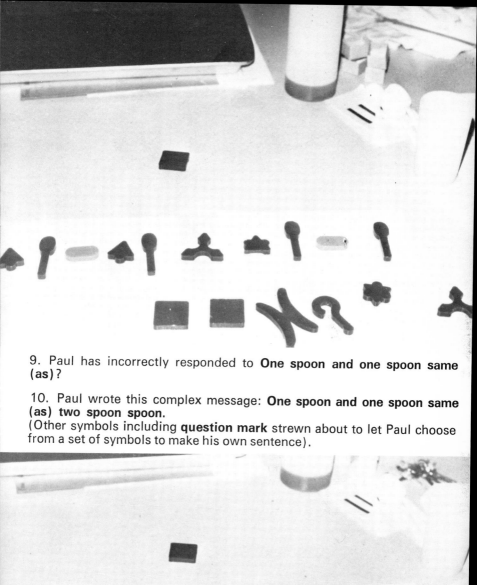

9. Paul has incorrectly responded to **One spoon and one spoon same (as)?**

10. Paul wrote this complex message: **One spoon and one spoon same (as) two spoon spoon.**
(Other symbols including **question mark** strewn about to let Paul choose from a set of symbols to make his own sentence).

11. James writes two sentences:
Child clean teacher, which he thinks is very funny, and he carries this out.
Then he writes **Toy on radio color (of) red.**

12. Teaching is a time for closeness.

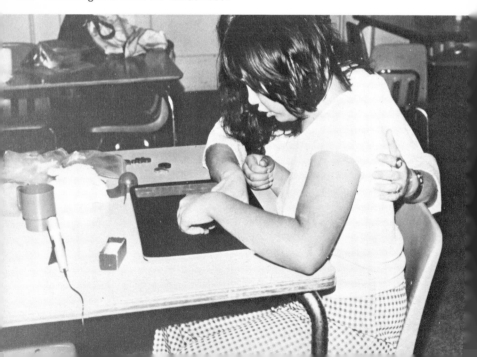

13. Lilly 'reads' and she must carry out **Child give cracker.**

14. Jane has just read the sentence and incorrectly gives the teacher a banana. (It should have been a ball).

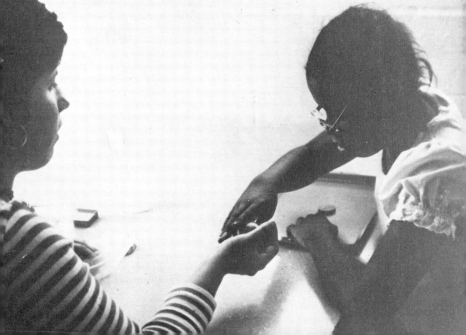

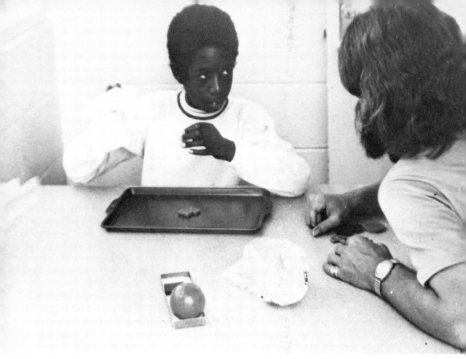

15. The teacher must learn not to give any cues to the children. Note Albert's questioning look at this teacher as he learns **clean.**

16. Sweet success! Bernie reads **Child give book (to) teacher** and does it correctly!

quently, reinforcement occurred only when a correct response was made.

By changing various strategies, Dr Savage-Rumbaugh found it was possible quickly to focus the chimps' attention on key brightness, colour and design. The four chimps rapidly learned to request desired food, which led Dr Savage-Rumbaugh to conclude that requesting is a more basic form of communication than is labelling. She also points out that at this juncture the chimp has learned an association, i.e. that a particular key goes with a particular food. However, this is a rote response and does not demonstrate that the chimp is doing any symbolic processsing. In later, more complex manipulations, the animals did display symbolism, though not the type anticipated by the experimenters. The chimps learned a simple strategy : if a sentence doesn't produce the food from the dispenser on the right, then it will produce the food from the dispenser on the left.

Dr Savage-Rumbaugh concludes that rote pairing of symbol and reinforcer is not an efficient method of teaching meaning, and that increasing the amount of control the animal (or human) has over its environment facilitates the learning of meaning.

In an associated study at the Georgia Retardation Centre, Dr Dorothy Parkel[22] has been working with a small group of profoundly retarded subjects using the computer-based system developed by the Rumbaughs. One nonverbal subject with the lowest mental age has made little progress; however, the other two present interesting case studies. Dr Parkel has chosen to compare the strategy of teaching a stock sentence, with teaching single elements which are then strung together much as a normal child acquires language.

The first subject described is a male (Cattell Mental Age of twenty-five months) who had some language use such as being able to identify a few common objects. This subject was taught the stock sentence, **Please machine give popcorn period**. (These were the top five keys on the keyboard and they were backlighted.) He was then taught to depress the key for popcorn in response to the experimenters question, **? what want**. This was presented in lexigrams on a projector and simultaneously spoken by the experimenter. The question was enlarged to **? what subject want**, and the response required was first, **Popcorn period**, and finally, **Please popcorn period**. After seventy-two sessions, this retarded man was able to read the lexigram (the experimenter no longer needed to say the sentence) and he was able correctly to identify objects from an array with 95 per cent accuracy. However, this subject has had some difficulty in mastering action words (**brush hair, comb hair, eat edible, want,** etc.) and seemed to have little interest in the task even when highly desired items such as ice cream were introduced. The introduction of slides projected to the subject upon request revived his interest in the task, and he has learned many new concepts in this way. In addition he now has greater control over his environment in that he can request particular slides.

The other subject in the study is a sixteen-year-old female with a Peabody Picture Vocabulary mental age of thirty months. This girl was normal at birth but intoxication caused by gas fumes from a leaky furnace resulted in considerable brain damage. She has great difficulty with fine motor control and makes many keyboard errors due to her impaired dexterity. She was first taught the simple elements **car** and **doll**, and when asked **what is this?** and presented with the object she responded accurately. By the fifth week she was reading the lexigrams with a 90 per cent accuracy. By the time she had mastered twelve lexigrams she was uttering not only words used in training but words for objects encountered on her way to the training room.

Her ability to acquire new words was demonstrated in her response when nine objects were placed on a table. Of the nine objects, she had previously learned the lexigrams for eight, She immediately noted the ninth item, an apple, and went to the keyboard and depressed the correct key (all nine lexigrams were backlighted). At the same time she vocalised an approximation of the word 'apple'. This girl had some difficulty in producing two-word strings but is now reliably producing two-word strings as well as some three- and four-word strings which have not been modelled for her. She also has on occasion attempted two-word vocalisations out of the training situation. In addition, she also demonstrated incidental learning. For example, she incorrectly depressed the key for **string** (which the experimenter pronounced) several times. Later when the experimenter tied her shoelaces the girl turned to the keyboard and depressed the correct lexigrams for **shoe** and **string**.

In summarising the advantages of computer-based systems, Dr Savage-Rumbaugh points out seven major assets :

(1) the motor response required is simple;

(2) brightening the keys and maintaining the illumination focuses attention. Additionally the image remains on the projector, thus counteracting short-term memory problems;

(3) the sequence is arranged to separate the act of communicating from the message itself;

(4) use of the computer allows for more reliability in environmental events;

(5) subjects can work at their own pace;

(6) interpretation of the response is always consistent (a teacher may vary in recognition of sloppy signs or vocalisations);

(7) the computer acts as the communicator, thus lessening the demand to please the teacher.

To this list we might add an eighth asset, namely that data collection is easier, more reliable, and more complete.

PREMACK'S SYMBOL SYSTEM

David Premack[23, 24] has successfully taught a chimpanzee, named Sarah, to communicate using plastic symbols to represent words. She can respond to questions and commands, describe objects, and ask for the symbols for new objects. Premack's study was of great importance for two major reasons. The first of these is that his theoretical approach to language was very different than the ones previously offered by psycholinguists. By approaching language from a functional base rather than from a grammatical base, he clearly delineated the specific functions which language serves, and showed that the chimpanzee could master these functions. Premack specifies the four functions of language : word (the idea that a symbol represents something), sentence, question and metalinguistics. All of these were mastered by the chimpanzee (to be discussed below).

The second major feature of importance in Premack's study was the use of plastic symbol language rather than spoken verbal English, which reduced the communication process from one of requiring production, (i.e. speech), to one requiring recognition of a symbol. This made it possible for Premack to break the language-learning process into three simple phases of discrimination, association and motor response. Each of these phases could in turn be broken into smaller steps. To use the Premack system successfully, it would require a chimp (or child) only to be perceptually aware of the symbols, to be able to match and discriminate between symbols and objects, and to be able to grasp the symbols and move them on to a board. The responses required are considerably less complex than are the demands placed by requiring a linguistic product, i.e. speech. The system builds upon behaviours already existing in the organism's repertoire, so that the organism, whether chimp or child, can be successful at each step. Premack's work has been reported in several different areas, but for an entertaining and easily read description, the reader is referred to *Why Chimps Can Read* by Ann J. Premack.[25]

In examining language functions, Premack points out that the difference in modalities (language is a primarily auditory skill, whereas learning about the objects represented is primarily a visual skill) facilitates learning which of the members of the system is the referent. Thus the child learns object knowledge (visual) and the symbolic process (aural and oral). In the Premack system both referent and symbol are in the visual modality and the chimp had to learn which object was the symbol and which object was referent. (In our work with retarded children none of them has ever made the mistake of confusing the referent and symbol).

The initial step in teaching Sarah her first word was to place a piece of food between the chimpanzee and the trainer and encourage the chimp to take and eat the food. Very little encouragement is needed for this act and it established a pleasant and rewarding transaction scenario. After this transaction had taken place several times, the trainer placed a piece of plastic (the symbol) alongside the piece of fruit, the piece of fruit being somewhat further from the chimp's grasp than the plastic symbol. The chimp was then induced to put the plastic symbol on the nearby magnetic language board, after which she was immediately rewarded with a piece of fruit. Sarah quickly became proficient at this task, because it fell within her behavioural repertoire—unlike the task of imitating the sounds of the human voice, which was beyond the physiological capacity of the chimp. The rest of the training was similar : for example, two different kinds of fruit would be placed in front of the chimp with only one symbol, and the chimp's task was to place upon the board the piece of plastic associated with a specific fruit. These simple procedures were carried out until the chimp could choose the correct fruit eight times out of ten trials. In addition, the chimp was taught the reverse task as well : when one piece of fruit and two symbols were presented, the chimp had to choose the symbol correctly and place it upon the board before taking the fruit. In this way, the chimp was taught the relationship between the symbol and the food to which it refers.

The names of persons working with the chimpanzees were taught next. For example, if the trainer was 'Mary', the symbols **Mary apple** had to be placed on the board in order for the chimp to receive a piece of apple. Teaching the classes of donor and recipient followed essentially the same pattern. The trainer would write **Mary apple Sarah** and give Sarah a piece of apple. If two or more people were present this pattern could be varied, as for example, **Mary apple Tim**. The verb **give** was taught in a similar manner. Note that the chimp is taught correct sequencing, and must produce symbol strings in the correct sequence.

Among the other functions of language that Sarah learned were symmetrical and asymmetrical relationships. As an example of a symmetrical relationship consider the sentence, **Tom and Bob are playing**. The order of Tom and Bob is interchangeable because the action is symmetrical, i.e. if Tom and Bob are playing together, Tom is playing and Bob is playing. There are, however, other relationships that are not symmetrical. Premack referred to these as closed relationships. Examples of closed relationships are such sentences as 'Bob put on his hat'. One cannot have the 'Hat put on Bob'. (This problem was discussed in Chapter I.) That Sarah mastered these relationships was demonstrated by her ability to place coloured chips (which give no size or position clues as to which placement would be correct) in the correct order. For example, when the sentence, **Red** (chip) **on green** (chip), was constructed, Sarah could successfully place the red colour chip on the green colour chip. In addition, Sarah could construct such sentences and then execute them.

The teaching of a hierarchical organisation in sentence structure was somewhat more prolonged and involved the teaching of substeps. This was done by teaching first two simple sentences, such as, **Sarah insert banana pail**, and **Sarah insert apple dish**. The trainer would write each sentence on the board (in the chimp's preferred vertical construction), at the same time offering all the objects to be inserted in the containers, and Sarah was required to place the designated fruits into the designated containers. In the next step the sentences were placed side by side in the manner of a paragraph.

Sarah	**Sarah**
insert	**insert**
banana	**apple**
dish	**pail**

In a further step the trainer would place one sentence over another, so it would read :

Sarah
insert
banana
dish
Sarah
insert
apple
pail

And then the second subject was deleted so the sentence now read as on the left :

Sarah
insert
banana
dish
insert
apple
pail

In the next step the second insert would be deleted and the sentence would read as on the left :

Sarah
insert
banana
dish
apple
pail

Another language function which Sarah mastered was the use of the question mark, which was taught by using the concept of same and different. The question function was demonstrated by asking the equivalent of : 'What is the relationship between two things?' That is, are they the same or different? For example, two plums were placed in front of Sarah and the symbol for question mark would be inserted between the plums. The chimp was then taught to use a symbol for **same** when the two objects were the same, and a symbol for **different** to be used when the two objects were different. Sarah was able to demonstrate understanding of both the same–different relationship and the function of the question symbol.

Sarah demonstrated generalisation to non-taught items and she was also able to respond to the pieces of plastic in the same way as she did to the actual objects. For example, when presented with an apple she would choose correctly among the alternatives such as round versus square, square with stem versus plain, round versus square with protuberance, etc. When presented with the green triangle (representing apple) she responded in exactly the same way : round, having stem, and red, etc. This demonstrated that she knew the meaning of the symbol and the characteristics it represented.

In a later article Premack reported that Sarah demonstrated knowledge of concepts such as **all, one, none** or **several**. On varied trials she was required to select either a single cracker or several crackers from an array of crackers, according to what the sentence read. Premack notes an almost human incident when Sarah tried to cheat while being taught the three sentences, **Sarah insert all cracker dish**, **Sarah insert one cracker dish**, and **Sarah insert several cracker dish**. (Sarah was allowed to keep for herself the crackers or the candy that were placed upon the dish.) She carried out her instructions to her usual criterion of about 80 per cent correct, with one notable exception. When asked to place one cracker on the dish, Sarah managed to sneak a few candies on to the dish as well. Her trainer let her get away with this subterfuge because the sentence did not actually negate such an action. However, when Sarah was instructed to write, **Sarah insert one candy dish**, she terminated the lesson by taking all of the candies (something many of our retarded children have also attempted to do).

Sarah has also mastered more complex concepts, such as **if-then** relationships, that is, contingency relationships. Sarah was taught two sentences which describe the contingency situations, **Sarah take apple**, and **Mary give Sarah chocolate**. Sarah was given only one symbol to place between these sentences, the **if-then** sign, and she was induced to place the symbol between the sentences so the sentence read, **Sarah take apple if-then Mary give chocolate**. If Sarah then took the slice of apple, Mary gave her a piece of chocolate. After mastering this sequence, the next sentence taught was, **Sarah take banana, if-then Mary not give Sarah chocolate**, and if Sarah took the banana, she would be given only the banana and not any chocolate.

Studies based on Premack's work
Premack's work is beginning to have a great impact upon language intervention programmes, since the procedures are defined in steps

which the retarded child can master. Since the child does not have to produce the symbol but needs only to recognise it, the steps are simpler than in signing (which involves production as well as recognition). In the Premack system the association is one of object to another object, or of object to an action. This concreteness facilitates learning for the retarded child whose cognitive capacities are here-and-now oriented. Several investigators interested in the nonverbal intervention systems have successfully used Premack's system. (Eighteen such studies are referenced by Dr Macalyne Fristoe,[26] *Manual Communication for the Retarded*, and Dr L. Lloyd,[27] *Communication Assessment*.) We shall not attempt to deal with these in any great detail, with the exceptions of our own work and that of Dr J. Carrier. The interested reader is referred to the above references for greater detail.

DR CARRIER'S SYSTEM

Dr J. Carrier[28, 29] has described an extensive study devoted to teaching profoundly retarded subjects to communicate, based on the work of Premack. In developing his system, Carrier relied upon the disciplines of logic, linguistics, behavioural analysis and Premack's functional analysis. This blending produced a systematic programme which teaches syntactical rules apart from semantic content, an element Carrier regards as essential. He reports success in teaching a group of sixty retarded children to communicate by using this system. The group had no useful language skills (although some did try to imitate one-word utterances), and none had responded to conventional language therapy.

Carrier divided his programme into two separate procedures (labelling and syntactical learning). In the first procedure, the retarded child is taught ten symbols representing ten nouns (**boy, girl, man, baby, lady, dog, cat, bird, horse**, and **cow**). As in both our system and the Premack system, the 'words' are geometric forms, but these forms are marked with coloured tape to indicate grammatical class (articles have red tape; nouns, orange tape; auxiliary verbs, green tape; verbs, blue tape; and prepositions, black tape). A symbol is placed between the child and the

138   LANGUAGE WITHOUT SPEECH

response board and the child is then shown a picture of what the symbol represents. The child's task is to place the symbol on the response board. In the next step, the child is presented with a choice of two symbols (for example, a square for boy and a circle for girl), and must choose the correct symbol for the picture. When the child has responded correctly ten times, a third form is added (for example, a square for boy, a circle for girl, and a triangle for man), and pictures of the three are randomly presented until ten consecutive responses are produced. These procedures are randomised to ensure that 50 per cent of all the pictures will be of the noun that is being learned at that particular step, and 50 per cent are randomly selected from the previously learned nouns.

Carrier reported the children were able to learn the ten symbols in a training period of about two hours, ranging from a low learning time of 8.18 minutes to a high learning time of 512 minutes. He also reported that some of the children did not attend to the task or show responsiveness, and that these children were placed in a behaviour modification programme to establish clinical control of their disruptive behaviours. These children were then returned to the training programme and with this procedure Carrier reported some progress, although their progress was slow as compared to the group of sixty children who completed the programme.

The second procedure in Carrier's system (the syntactical procedure) is a rote learning of syntax through the use of colour and number discriminations. The sentence model to be learned is a seven-word declarative sentence for which Carrier uses a response board with seven coloured slots (eight in his ASHA article) as an analogue to the sentence. Thus, the model would be :

MODEL :	The	boy	is	standing	on	the	chair
GRAMMATICAL CLASS :	article	noun	auxiliary	verb	preposition	article	noun
RESPONSE BOARD CODE :	RED (1)	ORANGE (1)	GREEN	BLUE	BLACK	RED (2)	ORANGE (2)

The response required from the child is a rote sequence of placing a marker with coloured tapes in the slots marked 'red 1', 'orange

1', 'green', 'blue', 'black', 'red 2', 'orange 2'. (One or two stripes of tape are used to indicate sequences.) The symbols at this time are not associated with any semantic content and the response is intended only as a model for later operations, it does not function as a direct means of communication. An unusual feature of this procedure is that the last position ('orange 2') is taught first. Carrier reports this method was determined empirically to be more efficient (Carrier, 1976, *Nonspeech Language Initiation Program* —*NONSLIP*). The child is taught first to place a symbol with two orange markers in the last slot of the tray. This task is learned quite easily because every other slot is closed. In the next step, however, the last two slots are uncovered and the child is presented with two symbols, one with two orange markers and one with two red markers and the child's task is to place the red marked symbol in the first open slot on the tray and to place the marked orange symbol in the last slot. When this task has been learned, new geometric symbols of the same colour markers are presented to him and to complete this step the child must demonstrate generalisation to the new forms. A black marked symbol is then added and the next slot of the tray is made available. This process of adding forms is continued until the child can take any set of seven appropriately coloured symbols and place them from right to left into their correct slot. Carrier reports that most children reach criterion for the first lesson very quickly; however, Lesson Two requires more time, and Lesson Three requires still more time. Most of the children seemed to acquire the concept of sequencing, and the remaining sequencing tasks were learned in approximately three hours and nine minutes of training.

The third procedure in Carrier's programme is to combine the two previously learned procedures: the syntactical system (response board position), and the labelling system. The child has learned to select some nouns out of context and has learned to sequence seven symbols (which are designed to produce sentence order). The child is tested on the nouns previously learned in the labelling procedure, and if the child makes any errors in the programme, that lesson is repeated until the test criterion is met. In the ASHA article, only five noun symbols were used at this point.

In the NONSLIP programme, however, all ten symbols plus the six symbols (non-meaningful at this time) for other sentence parts were placed in front of the child. The child had to select the symbol for the first slot as taught in the previous procedures. To correctly place the symbol in the second slot, the child had to select the correct noun symbol for the picture that was presented to him/her. After filling the second slot correctly, the child filled the remaining five slots by using colour/number cues. The same procedure was used until the child could use each of the noun symbols correctly 100 per cent of the time. The mean time required to complete this portion of the training was one hour and ten minutes.

Carrier reports that learning verb symbols, particularly the first two verbs, is a major problem (for five verbs the mean time for learning was seven hours and one child required thirty-seven hours of training). In his NONSLIP manual, Carrier mentions a subroutine programme to aid the child in attending to the stimulus pictures. Additional sentence parts are learned in the same manner using the same sequencing.

To recap the cycle briefly: the first step is to learn the ten symbol noun names (the labelling procedure without any order); the second step is to learn the rote sequencing; and the third step is to combine these procedures by placing the correct noun in the correct sequence to describe a picture. Additionally, Carrier reported that as the children produced these responses and the clinician spoke the words, many of the children began to imitate the words. When the clinician's utterances were faded, the children continued to initiate speech responses. (In a personal communication, Carrier indicated that 180 subjects have learned to communicate with this system and verbalise fluently.)

BLISS-SYMBOLS

The Bliss system, or semantography as it is called, is a system developed by Mr Charles Bliss[30, 31] in cooperation with the Ontario Crippled Children's Center in Toronto, Ontario. The system was created for use with physically handicapped (primarily cerebral palsied) children who, due to their physical impairments, were not able to produce language; however, the assumption was that all of these children were able to process receptive language. A team consisting of the teachers working with the programme and a psychologist, linguist, occupational therapist, speech therapist and a rehabilitation engineer developed the system. The system is pictographic, ideographic and for some symbols, arbitrary. Examples of the symbols are as follows :

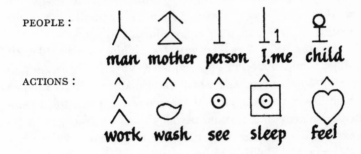

The children are trained to respond to pictures of symbols which are displayed on a communication board. The original board developed by Mr Bliss (and the centre staff) had thirty symbols which were used as labels for feelings, objects, place names and questions. The child would indicate a feeling or desired object by pointing to the symbol. The very first sentences the children produced tended to be short, one-word responses. It is interesting to note that as the system expanded (they now have 560 symbols available) and the children began constructing their own sentences, they tended to reproduce incorrect syntactical order although all teaching models were presented in correct syntactical order.

In the original project fourteen children were separated into three groups which met daily for thirty minutes. The children, ranging in age from four to nine years, had been selected because they were unable to use speech. Each subgroup was on the same academic level, although at a later date they were regrouped according to the level in learning the symbols. Due to attrition and other problems with the learning procedures, only six of the children remained in the programme in the second year. These six ranged in age from four and a half to nine years and the estimation of mental capacity ranged from educationally retarded to above average. The first symbols that were introduced were **hello, goodbye, man, lady, big**, and **little**, and then, **yes, no**. Twenty-one symbols had been introduced in the first six weeks and lesson procedures had been developed. The more representative and concrete symbols, such as those for **man. house, eye**, and **mouth** were the most easily learned, while those that were more abstract such as **opposite**, or those representing an action were more difficult to teach.

During the 1971-2 school year the children expanded their vocabulary and mastered approximately forty symbols. At present, a 100-symbol vocabulary board is available which is equipped with an electronic pointer, and the centre has plans for a computerised system which would permit the use of 360 symbols (to be expanded to 560 at a later date). On the basis of their first year's work, the children could use the symbols to express complex ideas and they communicated spontaneously with one another.

This symbol system differs from the other systems discussed in being a two-dimensional pictorial representation, and also in having a logic unit-concept so that symbols can be used together to produce new words. For example, the symbol for roof placed with the symbol for man means daddy, i.e. the man who livees in the house. Symbols for feelings are also used in this manner, i.e. a picture of a heart with an arrow up would represent happiness, with the arrow down, sadness.

The Bliss symbol system is also distinguished from others in that a symbol does not represent one particular thing on a one-to-one correspondence: the heart symbol, for example, may mean **happy, merry, joyous**, etc.—in short, a variety of things. Introducing the symbol for **opposite** immediately increased the number of responses available to the child, while the use of another symbol to represent the concept **part of** makes breaking larger elements into smaller units possible, such as

part of leg. The children have managed to create some of their own symbols, which are very entertaining.

Five retarded youngsters (all of whom were nonverbal) were trained to use the Bliss system.[31] Their lack of mechanical dexterity made the use of sign language inappropriate, while the Bliss system was an easier communication modality for them than was vocal communication. The mental ages of the children were not given except for one particular child who was noted as having an IQ of 56. The prerequisite behaviour for the five children for admission to the programme was that they could: (1) maintain eye contact; (2) attend; (3) pass all of Piaget's six sensory motor levels; (4) exhibit a desire for communication in some way or other; and (5) possess essentially no linguistic skills. The children were trained once weekly over an eight-week period for a total of 15 to 20 hours. The symbols were posted in all of the wards where the children lived, and the teachers in the wards were aware of the symbols and used them whenever possible. The symbols first used were **yes, no, goodbye, more, mother, teacher, toilet,** and **want**. The child was taught by a series of prompts to use a pointer to select the symbols referring to an exact object. All of the children were able to learn some of the symbol systems, and some of them learned to communicate quite well. In examining these studies one wonders why the use of an electronic device for the cerebral palsied child was not created long ago. In addition some of the children in the Bliss system seemed to be able to read, as the symbols also have the meaning written below.

Ms McNaughton[32] and the members of the Formative Evaluation study from the Ontario centre report that the symbol system is now being used in ongoing projects for deaf, blind, and autistic children as well as in pre-reading and remedial reading programmes. Additional uses cited were for programmes dealing with concept and language enrichment. Complete records were available for 130 subjects in twenty-one different settings. Positive changes occurred in thirty-two of these children in academic, social and psychological areas. Records for those who failed to improve tended to show the typical institutional problems faced by any innovative programme. These problems include: (1) changes in residence or instructor; (2) irregular instruction; (3) the subject was the only individual instructed in the system, thus limiting communication; (4) lack of acceptance by the family; (5) subject needed additional technical assistance to achieve access to the board; and (6) behavioural or emotional problems of the student inhibited progress with the system.

The Vanderheidens[33] have been involved in developing strategies for the nonvocal severely physically handicapped child using the Bliss system, and they have been instrumental in creating several ingenious devices to facilitate the use of the system for the extremely impaired child. Their work is also of note because they delineate the category of nonvocal children into four major components : the nonvocal mentally retarded, the nonvocal autistic, the nonvocal deaf, and the nonvocal physically handicapped. Each group is nonvocal for different reasons : (1) the physically handicapped child may have good input and cognitive processing, but lack the physical mechanisms to express himself; (2) the nonvocal retarded child may have auditory and expressive functions intact, but have severe cognitive and processing problems; (3) the nonvocal autistic child may lack some internal processing mechanism and have intact auditory, expressive and cognitive functions—although some investigators believe a large proportion of the autistic are also retarded; and (4) the nonvocal deaf child has intact expressive, cognitive and processing mechanisms, but lacks the input and model to process. To assume there is any one best system for all is fallacious; the system must be individualised to meet the unique needs of each person.

SUMMARY

Intervention programmes for the nonverbal retarded child are beginning to have a new look. Therapists have turned away from the traditional programmes which have had little success with the cerebral palsied, autistic, and the profoundly retarded population. The influence here comes from several directions, one of which is that of the communication systems developed for use with the chimpanzees. The impact of these systems is just beginning to be felt, but reports of successful studies using these systems for populations which previously experienced almost continuous failure are beginning to appear. For the child who has some minimal verbal skill and the dexterity to imitate signing, the future is promising. The use of signing as a facilitator of verbal speech for the autistic child seems hopeful : several studies[34, 35] have reported considerable success, with a more spontaneous use of language than achieved by traditional methods up to date.

For the handicapped child (such as a cerebral palsy victim) the Bliss symbol system[36, 37, 38] seems to offer a new way of communicating. These children lack the motor skills to produce either verbal or sign language, and some of these children have been erroneously labelled as retarded due to their limited capacity to handle language. There are other studies reporting on the use of a response board with alphabet or symbols to aid the cerebral palsied child. The work of Dr Eugene McDonald[39] at Pennsylvania State University is recommended to the teacher or parent of the cerebral palsied child.

For the severe to profoundly retarded child who has no language skills and who fails at signing, the work based on Premack's symbol system seems an excellent choice. This system intially reduces the skills needed to a simple association and rote learning task. In contrast to signing, the child does not have to create a response, which is conceptually more difficult, but needs merely to select a prepared response. Symbols and sentences may remain on the board, rather than vanish as the spoken word does, thus reducing the demand on short-term memory. The next chapter describes our pilot work on the Premack system.

5: The Pilot Study

'There was speech in their dumbness, language in their very gesture.' Shakespeare, *A Midsummer Night's Dream*, Act V, sc. 2, l. 14.
'Quand on se fait entendre, on parle toujours bien. . . .' Moliere, *Les Femmes Savantes*, Act ii, sc. 6.

As we described in the introduction, we decided after reading of Dr Premack's extraordinary accomplishment in teaching a female chimpanzee named Sarah[1] to communicate, to apply his system to a nonverbal retarded population. As far as we knew the only other application of the Premack system at that time was a study done by Drs Michael Gazzaniga and Andrea Velletri-Glass. Gazzaniga and Velletri-Glass[2] had used the Premack system with adult aphasic patients who had previous language skills but who due to stroke in the left hemisphere were severely language impaired. They were able to teach the system with varying degrees of success and competence to their entire sample of seven aphasic adults.

We contacted Dr Premack and arranged a visit to his facility which at that time was only 120 miles away from our offices.[3] Dr Premack greeted our interest with much enthusiasm and lent us symbols and a symbol dictionary he had developed. In addition we were able to meet and observe a most engaging young chimpanzee named Peony, during a training session. Then, with the blessing of Dr Premack and a small grant,[4] we started the study.

The pilot project was planned to have three groups. The group of major importance was composed of eight nonverbal non-deaf severely retarded children. This first group would be trained to communicate with the Premack symbol system. Since a second group of eight nonverbal retarded children of similar mental and chronological age was not available, we compared our training group to a group of severely retarded children (matched in chronological and mental age) with some limited language skills. This second group was used only for pre-post comparisons and did not receive any training on the Premack system. A third group of normal preschool children of a chronological age similar to the mental age of the nonverbal retarded training group was also trained to use the Premack symbol system. Since no data was available regarding normal acquisition rates, this third group was trained in order to supply some information about baselines for learning.

The first group, consisting of the eight nonverbal retarded children, received training in the Premack communication system for four months. These children were given two nonverbal measures of intelligence before and after training. The average mental age on the Leiter International Performance Scale for the group was 3·8 years, ranging from a low of 2·5 years to a high of 6·0 years; and the average chronological age for this group was 11·8 years, ranging from 7·7 years to 20·2 years. Table 1 reports group scores for all groups. On the Peabody Picture Vocabulary Test (PPVT), the mental ages ranged from unscorable to a high of 3·9 years. The PPVT, though a nonverbal test, relies heavily on receptive language processing and many of the children seemed to have deficits in this area. Discrepancies in Leiter and PPVT scores are given in Table 2. All of the children in the first group shared a common problem in that they had no expressive language skills. Despite several years of speech therapy, none of them had been reported to say a single word, nor did they produce any speech-like sounds. These children did differ on a number of significant variables.

The oldest, a young man of 20·2 years (Pete), had cerebral palsy and his motor skills were severely impaired. Pete's mental age as measured by the Leiter was 2·5 years (2·7 years on the Peabody Picture Vocabulary Test), thus his IQ was 15. Pete's difficulty in placing the symbols upon the magnetic communication board used throughout the study necessitated placing the board flat on a table rather than in the upright position we had intended to use. Despite his lack of communication skills Pete was good natured and presented no disturbing behavioural problems.

Only two of the group were female (the proportion of female to male subjects in the retarded population living at Pacific State Hospital is unequal, though not as extremely so as in our sample). The oldest girl, Linda, had no additional problem and had a Leiter mental age of 4·5 years (2·2 years on the Peabody Picture Vocabulary Test). The younger girl, Lorna, exhibited autistic-like behaviour as well as receptive language deficits. Her Leiter mental age was 3·3 years and on the Peabody Picture Vocabulary Test her responses were unscorable.

One of the boys, Mike, also had autistic-like behaviours and receptive language problems and his Leiter mental age was 2·5 years. The remaining four boys had no additional observable handicaps and few behavioural problems. The youngest child, Ben, had a Leiter mental age of six years giving him the highest IQ (64); his Peabody mental age was much lower (one year) though he seemed able to process direct, simple commands. Charlie (who proved to be the star of our programme) had a mental age of 3·8 years on the Leiter (3·9 years on the Peabody). One of the other boys, Jim, had a mental age of 3·5 years on the Leiter and 1·8 years on the Peabody. The last boy, Fred, had a mental age of 4·5 years on the Leiter and 2·3 years on the Peabody. None of these boys had any behavioural problems and all seemed responsive to social initiations.

The second group, which was our comparison group of eight retarded children, had an average Leiter mental age of 3·8 years ranging from a low of 2·5 years to a high of 5·3 years. The average chronological age for this group was 14·1 years ranging from 8·1 years to 26·8 years. These children had the same general behavioural characteristics as the training group although they did have some expressive speech skills.

The third group, which was composed of eight normal preschool children who also received training in the Premack system, had an average mental age of 4·9 years ranging from a low of 4·3 years to a high of 5·5 years. These children had been selected from a nearby nursery school[5] as being the youngest children available in the school. In some way this choice was unfortunate since they tended to have higher mental ages than we had expected. The average chronological age of this group was 3·8 years, ranging from 3·7 to four years.

Both the preschool children (third group) and the nonverbal retarded children (first group) were trained to use the Premack system and were tested for acquisition and retention of the system. The verbal retarded group (our second group) was not taught the system but was compared with the other groups so that we could evaluate the pre- and post-test measures.

In addition to collecting data on the acquisition of the system, we also recorded the training procedures from time to time on motion picture film. The films proved to be exceptionally helpful in training other research assistants and in demonstrating how to use the system.

The symbols read 'one and one same (as) two'.

TRAINING

The children were trained in individual sessions of ten to thirty minutes, twice a day, for five days a week at the beginning of the study. After two months of training, the children's attention span had increased so that the two daily training sessions could be combined into one daily session lasting forty-five to sixty minutes. (Not every child was seen daily, since many of them suffered from time to time from illness or fatigue.)

The training sessions for group one were conducted in almost any area we found available, often the dining room. None of the children lived in the same ward, so the teachers moved from ward to ward, taking the equipment with them. In good weather many of the sessions were conducted outside, which increased the attractiveness of the event for the child.

Our third group, the preschool children, were given the same training schedule as were the nonverbal retarded children. However, they were trained initially for the forty-five to sixty minute sessions and they completed the training programme in three weeks. Since all of the preschool children were in the same set of rooms and there were additional rooms available for teaching, the logistics for these sessions were much simpler for the teacher.

Procedures

The basic training procedure consists of requiring the subject to associate the symbols (which are the words of the system) with real objects such as **apple**, **box**, and **cup**, as well as more abstract concepts, such as **different**, **colour of**, **yellow**, and **give**. The next step in the procedure was to train the subject to construct and respond to meaningful sentences. The goal was to teach up to 39 such symbols of which 16 were nouns, five were verbs, and the remainder were connectors, classes, etc. By the use of progressive steps, the subjects were taught to use these symbols to construct three- to seven-word sentences where each word was represented by one of the symbols.

In pre-training sessions we observed that when the children were presented with only one symbol at a time, they did not learn to discriminate the distinctive features of the symbols, therefore all of the symbols were presented in sets of two or more.[6] Following Premack, the symbols were always placed on the board in a specific order, in this case from left to right. The syntactical order was always correct; however, the sentences were telegraphic in nature, that is they lacked articles and modifiers.

Training began with Set One, which consisted of the symbols representing **apple**, **banana**, and **cracker**. These items were selected because of their reinforcing properties, concreteness, and general availability. Any other readily available food item could have been used. The student sat at the table facing the magnetic board with the wide end towards him/her. The plastic apple, banana, and cracker were placed directly past the board. (Plastic fruit was used because real fruit proved too tempting to the children.) The symbols to be learned were placed on the student's preferred hand side. The teacher first demonstrated the task by picking up the appropriate symbol, tapping the symbol on the real object (for example, an apple) and then placing the symbol in front of the object but on the board. The teacher then guided the child through the same steps : (1) guided the child to pick up the appropriate symbol; (2) moved the child's hand (grasping the symbol) to the real object; (3) guided the child in tapping the real object; (4) moved the child's hand to the board; and (5) assisted the child in placing the symbol on the board. Since this was a correct move, the child was reinforced with a bit of the food. The same five steps including the demonstration were repeated for ten trials and the **apple** symbol was then placed with the three other symbols by the side of the board.

After completion of the ten trials, the teacher, by gesture and speech, indicated to the child that he/she was required to go through the five steps without guidance. If the child did the steps correctly he/she was immediately reinforced. If the child failed to do the task correctly, the original five steps including the demonstration were again repeated ten times. If the child indicated he/she wished to do the steps without guidance prior to the first ten trials, he/she was encouraged to do so.

If the child repeated the five steps to a criterion of 80 per cent correct without any prompting from the teacher, the child was then taught the symbol for **banana**, using the same general paradigm (one untaught symbol was also included in each symbol set to reduce the probability of a correct guess).

There are several important factors to be noted : (1) The teaching was errorless and the child thus experienced success and was rewarded. This was a unique experience for some of the children who had been exposed only to continuous failure and frustration. (2) The teacher talked to the student throughout the sessions, labelling the objects and symbols, and verbalising the required actions. This placed the teaching process in a natural context and had a second advantage of associating spoken words with the objects they represented, and with direct reinforcement. (3) Reinforcement occurred as soon as possible following the correct response. This is very important because it ensures that the child associates the reward with the desired response rather than with irrelevant or incorrect cues. Social reinforcement was paired with food reinforces at first and for most of the children social reinforcement, such as a hug, pat, or the expression 'good' soon became an adequate reinforcer by itself. (4) The learning criterion used throughout the pilot study was correct selection for each symbol eight out of ten times in succession. (For the preschool children the criterion of four out of five correct successive responses was used since they seemed to be bored with excessive repetition.) (5) As soon as a child had mastered a specific symbol, we moved on to the next symbol or lesson. There were frequent retests for retention to ensure the child had not forgotten any lesson.

After the child had learned the symbols for both **apple** and **banana**, the symbol for **cracker** was introduced and the same steps were followed. The next set of symbols taught was **teacher** and **child**. Again the symbols, including one that would not be taught, were placed on the child's favoured side. For this demonstration the teacher selected the symbol **teacher**, tapped the symbol to him/herself and then placed the symbol on the board. To guide the child through the motions the teacher : (1) moved the child's hand to grasp the symbol; (2) guided the child to tap the symbol on the teacher; and (3) guided the child in placing the symbol on the board. These three steps, including the demonstration, were repeated for ten trials. The teacher then indicated by gesture and speech that the child was to complete the same sequence without any guidance or prompts. The child was reinforced on every one of the guided trials and on every correct imitative trial. If the child could do this correctly to a criterion of eight out of ten trials, the teacher moved on to the next symbol, **child**. The same procedures were used for this symbol, except that the teacher demonstrated and guided the child to tap the symbol to him/herself.

Tests of learning

Tests were given after each lesson. For example, after learning Lesson One (**apple**, **banana**, and **cracker**) the teacher changed the positions of the real objects and then shook the four symbols in his/her hand and dropped them on the child's dominant side. (This ensured a random change of symbol position to control for any tendency to respond to position cues.) The teacher then pointed to the real banana and indicated (this time without any vocalisation) that the child should find the **banana** symbol and place it on the board in front of the banana. If the child did this, he/she was reinforced and the same procedures were carried out for **cracker** and **apple**. The position of the real objects was again changed and the sequence was repeated starting with **cracker**.

If the child failed to pass the retention test to a four out of six criterion, he/she was returned to the original guided demonstration task. If the child seemed to be bored with eight replications of the exact task, the symbols were alternated as follows: three trials for **apple**; four for **banana**; three for **cracker**; and so on until the eight out of ten correct trials were achieved for each symbol. This method was used on all subsequent lessons as well.

In the same errorless manner the symbols for the next set of objects (**candy**, **chip** and **cereal**) were taught. The child

The symbols read 'boy give (the) apple (to) girl'.

was at first reinforced for every correct move, but later reinforcement was given only for a completely correct act. The term 'move' is used to refer to any portion of the complete act the teacher desires. The behaviour is shaped by at first rewarding any correct approximation of the desired response. The moves required to receive reinforcement are gradually made more precise and complete, until the child must complete the entire sequence (act) to receive any reward. For example, at first the child would be rewarded for correctly selecting the symbol even if he/she failed to grasp the symbol and place it on the tray. Later, the child would be reinforced only if he/she selected the symbol, grasped it, and moved it to the tray. At a later point in time, the child would be required to place the symbol in a correct sequence, in order to receive any reinforcement. The gradual modification of the child's response is called 'shaping' the behaviour by gradual approximations of the desired behaviour. The tapping, which was used in the first two lessons, was faded out in Lesson Three. See Appendix C for more details of our more recent approach on individual lessons and retention tests.

We ran into our first problem with the next set of symbols,

give and **take**. We had developed an elaborate manual which described a step-by-tep teaching process for this apparently logical set. However, we were forced to abandon the lesson plan and change our approach. The motions involved in the act of giving or taking were apparently so similar that the children were confused. We therefore moved to an entirely new set of verbs, **eat** and **insert** (or **put in**) since these verbs involved distinctively different actions.

Prior to teaching the new verbs we had the children learn several other symbols (**ball, box, cup, dish, spoon, fork**) in order to construct meaningful relationships for **insert**. All of these were taught in the same manner as the other noun symbols. To teach **insert** the teacher placed the symbols **child, insert, apple, box** on the board and guided the child to perform the action. Since this was a correct action the child was reinforced. The teacher then guided the child through the procedures until the child could insert the apple into the box alone. Again the child was required to do this correctly to a criterion of eight out of ten trials. The teacher then constructed a new symbol combination **child, insert, cracker, box** and motioned the child to carry out the action. After the child had done this successfully to a criterion of eight out of ten trials, the teacher substituted the symbol **cup** for **box** and the child had correctly to place the cracker in the cup eight out of ten trials. In the last teaching session the teacher substituted the symbol **cereal** for **cracker** so the phrase read **child, insert, cereal, cup**. Again the child was required to do this to a criterion of eight out of ten trials.

To teach the verb **eat**, the teacher put the symbols **teacher, eat, candy** on the board and carried out the command. The teacher then replaced the **teacher** symbol with the **child** symbol and guided the child through the procedure. The above steps were continued until the child could renact the sequence of picking up and eating a piece of candy on his/her own. (Again to the criterion of eight out of ten trials.) The teacher then substituted the symbol **chip** for the **candy** symbol and went through the same demonstration and guided steps until the child correctly took a chip and ate it eight out of ten times. The teacher then substituted **cereal** for **chip** and went through the same guided steps until the child did this correctly eight out of ten times.

The retention test involved having the teacher construct the sentence, **child, eat, candy** and the child was required to carry out the command. The teacher then constructed the sentence **child, insert, cracker, box** and the child was required to carry out this command. The teacher then constructed the sentence, **child, insert, banana, cup** and the child was required to carry out this command. The last retention test required the child to construct a sentence after the teacher performed the action sequence. The teacher ate a piece of candy and indicated that the child was to construct the sentence describing the action. This lesson was considered learned if the child could do three out of the four retention tests correctly.

All remaining symbols sets were taught in a similar manner (for variations on this theme see Appendix C). It is very important for the parent or teacher to note that the retarded child will quickly pick up cues from the teacher, so the teacher must not only learn to randomise symbol positions to control for position learning, but must also learn not to give any visual cue by attending to the correct symbol.

Because our funds were limited we could not teach all symbols to every child. We therefore made a decision to teach some of the more abstract concepts to subgroups of children. We had found that the children differed in their attention and acquisition rate (see Table 2). So we stopped training the slowest two children, the two girls in our study, and used that additional time with the remaining children who seemed to learn at a faster rate.

RESULTS

All eight of the nonverbal retarded children were able to learn some symbols in the four-month training period. The range varied dramatically, however. The slowest, Lorna, learned only five symbols representing concrete nouns, and she required an average rate of 101 trials per symbol set. (Lorna and Linda were trained for only a three-month period.)[7] Linda, our second slowest child, learned fourteen symbols, but again all of these were concrete nouns. Because of her slow learning rate we did not try to teach her any of the verbs, which had been more difficult for the other children.

Charlie was clearly the star of our programme. He learned thirty-six symbols at an average rate of eighteen trials per set. The symbols included such abstract concepts as **food**, **colour of**, **question**, and the numbers **One, Two and Three**. Charlie was able to read sentences such as **One and One, and One, same, ?** and answered by replacing the **?** with the symbol for **Three**. Much of Charlie's learning was of a one-trial type. Pete, the young man with cerebral palsy, also proved to be an able student and learned twenty-eight of the symbols, including prepositions. All of the boys were able to construct three- to seven-symbol sentences. They could also carry out commands such as **child, insert, apple, cup, and banana, box**. When the groups were divided into fast, medium, and slow learners on the basis of the number of trials to learn the symbols, it was evident that the fastest learners also learned more symbols. The fast group learned thirty-two symbols averaging thirty-one trials per set, while the slow subjects learned 8·5 symbols averaging seventy-seven trials per set. Because of the small number of children in each of these sub-groups no statistical analysis was performed.

Group Three, the six preschoolers who went through the training procedures, learned all the symbols and were able to construct from three-to seven-symbol sentences in a three-week period. The retarded children needed a longer period of training, and on the retention test, administered one week later, the retarded group exhibited a retention knowledge of 88 per cent. They were given an average of thirty-five symbols, ranging from five symbols to forty-one symbols on the retention test. The Group Three preschoolers were given all of the symbols and had 74 per cent retention one week after training. Thus both of the trained groups did learn and have high retention. The higher retention for the retarded group may have been due to the fact that they were, on the average, tested on fewer symbols and therefore some of these children were tested on sentences which were less complex, and there was less interference in memory because there was less to recall. Additionally, the greater number of trials this group required to reach criterion may have resulted in some degree of overlearning. Again, the retarded children could furnish missing parts of sentences (**cup, same as, ?**), carry out commands (**child, put, ball, on, box**), construct sentences (**one and two is three**), construct sentences to guide their behaviour (**child, eat, candy, and, child, put, fork, in, dish**), and construct commands for their teachers (**teacher put cereal under cup**).

The child is incorrectly constructing the sentence
'apple give apple'.

There was an increase in scores on all of the pretest measures (Leiter, Peabody Picture Vocabulary, Adaptive Behavior Scale —positive behaviours); however, none of these changes were significant when compared with the changes in the nontrained verbal retarded group.

We had hypothesised a decrease in negative, acting out behaviours with increased communication skills; and retrospectively, this seems to have been a quite unrealistic expectation on our part. Since the children had no access to the symbols and no individuals in their ward were familiar with the symbol system, they could communicate only during the training sessions. Thus, there was no increased communication outside the training sessions and no resulting decrease in frustration.

Neither mental age, chronological age, nor IQ predicted which of the children would be a fast learner. Ben, the youngest child, had the highest mental age on the Leiter, and while he was a good student and learned many symbols (29), both Charlie and Pete, who had a much lower mental age and IQ, clearly excelled Ben's performance. The two girls, who proved to be our slowest pupils, did not have particularly low IQs or mental ages. Lorna had autistic-like behaviours, however so did Mike and he was able to master twenty-nine symbols. One of the factors that seemed significantly to influence the learning rate was how attached the child was to the teacher. The children who exhibited less spontaneous attachment to their teachers seemed to learn less.

The motion picture film shows the individual differences in attention span, attachment, social behaviour, and learning rates very clearly. At the beginning of the study, all of the children were highly distractable. When the lights and camera were turned on this distraction seemed overwhelming for some. Later filming sessions show that some children overcame this distractability while others did not.

While all of the children seemed to enjoy the training sessions, some responded in a more passive way than did others. For example, it was always necessary for the teacher to find Linda and lead her to the teaching sessions, whereas both Pete and Charlie would eagerly await the arrival of the teacher and in some cases, almost overcome him/her with welcoming hugs.

The film was also useful in demonstrating individual differences in response styles. Towards the end of her training, Linda is seen laboriously, but correctly, responding with the correct symbol when shown the actual object. In contrast, films of Charlie show him interacting with the preschool group and spontaneously constructing sentences for these children. Charlie was taken on a visit to the preschool on several occasions and he and the younger children enjoyed the encounter. We were able to film several interesting episodes as a result. In one scene, Charlie is working with Paul, a preschool child who constructed his sentences from the left to right direction. There was a brief moment of puzzlement on Charlie's face as he read **box, insert, cereal**, and **candy, eat, boy**. He then smiled and pointing with his finger, read the sentence in the opposite direction and correctly carried out the action. He subsequently reversed the direction of the sentences he constructed for Paul.

In another scene, Charlie is seen constructing sentences for a very pretty preschooler named Susie. Charlie constructed the sentence, **girl, eat, candy**. Susie flirtatiously looked at Charlie, blinked, fluffed her hair, pointed to the sentence and smilingly picked up a candy and ate it. It was difficult to get Charlie to construct any other sentence for Susie after he had observed her pleasure with this one, and it took a great deal of coaxing to get him to construct a more elaborate sentence for her.

The children showed a good knowledge of this artificial language and adapted it when necessary. They were also able to generalise to untaught items. For example, the symbol for **food** was learned with six **foods** (**apple, banana, cracker, candy, cereal**, and **potato chip**). The children were then later able correctly to label as **food**, items which had not been taught, such as **lemons** and **pears** and **grapes**. They were also able to choose a red apple and a red dish in response to **red, colour of, ?** which they were taught and they were then able to generalise to non-taught objects such as red wool and red pens. As another example demonstrating their knowledge of the use of the symbol system, Pete constructed the sentence, **child, eat, fork**, and laughed when he looked at what he had written. He then placed some cereal on the fork and ate it.

On the Concepts Test[3] which measured knowledge of concepts —such as 'same' and 'different'; 'on', 'in', and 'under'; 'large' and 'small'—previous knowledge of the concept did not seem to be related to mastering the symbol representing it. Some of the children understood none of the concepts at the beginning, and others knew ten out of the fourteen tested. Charlie, for example, did not know 'same–different' before training. However, he learned it in the symbol system and remembered it on the post concepts test. By contrast, another fast learner failed all of the items both before and after training.

Charlie also acted as a teacher for some of the slower children. We have films of Charlie helping Ben learn the concept **food**, and Charlie's delight as Ben begins correctly to identify food and non-food items is evidenced from his smiles and clapping. Charlie worked with four of the boys under the supervision of the teacher, and again it was evident that both Charlie and the other boys thoroughly enjoyed this situation.

As a test of comprehension, one of the teachers pretended to misunderstand Charlie when he constructed the sentence, **Teacher put candy in box**. The teacher started to eat the candy, and Charlie vehemently shook his head 'no', and pointed to the box, demonstrating the task to the teacher. This proved to be a useful variation to determine if the child understood the sentences he spontaneously constructed—we have several filmed scenes of Charlie correcting his teacher.

The results clearly show that the Premack system can be used to teach the severely and profoundly retarded child to communicate with a symbol system rather than a vocal language. Two of the children showed autistic-like behaviour yet they respectively learned five and thirty-one words. Except for the child who learned only five nouns, all of them demonstrated the learning-to-learn phenomenon, even though some of the symbols presented later represented far more difficult concepts. "Learning-to-learn" is a term commonly used in psychology to refer to the learning of a

F

'Child want eat cereal and banana.'

strategy rather than a specific response. For example, when Charlie learned the first set of symbols (**apple, banana, cracker**) he learned more than the symbols: he learned that specific real objects are associated with specific symbols, and thus on the following sets he immediately attempted to associate the symbols with the objects. Because of this effect much of his later learning was rapid: some symbols were learned on only one trial. (This was not true for our slow learning group, since they still required many trials to form the same type of association.) It did not suprise us that the children tended to learn faster as training proceeded, but other changes were unexpected. During the process of training, about half the children started to vocalise spontaneously, imitating the tonal quality and sentence length of their teacher. Thus, when the latter said, 'The dish is different from the apple', Charlie would vocalise, 'ta da ta da ta da'. However, the children didn't vocalise in other situations.

The children also showed increased attention span and this was so noticeable that the ward personnel reported the changes to us. But neither spontaneous vocalisation nor length of attention span were measured in any consistent manner in this project.

The large difference in the rate of learning in the retarded group underlines the heterogeneity of functioning in this group, and the error of labelling all of these children as having the same degree of retardation. Learning rates had no consistent relationship to mental age or IQ for the retarded subject. (This confirmed previous findings.) Learning rate for the retarded might thus be a better predictor of job performance than are traditional measures of IQ.

Predictable differences were found between the retarded children and the normal children, with the latter group learning the entire vocabulary in less than one quarter of the time required for the retarded children. The film clearly shows the differences in the retarded group before and after training.

A particularly satisfying outcome of the study was that Charlie's capacities were called to the attention of the staff. This child, who had not been responsive to any form of language therapy (including signing), was now given sign language training, and has been placed in the community in a class for trainable mental retardates.

CONCLUSIONS

Where traditional speech therapy has failed, nontraditional communication systems may be of use. If a retarded nonverbal child has not been able to learn through speech therapy, either a symbol system such as ours or a signing programme should be attempted.

In a previous chapter, those working with signing[9, 10] have pointed out several advantages for signing programmes. These are : (1) its greater flexibility as compared with communication boards or plastic symbols; (2) the ease of use and portability of equipment; (3) the spontaneity permitted the child; (4) the non-curtailment of creativity; and (5) the ease of teaching, by moulding the child's hands into the desired response. The advantages of a computer-based system were delineated by Dr Savage-Rumbaugh.[11] These are : (1) the motor response is simple; (2) brightening keys and maintaining illumination focus attention, and the image remains on the projector thus counter-affecting short-term memory deficits; (3) the sequence is arranged to separate the act of communicating from the message; (4) the use of the computer allows for more reliability in environmental events; (5) the subject can work at his/her own pace; (6) interpretations of a response are always consistent (teachers may vary in recognition of sloppy signs or vocalisations); (7) the computer acts as the communicator, thus decreasing the need to please the teacher; and (8) data collection is easier, more reliable, and complete.

In evaluating the Premack system in relationship to the above, it becomes obvious that the system has both pluses and minuses. Signing does indeed give the signer more flexibility, and the necessary equipment is always with the child, unlike a piece of baggage which can be misplaced. 1, Yet spontaneity and creativity need not be curtailed by the symbol system, and they can in fact be encouraged by teaching the symbols **name of** and **what is**. The children in our pilot study did build sentences spontaneously, and they demonstrated both creativity and humour. Their spontaneity was limited to the training sessions, but this difficulty could be easily overcome by placing symbols in all wards where the children live, and by teaching ward personnel and other children the system. 2, Also, not all children have the dexterity accurately to reproduce signs, while the responses required by the symbol system, as by the computer system, are simple enough to fall within the behavioural repertoire of most retarded children. 3, The symbol, further, remains in view, as does any written sentence, thus decreasing demands on short-term memory. 4, If symbols are placed in the wards each child can work at his/her own pace. 5, The interpretation of the response is much clearer than it is in signing or vocalising and therefore the teacher is less likely to reinforce inappropriate behaviour. 6, Since the child's response to the teacher seems to us to be a critical factor, we are not sure that we would wish to eliminate the demand of pleasing the teacher, as Savage recommends.

To summarise, the Premack symbol system does have some disadvantages. It is less flexible than is signing, and the child who can sign enjoys the possibility of enhancement of spontaneity and creativity. For the profoundly retarded child, however, the demands of signing may be too great, as there is a greater reliance on short-term memory and the response required is a relatively complex one. The child must accurately produce a sign, whereas in the Premack system the act is one of recognition, discrimination, and a simple motor response. We would certainly recommend that any nonverbal child be taught to sign in preference to using the symbol system if the child has the potential to learn signing. But since it would seem that signing requires a high degree of dexterity and a higher level of functioning than does Premack's system, for the child who does not have these abilities, the Premack system seems to be a simpler method of communication. It can be taught fairly easily and rapidly and may facilitate an advance either to speech or signing.[12] The Premack system is less expensive and elaborate than the computer system, and is also a great deal easier to carry around. In addition, it has the virtue of encouraging the development of positive social behaviour with the teacher and others.

In our pilot study we demonstrated several important things: (1) low functioning retarded children can learn the system; (2) the ease with which they learn the system varies; (3) mental age alone does not predict learning rate; and (4) use of the system may facilitate other communication modes.

However, several other questions must be answered. Can even

lower functioning children, those with a mental age below two years, learn the system? If the children have free access to the symbols, will they use them to communicate with one another? If the symbols are colour-coded for grammatical class, will the children learn faster?

To answer these questions and to demonstrate that para-professionals could use the system, a larger project was devised. In the next chapter we will describe our ongoing project at Pacific State Hospital, in which an entire ward of low-functioning retarded children will be taught to use the Premack symbol system.

TABLE 1

Pre- and Post-training: Mean group results: (n = 8 per group) for pilot study

Group		Leiter Chronological age	Mental age	IQ	PPVT Raw score	Mental age	IQ	Concepts test	AAMD* A	B
Nonverbal	Pre-	11·8	3·8	37·4	11·0	1·8	10·5	2·1	278·9	53·0
Retarded subjects	Post-	12·3	4·2	37·7	16·1	2·7	17·8	3·5	295·0	58·5
Verbal	Pre-	14·1	3·8	30·0	19·4	2·5	19·8	5·7	316·0	53·2
Retarded subjects	Post-	14·4	4·1	32·0	28·8	2·9	24·2	5·9	321·5	54·6
Preschoolers	Pre-	3·8	4·9	131·0	45·7	4·7	112·0	13·8	—	—

* American Association for Mental Deficiency.
A = positive behaviours (independent functioning etc.).
B = negative behaviours (aggression, tantrums etc.).
PPVT: RS = raw score.

TABLE 2

Learning Rate of Nonverbal Retarded Subjects in the Pilot Study

	Subject							
Subject Number	1	2[a]	3	4	5[b]	6	7	8[b]
Leiter MA	3·8	2·5	6·0	3·5	2·5	4·5	4·5	3·3
Leiter IQ	38	15	64	26	21	38	53	43
PPVT MA	3·9	2·7	1·0	1·8	0·1	2·2	2·3	0·1
Concept	*Number of Trials to Criterion*							
Apple, Cracker, Banana	13	40	11	58	76	149	51	95
Subject, Trainer	8	15	8	20	20	20	48	108
Candy, Chip, Cereal	8	20	34	17	8	30	34	—
Ball, Box, Cup, Dish, Spoon, Fork	8	8	11	8	10	12	8	—
Eat, Put in	20	34	36	35	270	—	227	—
Clean, Give	22	10	38	28	108	—	40	—
Same, Different	325	309[c]	673[d]	161[c]	220[c]	—	—	—
Question (?)	36	—	—	—	—	—	—	—
Food	12	40	35	38	36	—	33	—
Red, Blue, Yellow	12	40	69	73	39	—	180	—
Colour of	11	—	—	—	—	—	—	—
Numbers 1, 2	—	10	46	18	39	—	120	—
Numbers 1, 2, 3	20	—	—	—	—	—	—	—
Adding (and)	23	—	—	—	—	—	—	—
On, Under (in)	—	170	97	—	17	—	—	—
Boy, Girl	e	e	e	—	—	—	—	—
Small, Large	19	—	—	—	—	—	—	—
Size of	19	—	—	—	—	—	—	—

[a] this subject had cerebral palsy; [b] autistic-like behaviour; [c] not learned; [d] first taught verbally; [e] known by recognition (symbols were appropriately shaped); dashes indicate the symbol was not taught.

6: The Ongoing Project

'It is only by amusing oneself that one can learn.' E. Kasner and J. R. Newman, *The World of Mathematics*, 1956.

The pilot study demonstrated that the retarded child could use the Premack language system, and that for some the system facilitated use of other communication modes. Our ongoing study at Pacific State Hospital[1] on the other hand was designed to answer several specific questions raised during the pilot work. These were :

(1) Could an entire unit of children be taught to use the Premack system?

(2) Would the children use the system to communicate spontaneously with one another and with staff members after they had learned it?

(3) Is the system suitable for children who function at a very low developmental level?

(4) Does colour coding to represent classes of words (nouns, verbs, prepositions etc.) facilitate learning?

(5) Can the nonprofessional use this system to teach the retarded child?

(6) Was the increased vocalisation we observed among the children due to learning the Premack system, or was it simply due to individual attention accompanied by a vocalising model?

In an attempt to answer these questions, an entire ward of primarily nonverbal children[2] are currently being taught to use the Premack system. One third of the children have some language skills, ranging from single words to very simple speech, which is in general unclear. The child with the highest speech level is a young boy who has approximately the vocabulary and language use of a five-year-old. No other child is near this level, as the other vocal children have very limited language.

The children in this ward range in age from nine years to seventeen years, with the average age being about twelve years. Ten of the children were randomly chosen from matched pairs to act as control subjects, as were ten children from another ward. The first control group was used to determine how much of the Premack system these children would learn from the children who were directly taught the system.

Both groups of control children were given the same amount of one-to-one interaction, with modelled vocalisations. The primary purpose of this strategy was to see whether it was the use of the Premack system that had facilitated the increased vocalisation we found in the pilot, or whether, because of the reinforcing properties of the one-to-one vocalising model, vocalisation itself had become more reinforcing. The effects of modelling upon facilitated vocalisation would be consistent across trained and control groups, and thus if the trained groups do tend to vocalise more than the control groups, the use of the Premack system as a facilitator of language would be clearly demonstrated. A secondary purpose was to assess change in attention in the same manner. The children in the pilot study had also become more attentive, but we could not ascertain if this increased attentiveness was due to the one-to-one interaction, or facilitated by learning the Premack system.

In the original pilot study, it was hypothesised that there would be a decrease in negative behaviour as measured by the Adaptive Behaviour Scale, and this decrease was not found. Retrospectively, we realised that it had been naïve of us to hypothesise this, when the children were not able to use this communication system outside of the training situation. In the current study, we hope to discover if availability of the symbols outside the teaching situation will facilitate communication and reduce negative acting out behaviours. After the children have learned to use the system, the symbols will be available on the ward, and the children will be able to construct communication for their caretakers and peers if they wish to do so. Thus, in this study, we will be able to assess spontaneous use of the Premack system and to see if this communication has any direct relationship to frustration-induced negative behaviour.

The children in this ongoing study are a much lower functioning group than those in the pilot study. Due to large shifts within the hospital assignment, the unit population has become dramatically lower, so the group under study have extremely low mental ages and a large number of behaviour problems. For most of this sample, the tests of mental age used in the pilot study were not appropriate. We attempted to use the Leiter and the Peabody Picture Vocabulary Test; but most of the children could not pass any of the items and were therefore given the Kuhlmann-Binet (KB).[3] The twelve- to eighteen-month items from the Kuhlmann-Binet include:

(1) Can the child take a drink of water?
(2) Can the child take a drink of milk?
(3) Has anyone reported the child ever was able to take a drink?
(4) Can the child spit out distasteful food?
(5) Can the child feed her/himself with a spoon?
(6) Can the child feed her/himself with a fork?
(7) If presented with a picture, does the child gaze at the picture?

On the basis of our testing, the children fell into two mutually discrete groups. One group, the low functioning group, was composed of thirty-two children who were tested with the Kuhlmann-Binet (one was given the Stanford-Binet). The majority of these children were non-verbal, having expressive language skills ranging from grunts, clicking sounds, speechlike sounds (ahh, uum) to a few who have words and some word combinations. The average Kuhlmann-Binet mental age for the group was one year five months, ranging from a low of eleven months to a high of twenty-four months. The average IQ was 13, ranging from a low of six to a high of 30.

The second group of higher functioning persons, was given both the Leiter and the Peabody Picture Vocabulary Test. The mean Leiter Mental Age for this group was four and a half years, ranging from a low of two years nine months to a high of seven years six months. The average IQ for the group was 43·5, ranging from a low of 36 to a high of 64. (See Table 3 for individual scores). For the Peabody Picture Vocabulary Test the average mental age was three years, ranging from a low of 2·5 to a high of 7·3 years.

No direct comparison of the colour coding nor random use of colour for the symbols was planned. A comparison of the acquisition rates for the higher functioning group with the acquisition rates from our pilot group would allow some comparison; but since the symbols used in this study are sometimes representational, only a comparison of word classes could be made. If for example the second and third members of a class such as verbs are learned much more rapidly than were second and third verbs in the pilot study, this would tend to indicate that colour coding facilitates learning word-class codes. Since we are using volunteer aides as well as college students, we will be able to evaluate the ease of teaching the system for the nonprofessional person.

In addition to the intelligence tests or developmental tests, the children were rated on language skills. The expressive language test contained items such as the following :

(1) Does the child respond to questions? (The teacher holds up a piece of candy and asks, 'Do you want candy?')
(2) Can the child imitate sounds? (Say 'mm', say 'pp', say 'eeh')
(3) Can the child imitate words? (Say 'ma-ma', say 'pot')
(4) Does the child say anything spontaneously?
(5) How clear and understandable is the language?

To test for receptive language, three requests were made by the teacher under three conditions. The child was asked to 'sit down', 'come here', and 'give me a pencil'. In condition one, the teacher gave no clue as to the meaning of the request; in condition two, the teacher accompanied the vocalisation with the appropriate gesture (gesturing to come towards chair, and pointing to the pencil); and in condition three, the teacher gave false clues by pointing to a different object and saying 'give me the pencil'.

Separate scores were obtained on the three, since indication of confusion under condition three could indicate that the child understood both the vocal and gestured message; but there were also indications of confusion in response to the direct commands.

Using this system of rating receptive and expressive language, our lower functioning group of twenty-two children[4] who remained in training included two who had a few words, such as 'baby', 'candy', 'choo-choo train'; one who said phrases such as 'want my baby'; two who babbled; and three who made noises other than grunts. The remaining fourteen had no speech or speech-like sounds. The higher functioning group all had some verbal skills, ranging from single words to limited sentences.

In the area of receptive language, our groups did not differ as much. The higher functioning group all had some receptive language skills, such as demonstrated by responding to our questions, while the lower functioning group varied far more. Eleven of the low functioning group had about the same level of receptive language skills as did the higher functioning group. Six had essentially no receptive language (they were, however, non-deaf); and the remaining eight had a mixed level of skills, responding only to familiar commands such as 'sit', and 'come here'.

Each of the children was rated on an attention test covering items such as interest and responsiveness, eye contact, and body motion. Attentive behaviour seemed to be related to speech level, in that the children who had meaningful speech had high levels of attention (85 per cent of the time); those who had some speech (Level Three) were attentive about 67 per cent of the time; and the nonvocal children were attentive about 55 per cent of the time.

To summarise the plan for the study, there are three groups of children. Group one is receiving training in the Premack system. Within this group, there are two naturally discrete groups, one of which functions at a higher level than the other and tends to have some verbal skills. Group two is a matched control group living on the same unit, who are not receiving any direct training in the Premack symbol system. The third group of ten children are residents of another ward at the same hospital, and they also are not receiving training in the Premack system. All three groups were given several measures at the beginning of the study. The same measures will be administered at the end of the study. The children were tested for mental age (Kuhlmann-Binet, Leiter, PPVT), for concepts knowledge, for expressive and receptive language, for attention span, and on behavioural measures of positive and negative behaviours. All groups were video-taped to assess any gestural or vocal response to the question, 'Would you like a candy?' in order to evaluate not only increases in vocalisation, but any increase in attempted communication, such as meaningful gesture.

TRAINING PROCEDURES

For the children who had low levels of attention, and did not respond to the symbol teaching, a training procedure to develop eye contact, awareness of surroundings and task attention was instituted. This programme used behaviour modification principles to develop habits such as sitting at the table and attending to the lesson. This included presymbol training in which the child was trained to : look at objects, reach for objects, follow instructions, respond to social reinforcement, and imitate movements. One of the children was unable to grasp the symbol, so a grasping programme was developed in which she was taught first to grasp larger objects, and later, smaller objects such as symbols. We also found that it was necessary to train some of the children to match-to-sample (i.e. they learned to match an apple symbol to another apple symbol, or a banana symbol with another banana symbol). In this way, the child was trained to discriminate and recognise the symbols and objects and to respond to objects which were the same.

The training procedure we are now following is essentially the same as used in the pilot study, with the exception that for the very low functioning children many additional intermediate steps are required. The symbols are again of varying shape and made of plastic, and they are colour coded as follows : nouns are red, verbs are blue, adjectives and adverbs are green, colour names

are grey, and other speech parts are yellow. Some of these shapes
are representational.

The student and teacher sit at a table with the student facing a
12″ by 18″ framed board, with the wide end parallel to her/him
(a framed board is required since many of the children have
poorly coordinated perceptual and motor movements, and tend
to displace symbols, sometimes causing them to fall on the floor.
A smaller board was used later, and these seemed even more
effective in framing the area.) Directly beyond the board are two
or three real objects and some food reinforcers such as candy (or
whatever has been found to be reinforcing to the student). The
symbols to be learned, plus one which will remain unfamiliar, are
placed on the left or right side of the board according to the
child's preferred hand dominance.

The teacher starts by tapping the appropriate symbol to the
real object (for example, the apple), and then places the symbol
directly in front of the object, but on the board. The teacher then
places the symbol in the child's hand and moves the child's hand
to tap the symbol to the object and then place the symbol on the
board. The child is immediately reinforced, since this is a correct
move. Reinforcement should be of both a tangible and a social
type. The teacher verbalises the procedure and says the sentence
as he/she carries out the act. The exact procedures were discussed
in Chapter 5, and are detailed in the manual in Appendix C.

To aid one of the children who had difficulty in learning 'same'
and 'different', we first taught the child to respond to an 'oddity',
or 'difference' task. To do this, the teacher placed three objects,
two of which are alike, on the board (cup, spoon, cup). A candy
was placed under the odd member of the set. The teacher demonstrated the task by picking up the odd member of the set (spoon)
and taking the candy. The same set was placed on the board
again, and the child was required to select the odd member of the
set (and thus reward himself/herself). When the child did this
correctly, the teacher switched to a different set (two spoons and
one cup) and repeated the demonstration. When the child did this
correctly, the teacher continued the test through several variations,
using different objects until the child had selected the odd

different member of four sets correctly. If the child did not perform this step correctly, the teacher demonstrated again, and once
more guided the child through the correct steps.

The teacher then went through the same sequence, except that
this time the symbol for **different** (odd) was placed under the
odd member of the set and the child received a reinforcement after
picking up the symbol for **different** and placing it on the board.
After the child had mastered this task successfully, the teacher
moved to the next step.

The symbols for **same** and **different** were now both available, and the teacher placed two dissimilar objects on the board,
such as an apple and a banana. The teacher then placed the
symbol for **different** between the objects, and took the candy.
The teacher then guided the child through the same task, having
the child place the symbol for **different** between the two dissimilar objects. When the child did this correctly, he received a
candy. The teacher used a variety of sets to demonstrate this, and
when the child had mastered seven sets successfully, the teacher
moved on to the next step: 'sameness'. The procedures were the
same as those for teaching 'different', except that the child was
presented with sets of identical objects, and the symbol for
same was used. Finally, the teacher wrote a series of phrases,
using symbols, rather than objects: **apple —— apple**, **apple
—— box**, etc., and the child had to place the correct symbol
(**same** or **different**) between the objects. For the test of
learning, the child had to respond correctly to phrases such as
apple same ——, **child —— teacher**, **red box same ——**;
so that the completed phrases would be **apple same apple**,
child different teacher, and **red box same red box**.

RESULTS

After four months of training, many changes were evident in the
children's behaviours. The majority of the children gained some
use of the Premack system, but the rate of learning varied widely.
The three higher functioning children, with mental ages of over
five years, learned the most and progressed the fastest. They are

now at the level of writing sentences and answering questions with the symbols. However even the low functioning group began to carry out written commands.

The higher functioning group have learned an average of twenty-five symbols, ranging from a low of thirteen symbols to a high of forty symbols. The child who has learned forty symbols after four months mastered such difficult concepts as same-different, numbers one to three; adding; prepositions such as in, on, under; sizes; size of; small, large; and question mark. This child is an unusually interesting case because he was diagnosed as retarded at an early age, and was living at home and taking special classes for the retarded. A few years ago, he was injured in an automobile accident. After this injury he lost all speaking abilities for a period of time. Now he can speak, but his expressive language skills are far more impaired. He has some words and limited sentences, but they are very difficult to understand. He has responded to the symbol system with a variety of emotions, at first treating it almost disdainfully as if the task were too easy for him. As he progressed very rapidly through the lessons, learning many of the symbols in relatively few trials, his attitude towards the training sessions has improved to the point where he responds to his favourite teacher and eagerly waits his turn. He prefers a non-tangible reinforcer of 'stars' which are traded for candy later.

The other two high functioning boys have also mastered most of the same symbols and enjoy their lessons very much. They also tend to defer the immediate reward of candy for stars and a later, larger reward. One of these children is particularly interesting because he will construct an incorrect sentence, correct it, and then ask for a star. This boy also became very upset when we were teaching the symbol **no**. He would rephrase the sentence to require a **yes** response. For example, if the question was of **colour of** (red) **dish blue?** he would change the **blue** to **red** so that he could respond **yes**, rather than use the **no** as a response (parentheses used to indicate true colour).

For the faster learning group, mental age as measured by either the Leiter or PPVT did seem to relate to the amount learned. The three boys with the highest mental age (5·9, 5·0 and 7·6 years) learned many more symbols than the three with the lower mental ages (3·2, 2·5 and 2·9 years). The data for the number of trials to learn the symbols (on an average) has not been analysed, but a cursory glance at the figures reveals the same general pattern.

The children with a developmental age between one and two years have shown very slow learning rates. They learned an average of seven symbols in the four-month period, ranging from those who know only the first food symbols, such as **apple** to those who can write simple phrases such as '(**child**) **give apple** (teacher)' (—the parentheses in this case indicate implied words). All of these children learned the symbols for 'teacher' and 'child' more rapidly than the other noun sets. The teachers and ward personnel have reported an increase in attention span and vocalisations for this group, and it was actually a surprise to many of the teachers and caretakers when some of the very low functioning children did begin to learn the system.

PROBLEMS

Three children were transferred out of the unit, and new children took their places. We have attempted where possible to give additional training to the new children to give them the same number of sessions and trials as the children in the present group. Where this has not been possible (in one case a child was moved into the unit four months after the programme started), the data will be evaluated separately at the end of the study. We also dropped four children from the programme.

Of these, one had a bout of prolonged illness and was placed in the infirmary section of the hospital for an extended period. Another was dropped because of violent attacks upon the teachers. This behaviour did not decrease despite behaviour modification procedures. However, it must be understood that the strongest negative reinforcer we could use was restraining the child's hands with a loud 'NO.' 'Time-out' procedures were also used to decrease negative behaviour for other children, and the method was generally quite successful. In 'time-out' procedures, the teacher refuses to interact, or engage in eye contact, or watch behaviour until the child stops his attention-getting behaviour. A third child was dropped because we could find no effective reinforcer, nor was the staff able to find any apparent preference for any food or drink or any responsiveness to social stimulation. Finally, after two months of training a fourth child on grasping, we decided to use our time more profitably with the other children. She had learned to unclench her hand to grasp, and could very slowly go through the procedure of picking up a symbol to place it on the board. However, every time there was a change in the staff personnel or she went home on a visit, she became highly distractable and the grasping programme had to be reinstated.

The high rate of turnover in the hospital personnel is probably not unusual for this type of facility, but the children tended to react negatively to such changes, and so did we. We would eagerly explain our methods and receive much enthusiasm and cooperation from staff members, only to discover that we needed to explain all over again as they were replaced by new people. We were, however, impressed with the sincere and willing effort the staff made to facilitate our study. Wherever possible, they took time to make our job easier by scheduling busy times around our teaching schedule.

There were noticeable behaviour changes that were not qauntifiable. One girl who was an aggressive behaviour problem now smiles and responds to social reinforcement. All of the children now want to come to the sessions, and the staff has found that they can control children who misbehave by not allowing them to attend. The children now have longer attention spans and are more responsive to social contact. Other examples of noticeable change include one somewhat verbal low functioning girl who used to hit herself and shout 'Stop it, Mary,' now shouts 'Good girl, Mary.' Some of the children who were considered mere 'blobs' at the beginning of the study are responding, and the staff and teachers have noticed the increased attention and responsiveness. One former 'blob' recently sat down spontaneously, placed the symbol for 'give' on the board, and carried out the action, smiling.

We have also noted that when the medication levels for a child

are increased, he or she tends to become less attentive and sometimes cannot respond even to lessons previously learned. The reverse may also occur, where a lower medication level leads to
higher distractability.

We came upon several unique problems with the low functioning group. The first major problem occurred when we discovered
they could match the symbol to the object correctly, but did not
understand the reverse task: that is, they were unable to match
the object with the symbol. We had to train them to shift from
one learning technique to the other; that is, after teaching that A
goes with B, we also had to teach that B goes with A. This was
not a necessary step for the children with a mental age of over
two.

We assumed that the children would then be able to transfer
this learning to a new set, and we would not have to teach shift-
learning for each symbol. However, we were wrong! It was necessary to teach symbol-object and then object-symbol for each item.
To illustrate the problem, consider Mary's responses. After many
trials, Mary learned that the symbol **apple** goes with the real
(plastic) apple; that is, she reliably (over 80 per cent of the
time) picked up the apple symbol, touched it to the plastic
apple, and then placed it on the board in front of the apple.
When presented with the actual apple and required to move it
to the symbol, **apple**, she could not do so. This step (called a
shift) must be taught separately. Having learned this shift, we
proceed to the next symbol, **banana**. Mary reliably (over 80
per cent of the time) tapped the **banana** symbol to the real
(plastic) banana, and placed the symbol on the board in front
of the real banana. When presented with the real banana and
required to move it to the symbol, she was unable to do this and
had to be taught this shift.

This same procedure must be used for each symbol even when
the child has mastered eleven other symbols and shifts. Shift learning seems to occur more quickly than the original pairing, but it
takes many guided repeated trials.[5] In other words, when the child
learns that A goes with B, he does not automatically learn also
that B goes with A; and having learned that A goes with B, and

B goes with A, he cannot transfer this to a new task. Therefore, when he learns that C goes with D, they must also learn that D goes with C, and so on. This represents an unusual conceptual deficit which we have never seen referred to in the literature.

We have now had many instances in which, for the group with a mental age below two years, it is necessary to break lessons into extremely small steps: first the match-to-sample task for both symbols and objects; and next, the association of a symbol with an object and then the reverse, the association of the object with the symbol. The children do not seem to make even the smallest conceptual leap or deduction. Thus any procedures requiring an inference or deductive process must be broken into additional training procedures.

This low functioning group has also had great difficulty in learning verbs. In the pilot study, we had a problem with verbs. We had initially selected two verbs, 'give' and 'take', which confused the children because they required essentially the same motions. In this study, we decided to pick verbs which had completely different motions, and we chose **clean** and **give**. The sentence **Child give apple teacher** was placed on the board. Note that the child already knows the symbols **child**, **apple**, **teacher**, and that **give** is the new symbol. The child was then guided through this procedure many times. We repeated this type of lesson over and over, but the children did not seem to learn. After several weeks of failure we decided that we would simplify the task and teach **clean** as a one-word sentence. Two real objects for which the symbols had not been learned (a bowl and a spoon) were placed on the table. The two symbols **give** and **clean** and a small cloth to be used for cleaning were also placed on the table. The teacher placed the bowl and cloth above the tray, placed the symbol **clean** on the tray, demonstrated the task by picking up the cloth and bowl and wiping the bowl with the cloth, and then reinforced himself/herself. The teacher continued to do this for as many times as needed to meet an 80 per cent correct criterion, and then proceeded to teach **give**.

To do this, the teacher used the same objects as in the **clean** lesson to be sure that the child associated the symbol with the action and not an object. The teacher placed the symbol **give** on the board and guided the child in giving the bowl to the teacher. This was repeated until the child could reliably (to a criterion of 80 per cent correct) clean the spoon when the **clean** symbol was on the tray or give the spoon when the symbol **give** was on the tray. The learning test involved variations of the above.

If the child did not master this, the teacher then proceded to go through the same steps with two other unfamiliar items. If the child had mastered the task, the teacher then proceeded to move to word sentences.

The previously taught words, **ball, box,** and **cup** were placed behind the tray with the cloth for cleaning. The teacher then wrote the two-word sentence **clean cup** and the child was required to clean the cup. The teacher then constructed a series of two-word sentences. The learning test required the child to achieve to the same criterion of 80 per cent correct, variations of two-word commands using **clean** (or **give**) the **ball** (or **box,** or **cup**).

At this point, some of the lower functiong group have reached this second stage. The children have proved able to learn the first part, the one-word sentence and the connection between the symbol and action, but seem overwhelmed when faced by a two-word sentence. We are in the process of trying new approaches, which seem to be working. In order to make the symbols more salient, we have added variations such as dots to the symbols, or used pictures to depict action. Our final report, which is to be available in 1978, will give information on the success of this technique, as well as more specific analyses on the time and number of trials required to learn each symbol set.

We have discovered other unique problems with our low functioning group. At first one of the children became so excited when he was right that he became distracted. He then performed incorrectly and was very frustrated—or so we surmised from an unusual display of temper from a usually passive, easygoing child.

Working with a large group has resulted in problems which can be readily resolved when smaller groups are taught. Some of the volunteers we originally used proved to be unreliable, often not showing up for sessions, or when they did appear, not reading the instruction manual before starting to teach. On the other hand, other volunteers were extremely reliable, followed instructions carefully, and worked well with the children. Based on their effectiveness, we can say that the system can be used by an interested person who is willing to take the time to follow the step-by-step procedures. The parent, teacher, caretaker, or grandparent of a non-verbal retarded child can use this system, and where necessary, improve it to meet the needs of the individual child.

A variety of Christmas events, including a temporary break for our teachers, led to disruption in the learning process, and many of the children needed to review materials they had previously passed, after the break. An even more serious problem has occurred with an outbreak of hepatitis on our control ward. This meant that we had to stop teaching for a while until the incubation period was over.

We have noticed that our teachers occasionally get discouraged when the children get stuck on a particular step. Yet they are always eager to try new methods to help the children over these obstacles. And they are always delighted with the evident blossoming of some of the children, and are proud of them when they do learn.

Among the interesting side factors we discovered was that we were never able to phase out food reinforcers for the lower functioning group. The faster learning group prefer tokens or stars as more rewarding than such immediate reinforcers as candies, but our lower functioning group tend to become upset when we give only verbal and social reinforcement.

One of the children was distracted by having three foods available (candy, chip and cracker) and would push away the symbol he was to learn to grab the candy symbol. Others seemed overwhelmed when many symbols were placed on the table, and could not respond to symbols they had recently learned. The answer to this problem is to reduce the number of symbols on the board.

Sometimes the children will put a symbol representing a food item into their mouths; however, they never do this for non-food items. Thus they evidently know which symbols represent something edible.

It would seem that even the very low functioning developmentally disabled child can master the labelling functions of the Premack system. Although the learning is slow, it is taking place. We now wish we had additional time, since the six-month period with its disastrous delays may not be of sufficient length to teach some of the low functioning children to build sentences. Some of the children who did not seem to be learning at first are now doing so, as we have seen by examining the slow drop in their error rate. And the staff have been surprised at the unexpected capabilities of some of the children who were considered hopeless. For these children it is important to break the learning task into mini-steps, and in some cases to build additional pretraining steps before the child can learn. It is very important to repeat learning trials many times before abandoning a particular lesson. Even for the child who has a low initial attention span it is worthwhile to attempt training. Three of the children who were considered the most distractable have improved significantly, to the extent of showing their distractability only between learning trials.

We are filming our training procedures again, and the film has many enlightening sequences showing the delight of the children with their new-found success. Some scenes are also of failures, as the children attempt unsuccessfully to respond to the difficult verb and object sequences.

CONCLUSIONS

At this point, we can state that the Premack symbol system can be used to some extent with even the low functioning child with a mental age below two years if he/she is taught on a one-to-one basis. In reviewing the conceptual and perceptual prerequisites for learning the symbol language, the low functiong group does seem to have the necessary skills : they can discriminate and respond to shape, size and movement; none are deaf and they do respond to sound (though the system does not require the ability to hear); they also [6, 7] have a hierarchy of food preferences; and they respond to touch and texture differences.

Premack[8] has commented on the chimp who did not distinguish the function of the referent (symbol) from that of the object it represents, as demonstrated by smearing a piece of apple on the board. All of our subjects seemed to differentiate between the class of real objects and the class of symbols. No child, not even the lowest functioning, attempted to smear candies to represent symbols. So perhaps we can conclude that children are, in some sense, preprogrammed for language function.

Our work has confirmed some of the previous findings. We have found that for some of the low functioning group (particularly those with a mental age below two years) separate, discrete, pretraining programmes may need to be given such as match-to-sample; attention shaping programmes; grasping programmes; and shifts. Our study has tentatively supported the view that this symbol system acts as a facilitator for other communication systems such as vocalisations and signing.

Our final report will be able to give information as to which children had specific problems and if there are pretraining criteria which might predict such difficulties. We shall also be able to state which words, procedures or concepts were difficult for all the children. At present, it seems safe to say that verbs are more difficult than nouns for this low functioning group to master. The inability of the low functioning group to respond to two-word and three-word sentences may be a limitation of their developmental stage or an artifact of our procedures. Our modifications of the planned lessons for the verbs 'give' and 'clean' should give us some indication.

The Premack system seems to be a useful predictor of which retarded child will be successful in moving into other communication systems. In view of our previous findings with the pilot group, the Premack system may be a much better indicator of learning ability than is mentage age.

Indirectly, the use of the system has affected the children. As the staff members have seen previously untrainable children progress, they have started to spend more time with the children. The system has also increased the children's responsiveness and social interaction. The system would be of greater value in a situation where the children were of about the same functional level. The range of abilities is so very disparate in our study that the progress made by the very slow can be easily overlooked in comparison with the rapid learning displayed by the higher functioning children.

Additional work is needed to compare the system advocated by Carrier with the Premack system, in order to evaluate the strengths and weaknesses of each. Carrier's system varies in teaching the rote sequence of a seven-word sentence model prior to starting actual language teaching. The children in our pilot study and the higher functioning group in our present study learned syntactical order without any direct teaching. They progressed from one-symbol labelling tasks to stringing fairly long and complex chains. We are therefore not convinced that this order sequencing is an important step, but we do not have any comparative data to back this up. Ideally, we should randomly assign matched subjects to be taught on one of the two systems, and later evaluate their progress in learning the systems and in increasing vocalisations.

Another distinction between Carrier's system and ours is in the use of pictures rather than real objects. The pictures Carrier uses are examples for the whole sentence and not for a particular symbol. It seemed to us that the manipulation of real objects was an important sensory input for these low functioning children, and in any case many of them did not show any significant response to pictures at the beginning of the study.

Carrier's subjects do all of the writing, which may be a significant factor, for they are therefore more actively involved in the system before our children are. Another difference which may greatly influence the more rapid learning rate he cites may be the randomness and cumulative nature of the way nouns are taught: the programme starts with only two nouns, the order of the nouns is randomised, and new nouns are added in a cumulative fashion, except that the noun being taught is always present at least 50 per cent of the time. This technique is quite important, since perseveration is not reinforced and continuous review is provided.

New words are also learned in the context of old words. Another difference is that we have required a fairly stringent retest for knowledge of symbols before moving to the next set, thus slowing down apparent speed of learning.[12]

Additional factors that may well influence the learning rate are the amount of control the system gives to the child. If the child can use the Premack system to obtain desired items, to make his/her needs and emotions known, and if these expressed needs are met, the system acquires greater value for the child. For the caretaker, parent or teacher little memorisation is required to learn the system since each symbol can be appropriately labelled. Although initially the child must have access to the symbols, as a final step potentially useful word symbols (which occur fairly late in our system), pictures of symbols, and/or a wall painting showing particularly significant symbols, could be made available to all of the children. This would overcome the availability problem. We do not yet know whether the children would respond to pictures of the symbols as they do to the symbols, but in the last phase of our study we will be looking at this question by examining evoked potential responses to pictures of the symbols.

For the parent or teacher interested in working with a particular child, the debate about the superiority of one system over another is less important than the fact that there are now systems available to teach the child who cannot make speech sounds to communicate. If your child can be taught to speak, no matter how clumsy the speech may be, it would seem best to place your primary efforts there. If your child cannot speak but has the dexterity and mental capacity to learn sign language, it is a far more viable system to use. It is important to know that neither signing nor symbol language will inhibit speech, but will rather facilitate oral language.

If your child cannot learn the signing, you should investigate the use of a symbol system. You have no need for an expensive set of symbols, but can make your own of any durable material (plastic, hardboard etc.) If, however, your goal is to teach a group, as in a school situation; or if your goal is to enable the child to communicate with more than a select few, it would be of greater value to use the same system for all children. Select the words that are most important to your child and those that will give him/her the greatest amount of control over his/her environment. Then teach the symbols consistently, preferably every day, at a quiet, unrushed time and follow the procedure we give in our manual (see Appendix C). There is no need to start with **apple**, **banana**, or **cracker** if, for example, your child's favourite food is a pickle. Teach him/her **pickle** first, and then proceed to other highly desired items. This will make learning the system itself rewarding.

The initial step-by-step procedures outlined in our manual will greatly aid you in your teaching. The particular items selected for teaching can be decided upon by you and your child. Just substitute those items for ours and use the same procedures. We hope that learning this system will facilitate other communication modalities for your child.

Good luck in teaching.

TABLE 3

Individual Learning Rates and Pre-Test Data for the
Training Group (No information is given for controls)

Subject	Kuhlman-Binet MA	IQ	Expressive language level*	Number of symbols learned as of 2/4/77
1	1–2	14	0	8
2	1–0	12	0	2
3	1–1	22	0	5
4	1–4	15	0	3
5	1–2	14	0	1[a]
6	2–4†	19	1	13
7	1–4	10	0	11
8	0–11	6	0	0[b]
9	1–4	8	3	8
10	1–5	10	0	1
11	1–10	16⁓	0	13
12	1–10	18	0	0
13	1–10	32	2	13
14	1–6	17	1	9
15	1–7	21	1	13
16	1–6	13	0	13
17	1–10	18	3	1
18	1–4	15	0	1
19	1–10	16	0	8
20	1–11	19	3	11
21	1–8	24	3	2
22	1–7	11	1	13

continued overleaf

Table 3—(continued)

Higher Functioning Group

Subject	Leiter MA	PPVT MA	Leiter IQ	Expressive language level	No. of symbols learned by 2/4/77
23	(3–2)c	2–3		3	13
24	2–5	1–10		4	13
25	2–9		36	3	13
26	5–9	7–3	50	3	40
27	5–0	5–4	47	4	38
28	7–6	3–8	64	4	33

* Key: 0 = no sounds; 1 = noise; 2 = speech-like sounds; 3 = some words; 4 = meaningful speech.

† Estimated.

a This child needed additional work on grasping.

b Later dropped from programme due to medication interfering with training.

c This score came from the Stanford-Binet and not the Leiter.

TABLE 4

Group Data on Pre-Test Measures

Group	Leiter MA	Leiter IQ	Kuhlman-Binet MA	Kuhlman-Binet IQ	Language skills*	Average number of symbols learned as of 2/4/77	Range
Low functioning N = 22	—	—	1–5	15·4	2	6·8	0–13
High functioning N = 6	4–6	43·5	—	—	3	25	13–40

* Expressive Language Scale:
   0 = no sounds
   1 = noise
   2 = speech-like sounds
   3 = some words
   4 = meaningful speech

7: Recapitulation and A Look Ahead

Success in using human language to communicate with other primates has opened up a promising new approach to help the language deficient and handicapped.

In this book we have discussed the technique of teaching a symbol system to those who have varying degrees of language impairment, and we have set this technique within the framework of language and its development.

We started with language and communication : a person's need to communicate is evident in the myriad ways he expresses himself, whether by movement, music, pictures or language. Of all these modes, language is most crucial to meaningful communication and to normal human development.

The significance of communication in the development of normal human functioning is difficult to exaggerate. When physical handicaps or developmental delays are accompanied by language deficits, a child's disabilities are severely compounded. The lack of functional speech causes both emotional and developmental difficulties. It interferes with language acquisition, and blocks the development of thought processes and of higher intellectual functioning.

Without the ability to express consent, dissent, needs, emotions, and ideas, individual autonomy is arrested, and emotional frustration results. Those who do not communicate are diagnosed and treated differently from those who do. If a person communicates, he is more likely to be treated as capable of comprehending, and at the same time he is provided with greater stimulation and met with more normal expectations. Recall the examples we cited of the cerebral palsied men. When they could not communicate, few bothered to teach or talk to them since they were, after all, literally 'dumb'. Yet once they were given a way to express themselves nonvocally they astonished others with their 'intelligence'. Because the consequences of language deficits are critical to healthy social, emotional and intellectual development, it is clear that one must provide forms of language stimulation adapted to individual needs and abilities.

Lack of language can mean temporary feelings of isolation, as when we visit a foreign country whose language is incomprehensible. Feelings of isolation can also be more permanent and more devastating: for stroke patients who suddenly find themselves unable to communicate; for the cerebral palsied who are frustrated from the beginnings of their lives; for all the other language deficient who search for some way to make their needs, wishes and ideas known.

When the means for ordinary communication are not available, some learn to adapt by miming. One of the children in our present programme is a past master at this. He makes eating motions to show he is hungry, rolls on the floor to imitate his friend's epileptic attack, and rolls his eyes to mean 'this is really silly!'

Others show maladaptive and negative behaviours, such as hitting themselves and others. When the doors of language are opened great changes may occur, as indeed happened with Helen Keller. This destructive hellion of a child became joyous, manageable and constructively curious about her environment once she made the illuminating connection between word and thing/idea —'everything has a name'.

Children like these are examples negating the generally accepted idea that language is acquired spontaneously by all unless they are deliberately prevented from doing so. Those who do not learn spontaneously, or those who by some accident have lost the facility to use language, are the ones who need to be taught to express themselves vocally and/or nonvocally.

However, most children do learn language spontaneously. It is this spontaneity, together with the fact that developmental stages and types of grammatical constructions are the same across different cultures, that has led psycholinguists, most notably Chomsky,[1] to posit an innate basis to language acquisition, i.e.

a 'universal grammar'. Whether the latter exists or not, we do know that innate capacities for auditory analysis, perceptual learning and so forth, do exist. So we feel it is not unreasonable to assume that there exists an innate capacity for generalisation and abstraction which helps the child as he/she acquires language.

We defined language as including the ability to convey concrete and abstract information (such as ideas, needs, and feelings), and to develop and form new concepts. This means that the person must be able to use language spontaneously and in different contexts, and to express himself by means of speech, or other nonvocal forms such as signs, writing or other symbols.

In this sense chimps have shown that they have learned human (nonvocal) language, although so far it seems that their level of sophistication and abstraction remains at the level of a young child's.

We gave many examples, including the findings of chimp communication, to show that thinking seems to occur prior to language. However, once language develops, it becomes intertwined with cognitive development, and helps expand thinking possibilities enormously. Because thinking can exist prior to language, one can, as in the case of chimps, build on concepts already present, no matter how primitive. From this base one can expand both expressive and receptive language, and also teach more complex concepts.

We next looked at the normal course of development and saw that, whether one looked at physical, mental or linguistic development, there were certain capacities which appear and reappear within fairly predictable age ranges, regardless of culture, class etc.

What parents have observed in watching their offspring, has been observed in more quantified detail by numerous professionals such as Gesell,[2] Bruner,[3] and Bower.[4] From infancy to childhood predictable increases in abilities and competencies inexorably occur, unless trauma intervenes and/or the child is handicapped in some additional way.

Although competencies are ever-increasing in the long run,

people like Bower have shown that throughout childhood there are apparent retrogressions. For example, the eighteen-month old child cleverly judges a ball of clay to be of the same weight, regardless of whether it is deformed into the shape of a long sausage, or rolled into a nice round ball—that is, the child has the concept of conservation of weight. Two years later the same child is not half as clever, and usually rates the sausage as heavier because it is longer. This ability to judge, to know that weight is 'conserved', fluctuates throughout childhood, and only becomes a stable part of one's bag of tricks by the time the child is about thirteen or fourteen years old.

Despite such apparent fluctuations, which are not as retrogressive as they seem, the child's constant learning permits him to build an ever-increasing repertoire. Those who are slower at learning come to be progressively further and further behind, since their learning base is so much slower and narrower.

A look at physical development showed the crucial importance of the young person's active interaction with the environment. Movement in space permits feedback from one's surroundings. When active interaction is not possible, feedback is limited, and there is a drastic curtailment in normal development.

In the normal child vision comes to play an increasingly important role. Some like Fowler[5] have suggested, not unreasonably, that perhaps 80 per cent of everyday problem solving and coping depends on vision, and indeed Arnheim concludes that problem solving is related to a 'reordering' of perceptual images,[6] and 'vision is the primary medium of thought'.

What cannot be predicted very well in the normal infant is his later IQ. Longitudinal studies have shown that very few indices of early development give a clue to later intellectual promise, or lack thereof. This is probably due to the fact that early tests of 'intelligence' are largely measures of motor ability which certainly cannot be equated with IQ.

Development does not occur in a vacuum, nor do individual functions proceed separately, one at a time. Indeed physical, mental and cognitive development occur more or less simultaneously, although in the first eighteen months, sensory-motor functions tend to take precedence. After that language becomes increasingly important, as well as inextricably intertwined with other effects of development, most noticeably that of cognition.

We suggested that, of the enormous amount of learning which occurs in early childhood, some can readily be explained in simple associative terms, i.e. a linking of stimulus to response in a more or less rote fashion. However, most learning probably involves cognition, and can be most economically explained as the product of hypothesis formation. This involves making decisions and responding on the basis of information, whether this is pictorial, linguistic, or whatever.

The young child, the mature adult, the dullard, the genius, and even nonhuman animals, can all be viewed as forming hypotheses and coming to conclusions based on them, regardless of the validity of either hypotheses or conclusions. Nonetheless, it is obvious that the more intelligent, and/or the more experienced, are more likely to be effective here. We concluded that hypothesis formation is a fruitful and flexible concept, since it can refer to most levels of response complexity, as well as clarify many aspects of learning, perception, and language acquisition.

Such acquisition starts from birth. We have distinguished carefully between expressive language (speech) and receptive language (comprehension), and between competence and performance. The distinctions are important, particularly when one deals with the language-handicapped individual. Recall the poor cerebral palsied man whom nobody wanted to teach at first because he could not talk. Hence he could not, by illogical deduction, comprehend what others said.

The normal child develops expressive and receptive language spontaneously. This is in contrast to others such as the retarded, autistic, aphasic, and the many cerebral palsied who show language impairment. These cases require much laborious teaching and a variety of approaches in order to stimulate language. As we have seen, some approaches are more effective than others in reaching a particular individual or diagnostic group.

Stages of language acquisition were seen to proceed from cooing, to babbling, to the development of single words, and then to two-, three- and multiple-word sentences. By the age of four the normal child has acquired basic grammatical operations, regardless of language, culture or social setting. Yet more sophisticated linguistic development continues into adolescence.

We suggested that before the child begins speaking, he is already able to think. But before the child can use mental symbols meaningfully to represent objects, he must, according to Piaget[8] and others, begin to form a concept of self which is separate from the objects surrounding him. Such a concept appears roughly at the age of one and a half years.

The careful studies of such psychologists as Brown[9] and Bloom[10] have put in quantifiable form many observations which intrigue and amuse parents as they listen to their children's developing speech. According to Slobin[11] and others, child speech is not merely a 'baby' version of the adult's. Child speech has its own unspoken rules and, indeed, follows roughly the same pattern regardless of which language is learned. We showed that the young child's errors are not haphazard, but instead follow certain logical guesses about the structure of language. If 'he sings now' is correct, surely 'he singed before' is also correct, since the past tense is formed by adding '-ed.'

Not surprisingly, both expressive and receptive language increase with increasing age, although we know that the level of understanding receptive language is generally higher than ability to speak. Despite this, there are times when children fool us. We think they understand the full import of a complex sentence, whereas in reality they correctly sift out the gist of meaning, and/or understand meaning only by context. If we remain aware of such levels of understanding, we increase our chances of offering more appropriate teaching techniques to children of different ages and abilities.

External factors influencing language development were discussed in some detail, and included socioeconomic status, cultural values and parental attitudes. Internal factors included attention, impulsivity, response to irrelevant stimuli, verbal control of behaviour, memory, intelligence and age—all complexly interrelated. Last but not least, sex is a factor in linguistic development. At all stages of the developmental period females generally exceed males in verbal competence, except for verbal abstract thinking.

Since this book's emphasis is on teaching those with language handicaps, we are particularly concerned with internal factors which might help or hinder language development. Younger children, retarded, and most autistics were seen to have difficulty in paying attention, and in tuning out irrelevant stimuli. They also show limitations in memory, which is related to their inability to adequately label, to rehearse, and to organise the material to be memorised. Other internal factors include intelligence, which influences amount and speed of learning, learning and memorising strategies, and level of sophistication in language and conceptualising.

The handicapped, like the normal, show a wide range of individual differences. Despite this, their specific disabilities place them within recognisable diagnostic categories such as the cerebral palsied, autistic, retarded and aphasics.

Much of our knowledge of brain functioning has come from investigating those with specific disabilities, like the aphasics. Various theories attempt to explain what happens when specific parts of the brain are destroyed. We concluded that there was evidence for localisation of specific functions in the brain, and evidence for more global representation of functions.

Furthermore, factors such as extent and locus of injury, as well as the age at which injury occurs, have important effects on how well, or how poorly, a person functions after damage.

We noted that in the very young child there is equal functioning in both sides of the bain, i.e. both halves are symmetrical, undifferentiated, and unspecialised. With time, brain functions diverge, and one half generally assumes dominance over the other. At this point hand preferences have emerged, and, for most people, language functions are then largely represented in the 'dominant' left hemisphere, while nonverbal functions, such as spatial perception, appear in the right hemisphere.

Recent evidence on the functioning of the two brain valves has come from the famous 'split-brain' experiments of Sperry,[12] Gazzaniga,[13] and colleagues. Results from these and other studies using drugs, special viewing and listening techniques etc., have further enlarged our knowledge of language functioning and the brain.

When we looked at abnormal language development, we saw that such abnormality may represent delay or deviance, either of which can be related to a variety of factors.

Retardates show delay not only linguistically, but motorically and cognitively as well. Although such delays occur across many different functions, we emphasised that even among retardates there are large differences. This is particularly true when one compares borderline retardates (who, by definition, are close to normals in functioning) with the profoundly retarded, who generally show gross impairments which are often qualitatively different in all categories including language. In addition, retardates may show some characteristics of other diagnostic groups such as the autistic, the deaf and the blind. As a group, retardates have difficulty in learning, focusing attention, and ignoring irrelevant information, and as their IQ decreases their language development becomes progressively delayed.

Instead of the delays shown by retardates, there are other groups who show deviant language and/or cognition in acquisition, reception and expression. Deviant language appears in aphasics, for whom the problem seems linked to auditory sequencing and difficulties.

Deviancy has been shown in autistics, for whom such deviance is considered their prime disability. Their other problems include defects in visual and auditory processing, as well as in cognition. Defect in the latter seems related to an inability to perceive order and meaning in stimuli.

Regardless of the diagnostic category, those who are further handicapped by language impairment suffer doubly from this burden, both in how others react to them, and in how well they manage to cope with their environment.

Consequently effective programmes to help stimulate language or communication are always in demand. The results of successful language programmes with animals have suggested promising new approaches for the language impaired.

Prior to the communication work discussed in this book, animal research has had considerable impact on educational systems. Riesen's[14] studies of sensory deprivation led to an increased emphasis on early stimulation. Dr Harry Harlow's[15] work with Rhesus monkeys demonstrated the extreme effects social deprivation had upon such 'innate' behaviours as sexuality and mothering. B. F. Skinner's[16] operant conditioning work with the lowly rat and pigeon led to behaviour modification techniques and programmed instruction, which are now used in institutions for the blind, retarded, and mentally ill, as well as in normal educational institutions such as colleges, universities and elementary schools.

Following in this tradition is the work of Dr David Premack[17] in developing communication techniques for the chimpanzee. His conceptualisation of the functions of language, the necessary prerequisite behaviours for communication, and his revolutionary teaching technique opened new avenues of communication for such groups as non-verbal retarded, cerebral palsied, or post-stroke aphasic populations. By simplifying language requirements, eliminating the need for oral production so that the communicator need only make a motor response, Premack made a communication system available for those groups who were unable to benefit from traditional techniques.

Several studies[18] have successfully used the Premack system. Carrier[19] has used an adaptation of the system with nonverbal retarded children and reports a high success rate with facilitation of oral speech. Glass, Gazzaniga and Premack used the system successfully with adult aphasic post-stroke patients. In both our pilot and present study, severely to profoundly retarded children learned to use the system.[20, 21] Munsch[22] and McLean[23] were able to teach the system to autistic children with varying degrees of success. The practical uses of the system for a variety of nonverbal populations thus seems well documented.

The work of the Gardners[24] has stimulated interest in using signing for non-deaf populations, and many recent studies have reported considerable success with simultaneous signing and speech programmes for autistic and autistic-retarded populations.

Our work, based on that of Dr Premack, has been directed

primarily at the nonvocal retarded population. One of us (Hodges), with the help of a graduate student, used a variation of the Premack system with adult aphasic patients with limited success.[25] However, our focus has been on the retarded, and in particular on the severely to profoundly retarded child. Our first project clearly demonstrated that severely retarded children with no language skills could learn to use the system.

The basic techniques used to teach the system are described in Chapter 5 and in Appendix C. The interested and conscientious reader can duplicate our results if she or he will be patient and follow the procedures. However, the reader should keep in mind the need to use ingenuity and try individual modifications where necessary. Each child has a different level of skill, and for some children it may be necessary to break sequences into even smaller segments to avoid learning blocks.

Our ongoing study will answer additional questions the reader may have. At this time we can safely report that profoundly retarded children can learn to use the system. The level of skill in learning the system varies, and again, doesn't seem to be generally related to mental age or to prior language skills. Some of the lowest functioning children are doing as well as some who scored higher in testing, and it would thus seem wise to try the system with even the lower functioning child. As our study has progressed, we have become aware of multiple difficulties in attempting to teach such a large and diverse group without a full-time staff. In doing such a large project, there are occasional oversights, and sometimes errors creep into the programme. We would recommend using the system on small subgroups of six to eight children, where one individual can easily supervise or handle the teaching.

The symbol system has several specific, but not exclusive, advantages. No long attention span is required. There is no reliance on short-term memory during training, because the word or sentence remains on the board during the learning process. This is particularly important since young children and retarded individuals, among others, are impaired on immediate memory span. The technique builds upon responses already existing in the person's repertoire, divides the learning process into a series of discrete steps, and makes use of both tangible and social reinforcers. Lastly, a sensory-motor approach is stressed which utilises tactual and visual information. This technique is, however, differentiated from those which emphasise sequential sensory-motor training, such as those described by Kephardt (1960) and Montessori (1964).

Premack's system provides a distinct advantage to the parent/caretaker/teacher as well. The latter can communicate directly with his/her student without having to memorise the language. This can be accomplished either by referring to a Dictionary list itemising the words and their accompanying shapes, or by looking at the correct word which can readily be printed underneath or on top of each shape. This also means that the parent or teacher can communicate instantaneously with the student without requiring prior training (as is needed in signing).

The printed word on the symbol may also serve another function. It may serve to stimulate and/or facilitate actual reading. (Deich and Brown have a proposal to test this possibility, as well as to teach the symbol system to stimulate speech with language delayed, handicapped children.)

Other advantages of such a system include the following: the symbols do not require complex interpretation of meanings; the simplicity of use and design make the symbols much like children's other educational games; because the symbols are both durable and lightweight they can be easily manipulated by children who lack fine motor skills; and, lastly, the symbols are easily portable, and so can be used on any level surface.

We cannot, at this time, definitely say whether use of the Premack system will always facilitate vocalising or signing. We will have some statement on this question after evaluation of our final data. As of now, several studies, including ours and Carrier's, tend to support such facilitation. As noted above we also intend to investigate how effective a symbol system may be in facilitating speech in language delayed, handicapped children.

We are also investigating the possibility of reducing the three-dimensional plastic forms to two-dimensional pictures and symbols which would be the equivalent of 'reading' a printed symbol construction. This would, of course, reduce the awkwardness of the system and make communication to others in a different locale possible.

It is interesting to speculate on the use of such a system internationally, or as a computer-video system. However, in view of the limited conceptual capacities that most of these children have displayed (below a mental age of two years), such events seem improbable. On the other hand, if one considers the higher functioning nonverbal individual, the system may well work to permit communication with peers and others via such devices. The use of a communication system coupled with an intensive stimulation programme for lower functioning individuals might reduce the deficit to some extent, but no programme that we are aware of has significantly altered the intellectual capacity of the retarded. Certainly the Premack system does not do this, nor do we claim it does. Rather, the system allows the retarded individual to communicate, and thus increases the possibility of correctly evaluating his competence.

The limits of the system have not been completely tested as yet, and we welcome additional research and training programmes. As an example, the use of the symbol system for studying the development of preverbal concepts has not really been attempted. Such information would be of immense value in understanding the verbally deficient population. We encourage others to apply the system where other systems have failed. Most certainly speech training or signing should be attempted whenever possible. But if speech training or signing programmes fail, a symbol system may be of value, as a transition instrument or, for some children, as a final goal. We have introduced the parent or teacher to a system of teaching that may meet his/her individual needs, and one in which they can be involved in creating and expanding the communicative abilities of their students by following a consistent, simple procedure.

In conclusion we feel the symbol system has promise. It may well be feasible to use as an alternate nonvocal system in cases where other attempts at meaningful communication have failed. Such a system could be used either as a substitute or, more hopefully, as a real stimulus towards more adequate language expression. As we noted previously, we of course would not recommend substituting an alternate system whenever speech itself remains a possibility.

To recapitulate : Although we emphasised that the symbol system is nicely applicable to nonverbal retardates, we feel that there are also broader groups of handicapped nonverbal, or low-verbal, persons who might well benefit from our system. Such groups might include the person who can handle receptive far more readily than expressive language. (Since we talk of the handicapped, in the commonly accepted sense of the term, we naturally exclude those who, coping with a foreign language, are usually far more adept at understanding rather than expressing the foreign language.) Since communication with symbols does not require speech, the problem of expression is by-passed.

Others who might benefit from an alternate language system might include the autistic who cannot properly cope with meaningful material, nor properly structure and sequence such material. If some measure of conceptual ability exists, some of the autistic may benefit from using our symbol system. Additionally, the child who has difficulties encoding in the presence of irrelevant stimuli, and who has passed the critical age of five, may find that learning to communicate by means of a symbol system is a more salient yet less demanding task than that of learning language per se, which requires from the start both audio-visual and long-term memory involvement.

There is also the aphasic who may have no difficulties with vision, yet has problems in understanding speech and in correctly perceiving the order of auditory stimuli presented at normal speaking speeds. There is the aphasic whose brain damage prevents him from communicating via speech and who furthermore has lost the ability to write. Both types may find that their avenue of expression, at least initially, may be by means of a symbol system.

There are those with impaired short-term memory who may effectively bypass the problem by means of plastic symbol shapes. As we said, no memory is required since all symbols are, or can be, simultaneously visible on the learning board.

Lastly, there may be those who are otherwise handicapped, but who do have visual and tactile abilities available in their repertoire. If they do, they may benefit from the symbol system, since it is geared towards the visual and tactual rather than the verbal.

Needless to say, the person must also have some desire to respond, a minimal level of attention, and at the least some very primitive concepts, in order for learning to take place. If such basic and simple capacities exist, and these exist even in chimpanzees, then we feel it is worthwhile to attempt teaching a symbol system as a viable alternative when other modes such as speech therapy are not successful.

References

Chapter 1

1 Peter Farb, 1968, p. 234
2 Kendler and Kendler, 1961
3 Alexander, 1975, p. 158
4 Sinclair, 1975
5 Quoted by Steiner, 1975, p. 173
6 Itard, 1932
7 Montessori, 1964
8 Keller, 1905, p. 36
9 op. cit., No. 3
10 op. cit., No. 3
11 Hebb *et al.*, 1973, p. 56
12a op. cit., No. 11, whole article
12b ibid., p. 56
13 Gardner and Gardner, 1969
14 A. Premack, 1976
15 A. & D. Premack, 1972
16 D. Premack, 1971
17 Schiefelbusch, 1967, p. 50
18 Hartley and Scott, 1975
19 Critchley, 1975, p. 3
20 E. H. Lenneberg, 1975, p. 18
21 *Encyclopaedia Britannica*, 1942, v. 13, p. 696
22 in Schiefelbusch, 1967, p. 50
23 O'Connor, 1975
24 E. H. Lenneberg, 1975
25 Koestler, 1975, pp. 595–596
26a op. cit., No. 8, 1905, p. 36
26b ibid., p. 256
27 Deese, 1958, p. 291
28 Berelson and Steiner, 1964, p. 92
29 Penfield and Roberts, 1959, p. 226
30 D. Premack, 1972
31 Scott, 1962, 1972
32 Rumbaugh *et al.*, 1973
33 Chomsky, 1972
34 Parveen Adams, 1972
35 op. cit. No. 12a
36 personal communication, 1973
37 Von Frisch, 1967
38 op. cit., No. 31
39 Russell & Russell, 1971
40 Sinclair, 1975
41 Borgese, 1965
42 Gardner and Gardner, 1969
43 D. Premack, 1971, or see No. 13
44 op. cit., No. 32
45 Calder, 1970
46 op. cit., No. 12a
47a op. cit., No. 39
47b ibid., p. 164
48 op. cit., No. 31
49 VanLawick-Goodall, 1971
50 Harlow, Gluck and Suomi, 1972
51 in Alexander, 1975
52 Christophersen, 1973
53 op. cit., No. 25
54 op. cit., No. 33
55 in Yergin, 1972
56 Bellugi and Brown, 1964
57 E. H. Lenneberg, 1966, 1974, 1975
58 McNeill, 1970
59 Hartley and Scott, 1975, p. 11
60 Broadbent, 1970
61 Hebb *et al.*, op. cit., No. 12a
62 Condon and Sander, 1974
63 Maurer and Maurer, 1976
64 Bower, 1966
65 Haaf and Bell, 1967
66 Goren, Sarty and Wu, 1975

67 Fantz, 1966
68 Salapatek and Kessen, 1966
69 Hershenson, 1967
70 Pettigrew, 1972
71 James Adams, 1974
72 Furth, 1972
73 ibid., but pp. 56–57
74 Piaget, 1969
75 ibid., but p. 6
76 op. cit., No. 40
77 op. cit., No. 74, but p. 9
78 op. cit., No. 16
79 D. Premack, 1972
80 D. Premack and A. Premack, 1974
81 Webster's Collegiate Dictionary, Merriam & Co., Springfield, Mass., 1947, p. 208
82 Maier, 1949

83 in Ghiselin, 1961, p. 43
84 Koestler, 1975, p. 118
85 op. cit., No. 83, but p. 118
86 op. cit., No. 57
87 op. cit., No. 23
88 McNamara, 1972
89 Wepman, 1976
90 Gombrich, 1960, p. 90
91 Vygotsky, 1972, p. 180
92 Bruner, in Piaget, 1967
93 Stephens and McLaughlin, 1971
94 quoted by James Adams, 1974, p. 94
95 Piaget, 1969, 1970
96 op. cit., No. 91, but p. 183
97 Whorf, 1956
98 op. cit., No. 52
99 Whorf, 1947, p. 214

Chapter 2

1a adapted from Lenneberg, 1962b
1b Gesell and Amatruda, 1964
2   Bower, 1976
3   op. cit., No. 2, p. 40
4   Held, 1965
5   op. cit., No. 2
6   Bruner, 1973
7   Maurer and Maurer, 1976
8a Gesell, 1940, 1952
8b Fantz, 1966
9   in Pines, 1970, and op. cit., No. 6
10 op. cit., No. 7
11 Goren, Sarty, and Wu, 1975
12 Salapatek and Kessen, 1966
13 Mackworth's and Bruner's findings reported by Thomas, 1968
14 White, 1966
15 Birch and Lefford, 1963
16 Piaget, 1969

17 Bayley, 1968
18 Kagan, 1971
19 McCall, Hogarty, and Hurlburt, 1972
20 White, 1964, p. 205
21 Bayley, 1955
22 Haber, 1970
23a White, 1966
23b ibid., but p. 97
24 Hochberg, 1972
25 J. Kagan and N. Kogan, 1970, p. 1305
26 ibid., but p. 1293
27 Stevenson, 1970
28 McNeill, 1970
29 Fourcin, 1975
30 Renuk, 1977
31 Fowler, 1971
32 op. cit., No. 28
33 Wood, 1976
34 Lenneberg, 1967
35 Nottebohm, 1975

36 Ervin and Miller, 1962
37 Flavell, 1970, p. 1010
38 Werner, 1957
39 Werner and Kaplan, 1963
40 Piaget, 1957
41 Piaget, 1970
42a Lewis, 1977
42b ibid., but p. 717
43 Bloom, 1973
44 Bloom, 1975
45 Brown, 1974
46 Brown, 1973
47 Brown and Bellugi, 1964
48 De Laguna, 1927
49 Stern and Stern, 1907
50 Leopold, 1949
51 op. cit., No. 48, p. 90
52 Sinclair, 1975
53 op. cit., No. 43
54 op. cit., No. 44
55 Brown and Fraser, 1964
56 op. cit., No. 45
57 op. cit., No. 28, p. 1074
58 Slobin, 1966
59 op. cit., No. 46
60 Smothergill, Olson, and
    Moore, 1971
61 Bowerman, 1973
62 Bloom, Lightbown and Hood,
    1975
63 Cazden, 1965
64 Lenneberg, 1974
65 Cited in Bloom, 1975
66 Kratochwill, 1973
67 Looft, 1971
68 Donaldson and Balfour, 1968
69 White, 1964
70 Kagan & Kogan op. cit., No.
    25, but p. 1300–1301
71 op. cit., No. 69, p. 201
72 Bruner, 1964
73 Birch and Lefford, 1963
74 Zaporozhets, 1965
75 cited by White, 1964
76 Emerson, 1931
77 op. cit., No. 69, p. 204
78 Deich, 1971
79 Piaget and Inhelder, 1969
80 Whorf, 1956
81 Vernon, 1937
82 Bayley, 1955
83 op. cit., No. 69
84 Slobin, 1968
85 Slobin, 1971
86 Bloom, 1970
87 Bellugi and Klima, 1972
88 Lenneberg, 1974
89 Slobin, 1972, see also op. cit.,
    Nos. 84 and 85
90 Gray and Ryan, 1973
91 op. cit., No. 31
92 Lesser, 1965
93 Fowler, 1970
94 Bernstein, 1971
95 Loban, 1965
96 J. Kagan and Klein, 1973
97 Krauss and Glucksberg, 1969
98 Krauss and Rotter, 1968
99 Krauss and Glucksberg, 1977
100 Hagen, 1972
101 Lehman, 1972
102 Maccoby and Konrad, 1967
103 Pick, 1972
104 Gollin, 1960
105 Gollin, 1961
106 Turnure, 1971
107 Schreibman, personal com-
    munication, June 1976
108 Yussen, 1974
109 Kagan, 1965
110 Kagan, 1967
111 op. cit., No. 18
112 op. cit., No. 25
113 op. cit., No. 96
114 Parveen Adams, 1972, p. 9
115 Luria, 1957, 1959, 1961

116 Graham, 1968
117 Farnham-Diggory, 1972
118 Hagen, 1971
119 Miller, 1956
120 Farnham-Diggory, 1972
121 Potter, 1966

122 Appell *et al.*, 1972
123 Kingsley and Hagen, 1969
124 Estes, 1974
125 op. cit., No. 123
126 op. cit., No. 120
127 Belmont and Butterfield, 1969

Chapter 3

1 Goldstein, 1939
2 Sperry, 1968
3 Gardner, 1975
4 Geschwind, 1972
5 Gazzaniga, 1970
6 Luria, 1970
7 P. Milner, 1970
8 Sage, 1976
9 Kimura, 1973
10 Lashley, 1929, 1942
11 Pribram, 1970
12 John, 1976
13 Gazzaniga, 1974 p. 380
14 in op. cit., No. 4
15 op. cit., No. 4
16 Buck, 1976
17 Lenneberg, 1966, a
18 Vogel and Broverman, 1964
19 Ornstein, 1973
20 in Buck, 1976
21 op. cit., No. 19
22 op. cit., No. 20
23 Nottebohm, 1975
24 Bakan, 1971
25a Zangwill, 1971
25b Zangwill, 1975
26 Sperry, 1968
27 op. cit., No. 5
28 in Gazzaniga and Blakemore, 1975
29 Gazzaniga, 1968
30 Gazzaniga and Sperry, 1967
31 Sperry, 1961
32 Sperry, 1969
33 Gazzaniga, 1973

34 op. cit., No. 29
35 Ornstein, 1972
36 Ornstein, 1973
37 op. cit., No. 25a
38 B. Milner, 1971
39 in op. cit., No. 7
40 op. cit., No. 25a
41 in Sage, 1976
42 Kimura, 1973,
43 op. cit., No. 7
44 Moyra Williams, 1973
45 op. cit., No. 24
46 A. Smith, 1975
47 Samples, 1975
48 op. cit., No. 35
49 op. cit., No. 24
50 op. cit., No. 20
51 ibid.
52 op. cit., No. 3
53 op. cit., No. 7
54 op. cit., No. 3
55 op. cit., No. 25a
56 op. cit., No. 7
57 Kinsbourne, 1975
58 Geffen, 1971
59 op. cit., No. 24
60 op. cit., No. 38
61 op. cit., No. 3
62 B. Milner, op. cit., No. 38
63 op. cit., No. 25a
64 Gardner, op. cit., No. 3
65 op. cit., No. 25b
66 Herron, 1976
67 McCall *et al.*, 1972
68 Fowler, 1971

69 Buffery and Gray, 1972
70 Kimura, 1973
71 Waber, 1976
72 in Khanna, 1968
73 op. cit., No. 44
74 op. cit., No. 3
75 Marshall in Hinde and Hinde, 1973
76 Graham *et al.*, 1963
77 Lenneberg, 1974, p. 627
78 Boll, 1973
79 Boll, 1972
80 Goleman, May 1976
81 Hermelin and O'Connor, 1970
82 Tallal, 1975
83 Tallal and Piercy, 1975
84 op. cit., No. 81
85 Mittler, 1970
86 Hughes, 1975
87 op. cit., No. 82
88 op. cit., No. 83
89 Fact sheet received 4/75 from United Cerebral Palsy Research and Educational Foundation, Inc.
90 Austin, 1975
91 Furth, 1972
92 Jarvella and Lubinsky, 1975
93a Rimland, 1974
93b Rimland, 1975
94 Schreibman and Koegel, 1975
95 Hermelin and O'Connor, 1970
96 Schreibman: lecture given at Pacific State Hospital, June 1976
97 Reynolds *et al.*, 1974
98 op. cit., No. 96
99 Wing 1966
100 op. cit., No. 95
101 op. cit., No. 93, a and b
102 op. cit., No. 95
103 op. cit., No. 95
104 Park, 1972
105 op. cit., No. 96
106 op. cit., No. 93b
107 op. cit., No. 95
108 op. cit., No. 96
109 Reynolds *et al.*, 1974
110 Frith, 1970
111 Frith and Hermelin, 1969
112 op cit., No. 95
113 1974 Handsheet from Pacific State Hospital, California
114 Deich, 1968
115 O'Connor and Hermelin, 1971
116 Baumeister, 1967
117 Robinson and Robinson, 1970
118 Heal and Johnson, 1970
119 Schiefelbusch and Lloyd, 1974
120 op. cit., No. 115
121 Crosby, 1972
122 Belmont and Ellis, 1968
123 Simmons and Tymchuk, 1973
124 Hermelin and O'Connor, 1958
125 MacMillan, 1972
126 Belmont and Butterfield, 1969
127 Kessler, 1970
128 Denny, 1964
129 Deich, 1974
130 O'Connor, 1975
131 O'Connor and Hermelin, 1965
132 op. cit., No. 126
133 Deich, 1973
134 Heal, 1966
135 Stephens *et al.*, 1971
136 Bryant, 1965 a, b
137 Fowler, 1970
138 Karlin and Strazzula, 1952
139 Lenneberg *et al.*, 1964
140 Lovell and Dixon, 1967
141 Dodd, 1971
142 op. cit., No. 138
143 op. cit., No. 139
144 op. cit., No. 140
145 Byrne, 1959
146 Lackner, 1968

147   op. cit., No. 85
148   op. cit., No. 17
149   Renuk, *Los Angeles Times*, Jan. 4, 1977

150   Dalgleish, 1975
151   Gray and Ryan, 1973
152   Kephart, 1960
153   Bortner and Birch, 1971

Chapter 4

1   Gardner, R. A., 1969
2   Gardner, R. A., 1971
3   Fouts, R., personal communication, 1977
4   Fouts, 1976
5   Fouts, R., Couch, J. B., O'Neill, Charity, 1977
6   Seligman, 1974
7   Schaeffer, B., 1974
8   Schaeffer, B., Killinyas, G., Musil, A., and McDowell, P., 1976
9   Lovaas, 1968
10   Konstantareas, 1976
11   Konstantareas, 1976
12   Nelson, 1973
13   Kotkin, R. and Simpson, S., 1976
14   Language Intervention Systems for the Retarded: a catalogue of original structural language programmes in use in the United States, compiled by Macalyne Fristoe, Ph.D. and L. Lloyd, Ph.D., State of Alabama, Department of Mental Health, P.O. Box 2224, Decatur, Alabama, 35601, cost— $2.00
15   Lloyd, L. and Fristoe, Macalyne, 1977
16   Fouts, op. cit., 1977

17   Rumbaugh, D. M., Gill, T. V., Brown, J., von Glaserfield, E. C., Pesani, P., Warner, H., and Bell, C. T., 1973
18   Lindsay, P. H., and Norman, D., 1972
19   Premack, 1971
20   Savage–Rumbaugh, S., 1976
21   Savage–Rumbaugh, S., 1977
22   Parkel, Dorothy and Smith, S. Tom, Jr., 1977
23   Premack, D., 1970
24   Premack, D., 1972
25   Premack, A. J., 1976
26   Fristoe, op. cit.
27   Lloyd, L., op. cit.
28   Carrier, J., 1974
29   Carrier, D., and Peak, T., 1975
30   Bliss, C., Semantography, Sydney, Australia, Semantography Publications, 1965
31   McNaughton, S. and Kates, B., 1977
32   McNaughton, op. cit.
33   Vanderheiden, G. C. and Harris-Vanderheiden, P., 1977
34   Fristoe, Macalyne, op. cit.
35   Lloyd, K., op. cit.
36   Ontario Crippled Children's Centre, op. cit.
37   Bliss, op. cit.
38   McNaughton, op. cit.
39   McDonald, Eugene, 1977

Chaper 5

1   Premack, 1969
2   Glass-Velletri (1971)

3   Dept. of Psychology, University of California at Santa Barbara

4 The authors gratefully acknowledge the support of NIMH Small Grant NH 21994

5 Our thanks to Ms Marion Biddle, Director of the Claremont Methodist Nursery School and the parents of this organisation for their cooperation.

6 Except for 4 sets, which were taught individually (and, ?, colour of, food).

7 Two subjects were dropped from the study due to their inattention to the task

8 Deich, 1972

9 Fouts, 1977

10 Shaeffer, 1977

11 Savage–Rumbaugh, 1977

12 Carrier, 1976

Chapter 6

1 This study was funded by a research grant from the Office of Education BEH No. 6007603152. Dr Hodges' time was made available by the California State University, Los Angeles.

2 Not all children were directly trained in the symbol system. Ten randomly selected children from matched pairs formed a control group living on the ward. In addition to this, several children were dropped from the programme for reasons described in the main body of the text.

3 One of the children was given the Stanford–Binet and one also scored on the Peabody Picture Vocabulary Test.

4 Several children were dropped from the group as discussed in the main body of the text. A few children moved into the ward in the middle of the study. Data are presented only for those who were given the equivalent of four months training (i.e. they may have missed a few days, but had recent additional training sessions to compensate for this).

5 Data on number of trials to learn shifts has not been analysed at this point.

6 Glass, Gazzaniga, and Premack, 1973

7 Carrier, J., 1974

8 Premack, D., 1970

9 Hodges, P. and Deich, R., 1976

10 Deich, R. and Hodges, P., 1975

11 Carrier, J. K. and Peak, T., 1975

12 We are indebted to Dr Nancy Squires for suggesting some of these comparisons to us.

Chapter 7

1 Chomsky, 1972
2 Gesell, 1952
3 Bruner, 1973
4 Bower, 1976
5 Fowler, 1970
6 In Petersen, 1972
7 Arnheim, 1969, p. 18
8 Piaget, 1957
9 Brown, 1973
10 Bloom, 1973

REFERENCES

11 Slobin, 1971, 1972

12 Sperry, 1961, 1968, 1969

13 Gazzaniga, 1968, 1973

14 Riesen, 1950

15 Harlow and Suomi, 1970

16 Skinner, 1957

17 Premack, 1970

18 Fristoe, 1975

19 Carrier and Peak, 1975

20 Deich and Hodges, 1975

21 Hodges and Deich, 1977

22 Munsch and Reichart, 1976

23 MacLean and McLean, 1974

24 Gardner and Gardner, 1969

25 Hodges and Salameh, 1976

Appendix A

ANNOTATED BIBLIOGRAPHY FOR TRADITIONAL
LANGUAGE INTERVENTION

Allen, R. V. *Language Experience in Communication.* Boston :
Houghton Mifflin (1976).
> Utilises spontaneous language of children to develop language
> and reading skills. Enables development of reading skills at
> a rate commensurate with language development. Enables
> group interaction in language experience.

Alson, L. B. and Seindler, A. G., A pilot programme for language
development in the educable adolescent. *Lang., Sp. and Hrng.
Services in Schools*, VII, No. 2, 102–104 (1976).
> Report of a two-year pilot project coordinating speech
> clinicians and teachers to develop language skills for inde-
> pendent living in educable adolescent boys. Objective of the
> project was to transfer language skills from school environ-
> ment to independent living outside the school. Target skills
> included categorising, sequencing, and association. Func-
> tional telephone and newspaper skills were also developed.

Bereiter, C. and Engelmann, S. *Teaching Disadvantaged Children
in the Preschool.* Englewood Cliffs, New Jersey : Prentice Hall
(1966). Chapter 7.
> Contains suggestions for group exercises to develop language
> in pre-school culturally disadvantaged children. Basic con-
> cepts and structures for plural, negative, polar discrimina-
> tions, and polar deductions, prepositions, and classifications
> are included. Exercises can be modified for use with severely
> language delayed children.

Bricker, William A., and Bricker, Diane D. A programme of
language training for the severely language handicapped child.
Exceptional Children, 37, No. 2, 101–112 (1970).

Basis for operant language training technique to develop naming skills in the severely language handicapped child. Sentence production trained from 2-word 'pivot-open' structures. Provides a thorough basis and explanation of operant procedures.

Brookshire, R. H., Speech pathology and the experimental analysis of behaviour. *J. Speech Hearing Dis.*, 32, 215–227 (1967).

Discusses operant conditioning procedures in relationship to speech pathology. Explains terminology and operant theory. Progresses from establishing a response to a realistic consideration of the problems of carry-over.

Ferinden, W. E. Jr., and Cooper, J.M., Successful treatment of childhood autism. *Lang., Sp., and Hrng. Services in Schools*, IV, No. 3, 127–131 (1973).

Four-month study of $5\frac{1}{2}$-year-old autistic boy treated through strict operant procedures. Explains target behaviours, reinforcers, and schedules of reinforcement used. Traces the development of specific behaviours throughout the four-month period.

Haney, H. Russell, Child therapy. In L. E. Travis (Ed.), *Handbook of Speech Pathology and Audiology*. New York: Meredith Corporation 183–228 (1971).

Discusses child therapy as treatment for deviant or delayed language and speech development. Language and speech are seen in relation to the child as a whole. Points out the importance of communicative interaction in language development.

Hargrave, E., and Swisher, L., Modifying the verbal expression of a child with autistic behaviours. *J. of Autism and Childhood Schizophrenia*, 5, No. 2 (1975).

Report of research utilising the Monterey Language Development Programme. The Monterey Programme is an operant programme using token reinforcement for correct naming, grammatic, or syntactic responses (Gray, B. and Ryan, B., *A Language Program for the Nonlanguage Child*. Champaign, Illinois: Research Press, 1973). This programme is used to modify speech behaviours of a nine-year-old autistic boy. The programme was presented by live voice and also by Language Master. It was found that responses to the Language Master recordings were at least as strong as responses to live voice in this study.

Kent, L., Klein, D., Falk, A., and Guenther, H., A language acquisition programme for the retarded. In R. E. Schiefel-busch, J. F. Miller, and D. E. Yoder (Eds), *Language Intervention with the Retarded: Developing Strategies.* Baltimore : University Park Press 191–211 (1972).

Outlines operant programme for language acquisition in institutionalised severely retarded, nonverbal children. Language is developed in pre-verbal and verbal sections. Careful explanation of data-recording procedures, content inventory, training, and criteria for mastery are presented. Dr Kent uses a decimal identification system for goals and objectives in both pre-verbal and verbal sections.

Kleffner, Frank R. *Language Disorders in Children.* Indianapolis : Bobbs-Merrill Company, Inc. (1973).

Notes goals and problems of language training using conditioned response learning and reinforcement theory for remediation of language disorders in children.

Lovaas, O. I. A programme for the establishment of speech in psychotic children. In H. Sloane and B. MacAulay (Eds), *Operant Procedures in Remedial Speech and Language Training.* Boston : Houghton Mifflin 125–154 (1968).

Thorough presentation of reinforcement theory used to establish and modify language and speech behaviour in psychotic children. The training is described in two parts. Imitative speech in mute children is established in the first part. Labelling, prepositions, pronouns, and spontaneous language are established in the second part. Describes specific sequencing of tasks, stimulus fading, positive reinforcement delivery and withdrawal.

MacAulay, V., A programme for teaching speech and beginning reading to nonverbal retardates. In H. Sloane and B. Mac-Aulay (Eds), *Operant Procedures in Remedial Speech and Language Training.* Boston: Houghton Mifflin 102–124 (1968).

Describes operant procedures for teaching six language skills related to reading in non-verbal retarded children. Skills include recognition of new sounds, differentiation of 31 sounds, retention for the sounds, sound-blending, teaching words, and retention for words learned. Colour-coding for vowels is used, progressing from coloured rectangles to coloured letters matching the original sounds. A system of token reinforcement is described.

Matthews, Jack. Communication disorders in the mentally retarded. In L. E. Travis (Ed.), *Handbook of Speech Pathology and Audiology*. New York: Meredith Corporation 810–818 (1971).

Discusses incidence and types of speech problems in the mentally retarded. Considers attitudes towards therapy as well as evaluation of therapy. Describes approaches to treatment. Emphasises importance of incorporating speech therapy with other aspects of the child's training and environment.

Miller, Jon F., and Yoder, David E., A syntax teaching programme. In J. E. McLean, D. E. Yoder, and R. L. Schiefelbusch (Eds), *Language Intervention with the Retarded: Developing Strategies*. Baltimore: University Park Press 191–211 (1972).

Using Bloom's developmental data for normal children, Miller and Yoder have suggested an operant instructional model toward sequential goals in the acquisition of syntax for children with delayed language development. The Syntax Teaching Programme is divided into four stages, from single-word utterances to 3-word sentences. Useful examples of sequences from the Sentence-Training Programme are provided.

Mitchell, M., and Lubker, B. Language and academics for retarded children: An interprofessional model. *Lang., Sp., and Hrng. Services in Schools*. VI, No. 3, 139–145 (1975).

Describes Bimodal Instructional Programme used in North Carolina to remediate speech and language deficits of educable students through teaming of classroom teachers and speech clinicians. Uses the speech clinician within the classroom process. Provides examples of language awareness and development through group activities for reading, arithmetic, and language.

Myklebust, Helmer and Johnson, Doris. *Learning Disabilities.* New York : Grune and Stratton (1967).

Excellent discussion of disorders of auditory language (Chapt. IV). Provides educational procedures for teaching language concepts, syntax and memory skills to children with auditory disorders. Discusses disorders of reading, written language, and arithmetic.

Perkins, William H. *Speech Pathology: An Applied Behavioral Science.* St. Louis : C. V. Mosby Company (1971).

Considers realm of speech pathology from theory to application. Describes therapy for speech and language in terms of behaviour vs. insight approaches. Provides rationale and techniques for both approaches (Chapt. 16).

Ratusnik, C. M. and Ratusnik, D. L., A Therapeutic milieu for establishing and expanding communicative behaviours in psychotic children. *J. Speech Hearing Dis.,* 41, 70–88 (1976).

Uses interactive group language learning in psychotic children to improve generalisation of speech and language behaviours learned in individual training sessions. Verbal praise and peer approval supplement the use of plastic tokens in the group to earn time for art activities. Emphasises spontaneous expressive oral language in a group setting. Treatment milieu includes family, counsellors, and teachers.

Richardson, Sylvia. Language training for mentally retarded children. In R. L. Schiefelbusch, R. H. Copeland, and J. O. Smith (Eds), *Language and Mental Retardation.* Holt, Rinehart and Winston 146–161 (1967).

Presents techniques derived from Montessori to develop language in the mentally retarded. Stresses importance of method of presentation as well as necessity of orderly sequencing of tasks. Pre-verbal activities include exercises in coordination and care of person and environment. Recommends that "sense training", name recognition, and recall of object name all be utilised toward a verbal language objective within a single lesson.

Risley, T. and Wolf, M., Establishing functional speech in echolalic children. In H. Sloane and B. MacAulay (Eds), *Operant Procedures in Remedial Speech and Language Training.* Boston : Houghton Mifflin 157–184 (1968).

Functional verbal behaviour is established from imitative speech using operant techniques. Operant procedures are described for intervention in disruptive behaviours, control over imitation, transition from imitation to naming, development of labelling vocabulary, and expressive usage of phrases.

Sailor, W., Guess, D., and Baer, D., Functional language for verbally deficient children : an experimental programme. *Ment. Retard.* 11, 27–35 (1973).

Divides training of language skills into three parts : pretraining evaluation, vocal imitation training, and functional speech and language training. Outlines sixty-one steps representing a total language training programme from labelling to objection relations.

Sulzbacher, S. I. and Costello, J. M., A behavioural strategy for language training of a child with autistic behaviours. *J. Speech Hearing Dis.* 35, 256–276 (1970).

Writers use experimental analysis of behaviour as basis for language development in a six-year old autistic boy. Speech clinician, parents, teacher, and psychologist team to establish and maintain appropriate language behaviours of colour, picture and object-naming. Includes instructions for treatment in the home. Discussion relates this case study with previous research findings.

Stark, J., Rosenbaum, R., Schwartz, D., and Wisan, A. The nonverbal child : some clinical guidelines. *J. Speech Hearing Dis.,* 38, No. 1, 59–72 (1973).

Case studies help explain the use of the experimental approach to the modification of language behaviour. Stresses the need to match the reinforcer with the individual. Considers importance of utterance, normal language development, and child success in his programming of stimuli.

Templin, Mildred. *Certain Language Skills in Children*. Minneapolis : Univ. of Minnesota Press (1957).

Compilation of frequently cited norms for speech and language skills in normal children. Compares research findings in areas of articulation, auditory discrimination, verbalisations, and vocabulary in normal children.

West, R., Ansberry, M. and Carr, A. *The Rehabilitation of of Speech*. New York : Harper and Brothers (1957).

Consists of two parts. Book I considers pathology and rationale for treatment. Book II deals with remedial principles. Outlines general rehabilitation programme (Book II, Chapter XII). Good review of traditional remedial procedures (pp. 355–360). Specific therapeutic procedures suggested as possible starting points for therapy. Stresses need to fashion therapy design to fit the needs of the individual patient. Includes extensive glossary, tests for hearing and tests for articulation.

Winitz, Harris. *Articulatory Acquisition and Behaviour*. New York : Appleton-Century-Crofts (1969).

Production of speech sounds is presented in terms of learning theory, descriptive linguistics, and instrumental phonetics. Includes helpful tables comparing research findings in speech development. Suggests the use of teaching machines for remediation. Includes comprehensive bibliography.

Wood, Nancy E. *Delayed Speech and Language Development*. Englewood Cliffs, New Jersey : Prentice-Hall (1964).

One of the first to consider the importance of language disorder in children. Clear presentation of causal factors and differential diagnosis for language delay.

SPECIAL HANDBOOKS

Agranowitz, Aleen and Mildren McKeown. *Aphasia Handbook for Adults and Children*. Springfield, Illinois : Charles C. Thomas (1964).

Deals with language and speech disorders related to aphasia.

Provides specific diagnostic tests and materials for retraining of aphasic adults and development of language skills in aphasic children. Builds from non-verbal communication skills to verbal with specific training in the area of weakness. Such areas include visual recognition, auditory recognition, naming, formulation, articulation, reading, writing, and arithmetic for children. Includes re-training of motor speech patterns for adult aphasics.

Bender, M., Valletutti, P., and Bender, R., *Teaching the Moderately and Severely Handicapped*. Baltimore : University Park Press (1976).

Curriculum in three volumes, designed for use with handicapped students at all age levels. Includes objectives, with required performance levels. Suggests specific activities toward these objectives. Includes pre-verbal, self-care, gross and fine motor, non-verbal and verbal communication, as well as functional academic and consumer skills. Includes objectives and activities for socialisation, interpersonal skills, sex education, and drug education. Especially useful ideas and activities for functional reading and safety skills. All curriculum areas include extensive references. Useful volumes for teachers and clinicians working with handicapped individuals.

Bush, W., and Giles, M., *Aids to Psycholinguistic Teaching*. Columbus, Ohio : Charles E. Merrill (1969).

Specific exercises for language development based upon the language areas measured by the Illinois Test of Psycholinguistic Abilities (ITPA). Includes activities for grades 1–8 for most language areas. Useful ideas for clinicians and teachers.

Farrald, Robert R., and Schamber, Richard G., A *Diagnostic and Prescriptive Technique. Handbook I: A Mainstream Approach to Identification, Assessment and Amelioration of Learning Disabilities*. Second Edition. Sioux Falls, South Dakota : ADAPT Press (1973).

Designed for use with teaching disabled students, this handbook notes descriptors and observable behaviours for areas of disability. Teaching strategies are suggested for the areas of auditory reception, visual reception, and verbal expression. Discusses learning style. Includes annotated bibliography of instructional materials.

Heasley, Bernice. *Auditory Perceptual Disorders and Remediation*. Springfield, Illinois : Charles C .Thomas (1974).

Describes steps in building auditory perceptual skills using an operant framework. Explains remediation based upon single words and upon connected speech. Includes activities for development of auditory perception for gross sounds and vowel sounds. Stresses auditory discrimination, memory, localisation, and sequencing.

Meeker, Mary. *The Creative Learning Workbook*. Institute for Applied SOI Studies, 1800 Highland, Manhattan Beach, Calif. 90266 (1973).

Games and tasks designed for the pre-school and kindergarten child, using the Structure of Intellect model (Guilford, J.P., *The Nature of Human Intelligence*. McGraw-Hill, 1967). Divided into sections designed to train specific kinds of intellectual functioning. Very specific instructions for materials needed and teacher instructions to the child. Intellectual abilities include cognition, memory, evaluation convergent production and divergent production.

Valett, Robert E., *The Remediation of Learning Disabilities*. Second Edition. Belmont, Calif. : Fearon Publishers (1974).

Defines, illustrates, and suggests programme ideas for development of language and conceptual skills in teaching disabled students. Includes references for related programmes and instructional materials.

Appendix B

The shapes were derived from those used by David Premack and were cut out from solid, coloured plastic sheets. Colours varied, except that grey was used on symbols representing the colours red, yellow, and blue. Size varied between one and two inches

△	apple	⋈	girl
▭	banana		take
○	cracker	⇨	insert
	candy		eat
	cereal		?
	potato chips		and
	ball		on
	box		in
	child		under
	teacher	◇	under
	food	☆	one
	spoon		two
	fork		three
	dish		colour of
	cup		yellow
			blue
			red

per shape. Drawings above are approximate to original and not proportional to each other. All shapes are abstract, except those for boy and girl which were shaped to look like them.

SAMPLE SHAPES USED IN SECOND PROGRAMME

The shapes were designed by us to fit within the restrictions imposed from machining moulds from metal sheets. The moulds were then filled with coloured plastic resins which hardened to form the symbols. Symbols were colour-coded according to sentence part, i.e. nouns are red, verbs, blue, and so forth, except that symbols for colours red, yellow, and blue were coloured grey as before. Sizes were like those in the first programme. Some shapes are abstract, others look like the object they represent.

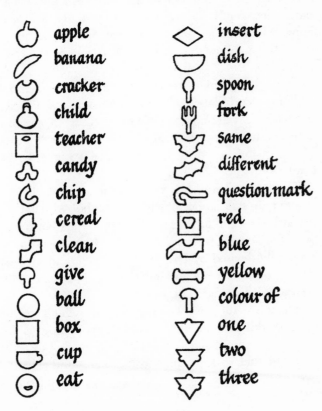

apple	insert		
banana	dish		
cracker	spoon		
child	fork		
teacher	same		
candy	different		
chip	question mark		
cereal	red		
clean	blue		
give	yellow		
ball	colour of		
box	one		
cup	two		
eat	three		

Appendix C

TEACHER/PARENT MANUAL OF NONVOCAL COMMUNICATION TRAINING

by R. F. Deich, Ph.D. and P. M. Hodges, Ph.D.

This manual is intended to teach a method of communicating without the use of verbal language and is intended for use with those nonverbal children or adults who have not benefited from speech therapy. Anyone (such as parent, teacher, caretaker or paraprofessional) can use the system. It is a step-by-step approach breaking each desired goal into a number of separate steps. If you follow the manual you should be successful in using the system.

The system makes use of a set of standard symbols each of which is clearly labelled to aid the teacher. These symbols are of plastic and are colour-coded according to speech functions. The symbols represent not letters but words—each symbol represents one word. Sentences are constructed by placing the symbols on the board.

The basic approach is very simple. The teacher teaches the student to associate a particular symbol with an object, and rewards the child for this act. The entire system is based on this very simple and easily done process. It is based on a technique originally devised by Dr David Premack and successfully used by the authors with low-functioning nonverbal retardates, as well as with autistic children.

There are 100 basic labelled symbols which are available to go with this manual. The step-by-step manual is divided into separate lesson plans. There is a word-symbol dictionary at the end, together with sample scoring sheets and retention tests. A few unlabelled symbols are also in the symbol kit. The un-labelled ones are few, since nonstandard symbols will prevent the students from communicating with their peers.

I. GENERAL APPROACH AND INITIAL TECHNIQUE

Student sits at a table facing a 12×18 framed board with the wide end parallel to him. Directly past the board are two or three real objects and some food rewards such as candy, or whatever has been found rewarding to student. The symbols to be learned, plus one which will remain unfamiliar, will be placed to the left or right of the board on student's preferred and dominant side. Teacher starts by tapping the appropriate symbol on the real object (for example, an apple) and then placing the symbol directly in front of the object but on the board. Teacher then places the symbol in student's hand and moves student's hand to make the same motions. Thus student, with teacher's guidance, taps the object, then places the symbol in front of the object on the board. Since this is a correct move, student is rewarded.

Colour coding is used as follows: nouns are red, verbs are blue, adjectives and adverbs are green, colour names are grey, other speech parts are yellow.

It is extremely important to reward (using food or social reinforcement) as closely as possible following the correct response. This insures that the student associates the reward with the desired response rather than an irrelevant and/or incorrect one.

The teacher talks to the student throughout the teaching process except when he is not allowed to give hints (see Lesson 1:B3). He labels and names what he wants the student to do, and speaks aloud the name or names of the symbol or symbols set out on the board. Speaking to the student puts the teaching process in a natural everyday context.

The tapping cues student to start making a connection between the symbol and the object. Once he finds the initial connection, and knows what goes with what, he has learned the basic rules of this game, then tapping is no longer necessary and is phased out.

All further teaching is based on variations of this relatively simple technique which offers a good deal of flexibility within its structure. Although the steps to follow start with some specific basic nouns and verbs, subsequent steps permit using whatever words seem most appropriate to students' individual needs.

The programme's first four learning sets include successively the symbols for: foods (*apple*, *banana* and *cracker*); names for *student* and *teacher*; foods (*candy*, *chip* and *cereal*); and two verbs (*give* and *clean*). This means that the student can produce simple sentences fairly early in the learning process.

Learning criteria: Student must be able to correctly select each symbol 8 out of 10 times in succession, unless otherwise stated in a lesson. With retardates this criterion of 8 out of 10 is necessary (see Lesson 1:C). If a student of normal intelligence learns this technique, the criterion for learning can be set at 4 out of 5, thus keeping the same percentage of successes.

As soon as student has mastered a specific word and/or lesson, go on to the next lesson. However, one must frequently retest for retention. This can be achieved by combining and recombining whichever symbols are currently in student's repertoire.

What if specific steps do not work? The specifics are intended as guides. If student fails at any point in the sequence of learning or retention, repeat previous steps (using specified symbols) until success is achieved. In addition, one can always improvise where a specific sequence does not seem to work with a particular individual.

II. SPECIFIC STEPS ORGANISED ACCORDING TO LESSONS*

Note: Teacher will hereafter be called *T*, and student, *S*. All other italicised words represent symbols.

LESSON 1: Learning 3 food names: *apple*, *banana* and *cracker*. *Apple* and *banana* should be good plastic representations so that

* *Remember*: As soon as *S* reaches criterion, go on to next word or lesson.

they will not be eaten during the training session. The cracker can be plastic if realistic-looking, or embedded in clear resin.

The real objects (banana, apple, and cracker) are placed just past the back of the board to the left, middle, and right position, respectively.

Four symbols—representing apple, banana, cracker and an unknown object—are placed to either side of the board. As previously noted, placement is to the left if *S* is left-handed, to the right if *S* is right-handed.

A. Learning: Criteria 8/10 successes. If *S* is bored, see Lesson 1:C.

(1) *T* selects the *apple*-symbol from the 4 symbols displayed, taps the apple with the symbol and then places the symbol on the board directly in front of the actual apple.

(2) Teacher: (*a*) gives student the *apple*-symbol; (*b*) moves *S*'s hand to the apple; (*c*) guides *S* to tap the apple 3 times; (*d*) guides *S*'s hand to place the symbol in front of the apple on the board. Student is then given a food reinforcement.

(3) Repeat steps 1 and 2 for 10 trials.

(4) The *apple*-symbol is put back with the 3 other symbols by the side of the board.

(5) In this step the tapping is faded out and will only be used once more in Lesson 2. *T* points to the real apple and to the symbols. Then, by gestures and speech, *T* asks *S* to place the correct symbol in front of the apple. *S* is reinforced with food *if, and only if,* *S* does this correctly. *Note:* If *S* starts to make the proper motions before the 10 trials are up (see steps 1 and 2), let *S* do so. This will avoid boredom.

(6) *If, and only if,* *S* cannot select the *apple*-symbol and correctly place it in front of the real apple, *T* repeats steps 1 and 2.

(7) Step 5 is repeated for a total of 10 times. *S* must be able to carry out the task correctly 8 out of 10 times, with no hints or cues given by *T*.

(8) Steps 1–7 are repeated, substituting the banana and *banana*-symbol for the apple and *apple*-symbol.

(9) Steps 1–7 are repeated, substituting the cracker and *cracker*-symbol for the apple and *apple*-symbol.

B. Retention: *S* need respond only once to each test. If errors, re-teach, but see Lesson 2.

T tests *S* for retention on all 3 food names by doing the following:

(1) *T* changes the positions of the objects so that the apple is now on the left, cracker is in the middle, and banana is to the right.

(2) *T* shakes the 4 symbols in his hands and drops them on the side of *S*'s dominant hand. This randomly changes the positions of the symbols so that *S* won't respond only to position cues.

(3) *T* points to the banana, gestures *S* to find the *banana*-symbol and place it in front of the banana. No hints are given by *T*. If *S* does this correctly, he is reinforced. *T* puts the symbol back with the other symbols.

(4) Same as B 3, substituting cracker for banana.

(5) Same as B 3, substituting apple for banana.

(6) *T* again changes the food placement with cracker to the left, banana in middle and apple at the right.

(7) *T* points to the *cracker*-symbol and gestures *S* to place it correctly. No hints are given. If *S* is correct, he is reinforced.

(8) Same as B 7, substituting *apple*-symbol for *cracker*-symbol.

(9) Same as B 7, substituting *banana*-symbol for *cracker*-symbol.

C. If S is bored doing 8/10 Criterion, alternate the symbols as follows: for example, on the above symbols, have *S* respond 3 times to the *apple*, 4 to *banana*, 3 to *cracker* and so forth, until 8/10 correct are achieved for each symbol. This method can be applied to subsequent lessons as well.

LESSON 2: Learning *teacher* and *child*. Symbols available: *teacher*, *child* and *unfamiliar*.

A. Learning: Criterion is 8/10 correct. If *S* is bored, see Lesson 1:C.

(1) T selects the *teacher*-symbol from the 3 symbols displayed, taps self with the symbol and then places the symbol on the board.

(2) Teacher: (*a*) gives student the *teacher*-symbol; (*b*) moves S's hand to the teacher; (*c*) guides S to tap the teacher 3 times; (*d*) guides S's hand to place the symbol on the board. Student is then given a food reinforcement.

(3) Repeat steps 1 and 2 for 10 trials.

(4) The *teacher*-symbol is put back with the 2 other symbols by the side of the board.

(5) In this step the tapping is faded out and will not be used in succeeding lessons. T points to self and to the symbols. Then, by gestures and speech, T asks S to place the correct symbol on the board. S is reinforced with food *if, and only if, S* does this correctly. *Note:* If S starts to make the proper motions before the 10 trials are up (see steps 1 and 2), let S do so. This will avoid boredom.

(6) *If, and only if,* S cannot select the *teacher*-symbol and correctly place it on the board, T repeats steps 1 and 2.

(7) Step 5 is repeated for a total of 10 times. S must be able to carry out the task correctly 8 out of 10 times, with no hints or cues given by T.

(8) Steps 1–7 are repeated, substituting the *child*-symbol for the *teacher*-symbol.

B. Retention: S need respond only once to each test. If errors, re-teach but see Lesson 1:C.

(1) T shakes the 3 symbols in his/her hands and drops them on the side of S's dominant hand. This randomly changes the positions of the symbols so that S won't respond only to position cues.

(2) T points to self, gestures S to find the *teacher*-symbol and place it on the board. No hints are given by T. If S does this correctly, he is reinforced. T puts the symbol back with the other symbols.

(3) Same as B 2, substituting *child* for *teacher*.

(4 & 5) Repeat step 2. *T* points to self. *S* must find and place
    teacher-symbol.
(6–8) Repeat step 3. *T* points to *S*. *S* must find and place
    child-symbol.
(9) Repeat step 2.

LESSON 3: (Involves learning more food names, See Lesson 1.)

LESSON 4: Learning *give* and *clean*. *Note:* At this point *S*
begins to form sentences. (Symbols available: those previously
learned, plus *give*, *clean* and another *unfamiliar*.)

A. Learning give:

(1) *T* places symbol for *T*'s name on the board and adds
    symbols for *give*, *apple*, and *child*. *T* gives the real apple to
    S and reinforces self. This is repeated 10 times.
(2) *T* writes: *S*, *give*, *apple*, *T*. *T* guides *S* to carry out command.
    If correct, go to step 3. If incorrect, repeat step 2.
(3) *T* writes: *S*, *give*, *apple*, *T*. *S* must carry out command
    unguided. If correct, go to step 4. If incorrect, repeat steps
    2 and 3.
(4) Same as step 3, substituting *banana* for *apple*.
(5) Same as step 3, substituting *cracker* for *apple*.
(6) Same as step 3, substituting *candy* for *apple*.
(7) Same as step 3, substituting *chip* for *apple*.
(8) Same as step 3, substituting *cereal* for *apple*.

B. Learning clean:

(1) *T* puts out symbols for *T*, *clean*, and *apple*, and demonstrates
    by cleaning real apple.
(2) *T* removes symbols and replaces with: *S*, *clean*, *apple*. *T*
    guides *S* through procedure. Steps 1 and 2 are repeated
    until *S* can do step 2 on his own. He then must do step 2
    to the usual 8/10.
(3) *T* places symbols for *S*, *clean*, *banana* and motions *S* to carry
    out command. Repeat for 8/10 criterion.

C. Retention of Give and Clean: Do each step from 1–6 only once. If errors, re-teach but follow Lesson 1:C. Step 7 is a test of spontaneity and there is no re-teaching involved.

(1) *T* writes: *S, give, apple, T. S* must carry out command.

(2) *T* writes: *S, clean, banana. S* must carry out command.

(3) *T* writes: *S, clean, apple. S* must carry out command.

(4) *T* writes: *S, clean,* ——. *S* must choose symbol and correct object and carry out command.

(5) *T* writes: *S, give,* ——, *T. S* must choose correct object and carry out command.

(6) *T* writes: *S, give,* ——, *T. S* must choose correct object and carry out command.

(7) TEST FOR SPONTANEITY: *T* writes for example: *T, give, candy, S* and carries out command. *T* takes sentence away and gestures *S* to write one.

    (*a*) Score '0' if *S* does not write, or '1' if he does.

    (*b*) Score 'I' if *S* imitates *T*'s sentence, and 'H' if his/her own creation.

NOTE: Manual is in process of being revised. Additional steps and techniques are being devised to encourage some learning by children with mental ages below 2 years.

Bibliography

ADAMS, J. L. *Conceptual Blockbusting*. W. H. Freeman, San Francisco, 1974.

ADAMS, P. (Ed.) *Language and Thinking*. Penguin Books, Baltimore, Maryland, 1972.

ALEXANDER, J. D. (Ed.) *Nature Science Annual*. Time-Life Books, New York, 1975, 157–164.

APPEL, L. F., COOPER, R. G., MCCARRELL, N., SIMS-KNIGHT, J., YUSSEN, S. R., and FLAVELL, J. H. Development of the Distinction Between Perceiving and Memorising. *Child Development*, 1972, 43, 1365–1381.

ARNHEIM, R. *Visual Thinking*. U. of California, 1969.

AUSTIN, G. F. Knowledge of selected concepts obtained by adolescent deaf population. *American Annals of the Deaf*, 1975, 120, 360–370.

BAKAN, P. The eyes have it. *In Psychology Today*, April 1971, 64ff.

BAUMEISTER, A. A. Learning abilities of the mentally retarded. In A. A. Baumeister (Ed.) *Mental Retardation*. Aldine, Chicago, 1967.

BAYLEY, N. On the growth of intelligence. *American Psychologist*, 1955, 10, 805–818.

BAYLEY, NANCY. Behavioural correlates of mental growth : Birth to thirty-six years. *American Psychologist*, 1968, 23, 1–16.

BELLUGI, U. and BROWN, R. (Eds) The acquisition of language. *Monogr. Soc. Res. Child Dev.*, 1964, 29, No. 92.

BELLUGI, U. and KLIMA, E. S. The Roots of Language in the Sign Talk of the Deaf. *Psychology Today*, June 1972.

BELMONT, J. M. and BUTTERFIELD, E. C. The relations of short-term memory to development and intelligence. *Advances in Child Development and Behavior*. In L. D. Lipsitt and H. W. Reese (Eds). Academic Press, New York, 1969, 4, 29–82.

BELMONT, J. M. and ELLIS, N. R. Effects of extraneous stimulation upon discrimination learning in normals and retardates. *American Journal of Mental Deficiency*, 1968, 72, 525–532.

BERELSON, B. and STEINER, G. A. *Human Behavior*. Harcourt, Brace & World, Inc., New York, 1964.

BERNSTEIN, B. B. Language and socialisation. In N. Minnis (Ed.) *Linguistics at Large*, Paladin Books, London, 1973.

BERRY, M. F. and EISENSON, J. *Speech Disorders: Principles and Practices of Theory*. Peter Owen, London, 1967.

BEVER, T. G. The cognitive basis for linguistic structures. In J. R. Hayes (Ed.) *Cognition and the Development of Language*. John Wiley & Sons, Inc., New York, 1970.

BIRCH, W. G. and LEFFORD, A. Intersensory development in children. *Mono. Soc. Res. Child Develop.*, 1963, No. 89.

BLAIR, N. and BALDWIN, A. A comparison of the effects of symbol versus speech training on the behaviour of autistic children. Unpublished manuscript, submitted to JABA, 1975.

BLISS SYSTEM: Year-End Report, and Manual; Ontario Crippled Children's Centre, Toronto, 17, Canada, 1973.

BLOOM, L. *Language development: Form and function in emerging grammars*. MIT Press, Cambridge, 1970.

BLOOM, L. Language development review. In D. Horowitz (Ed.) *Review of Child Developmental Research*. U. Chicago Press, Chicago, 1974, 4, 245–304.

BLOOM, L., LIGHTBOWN, P., HOOD, L. Structure and variation in child language. *Monograph of Society for Research in Child Development*, 1975, 40, No. 2, 97 pp.

BLOOM, L. *One word at a time: the use of single word utterances before Syntax*. Mouton, The Hague, 1973.

BOLL, T. J. Effect of age of onset of brain damage on adaptive abilities in children. In *Proceedings of 81st Annual Convention of the APA*, Montreal, Canada, 1973, 8, 511–512.

BOLL, T. J. Conceptual versus perceptual versus motor deficits in brain damaged children. *Journal of Clinical Psychology*, 1972, 28, 157–159.

BORGESE, E. M. *The Language Barrier: Beasts and Men*. Holt, Rinehart & Winston, New York, 1965.

BORTNER, M. and BIRCH, H. G. Cognitive capacity and cognitive competence. In (Eds) S. Chess and A. Thomas, *Annual Progress in Child Psychiatry and Child Development*. Brunner Mazel, New York, 1971, pp. 166–181.

BOWER, T. G. R. Repetitive processes in child development. *Scientific American*, November 1976, 38–47.

BOWER, T. G. R. Slant perception and shape constancy in infancy. *Science*, 18 February 1966, 151, 832–834.

BOWERMAN, M. F. Structural relationships in children's utterances: syntactic or semantic? In T. E. Moore (Ed.) *Cognitive Development and the Acquisition of Language*. Academic Press, New York, 1973.

BOWERMAN, M. F. Discussion summary: Development of concepts

underlying Language. In R. L. Schiefelbusch and L. L. Lloyd Eds) *Language Perspectives–Acquisition, Retardation, and Intervention*. University Park Press, Baltimore, 1974.

BRICKER, W. A. and BRICKER, D. D. A programme of language training for the severely language handicapped child. *Exceptional Children*, 1970, 37, No. 2, 101–112.

BRICKER, W. A. and BRICKER, D. D. An early language training strategy. In R. L. Schiefelbusch and L. L. Lloyd (Eds) *Language Perpectives–Acquisition, Retardation, and Intervention*. University Park Press, Baltimore, 1974, 431–468.

BROADBENT, D. E. In defence of empirical psychology. *Bulletin of the British Psychological Soc.*, 1970, 23, 87–96.

BROWN, R. Development of the first language in the human species. *American Psychologist*, February 1973, 97–106.

BROWN, R. *A First Language: the early stages*. Harvard U. Press, Cambridge, 1974.

BROWN, R. and BELLUGI, U. Three processes in the acquisition of syntax. *Howard Educational Review*, 1964, 34, 133–151.

BROWN, R., CAZDEN, C. and BELLUGI, U. The child's grammar. From I to III. In J. P. Hill (Ed.) *Minnesota Symposia on Child Psychology*. University of Minnesota Press, Minneapolis, 1968.

BROWN, R., and FRAZER, C. The acquisition of syntax. In U. Bellugi and R. Brown (Eds). The Acquisition of Language. *Mono. for Society of Research in Child Develop.*, 1964, 29, 43–79.

BRUNER, J. S. Pacifier-produced visual buffering in human infants. *Developmental Psychology*, 1973, 6, 45–51.

BRUNER, J. S. The objectives of a Developmental Psychology. *Developmental Psychology Newsletter*, November 1975, 41–50.

BRYANT, P. E. The effects of verbal labelling on recall and recognition in severely subnormal and normal children. *J. Ment. Defic. Res.*, 1965, 9, 229–236. (a).

BRYANT, P. E. The transfer of positive and negative learning by normal and severely subnormal children. *British Journal of Psychology*, 1965, 56, 81–86. (b).

BUFFERY, A. W. H. and GRAY, J. A. In C. Ounstead and D. C. Taylor (Eds) *Gender Differences: their Ontogeny and Significance*. Churchill & Livingstone, London, 1972, p. 123–158.

BUTTERFIELD, E. C. and BELMONT, J. M. The role of verbal processes in short-term memory. In R. L. Schiefelbusch (Ed.) *Language of the Mentally Retarded*, 1972, University Park Press, Baltimore, Maryland, 231–247.

BUCK, C. Knowing the left from the right. *Human Behavior*, June 1976, 29ff.

BYRNE, M. C. Speech and language development of athetoid and spastic children. *J. Speech Hear. Disord.*, 1959, 23, 231–240.

CALDER, N. *The Mind of Man*. Viking Press, New York, 1970.

CARRIER, J. K., JR. Application of functional analysis and a non-speech response mode to teaching language. In L. V. McReynolds (Ed.) Developing Systematic Procedures for Training Children's Language. *ASHA Monograph*, No. 18a, 1974, 47–95.

CARRIER, J. K., JR. and PEAK, T. *NON-SLIP: Non Speech Language Initiation Program*. Lawrence, H. & H. Enterprises, Kansas, 1975.

CAZDEN, C. B. Environmental Assistance to the Child's Acquisition of Grammar. Unpublished Ph.D. dissertation. Harvard U., 1965.

CHAPMAN, R. S. E. and MITLER, J. F. Analysing language and communication in the Child, paper presented at *Nonspeech Language Intervention Conference*, Gulf State Park, Alabama, March 1977.

CHOMSKY, N. Linguistic contributions to the study of mind : future. In P. Adams (Ed.) *Language in Thinking*, 1972. Penguin Books, Baltimore, Md., 323–365.

CHRISTOPHERSEN, P. *Second Language Learning*. Penguin Books, 1973.

CLARK, E. Some aspects of the conceptual basis for first language acquisition. In R. L. Schiefelbusch and L. L. Lloyd (Eds) *Language Perspectives—Acquisition, Retardation, and Intervention*. University Park Press, Baltimore, 1974, 105–128.

CONDON, W. S. and SANDER, L. W. Babies Respond to Adult Talk Long Before they Speak. *Psychology Today*, April 1974, 28–29.

CRITCHLEY, M. Language. In E. H. Lenneberg and E. Lenneberg (Eds) *Foundations of Language Development*. Academic Press, 1, New York, 1975.

CROSBY, K. Attention and distractibility in mentally retarded and intellectually average children. In *American Journal of Mental Deficiency*, 1972, 77, 46–53.

DALGLEISH, B. Communication Preference and the Social Conditions of Language Learning in the Deaf. *American Annals of the Deaf*, February 1975, 120, 70–77.

DEESE, J. *The Psychology of Learning*, 2nd ed. McGraw-Hill, New York, 1958.

DELAGUNA, G. A. *Speech: Its Function and Development*. Indiana U. Press, 1927.

DEICH, R. F. Incidental learning and short range memory in normals and retardates. *Perceptual Motor Skills*, 1974, 38, 539–542.

DEICH, R. F. Shifts in conceptual thinking by organically and familial retarded adolescents and adults. *American Journal of Mental Deficiency*, 1973, 78, 59–62.

DEICH, R. F. Reproduction and recognition as indices of perpetual impairment. *American Journal of Mental Deficiency*, 1968, 73, 9–12.

DEICH, R. F. Children's perception of differently oriented shapes : word recognition. *Perc. Motor Skills*, 1971, 32, 695–700.

DEICH, R. F. Concepts Test, unpublished test, 1972.

DEICH, R. F. and HODGES, P. M. Learning from Sarah, *Human Behavior*, May 1975, 40–42.

DENNY, M. R. Research in learning and performance. In (Eds) H. A. Stevens and R. Heber, *Mental Retardation: Review of Research*. University of Chicago Press, Chicago, 1964, 100–142.

DODD, B. Recognition and reproduction of words by Down's Syndrome and non Down's Syndrome retarded children. *American Journal of Mental Deficiency*, 1975, 80, 306–311.

DONALDSON, M., and BALFOUR, G. Less is More : A Study of Language Comprehension in Children. *British Journal of Psychology*, 1968, 59, 461–471.

DONOVAN, H. Organisation and development of a speech programme for the mentally retarded children in New York City Public Schools, *American Journal of Mental Deficiency*, 1957, No. 67, 455–459.

EINSTEIN, A. Letter to Jacques Hadamard. In B. Ghiselin (Ed.) *The Creative Process*. Mentor, New York, 1961, 43–44.

EMERSON, L. L. The effects of bodily orientation upon the young child's memory for position of objects. *Child Development*, 1931, 2, 125–142.

ERVIN, S. M. and MILLER, W. Language Development : phonology, language socialisation, language and cognition. In (Eds) H. Stevenson, J. Kagan, C. C. Spiker, *Yearbook of National Society for Study of Education*. University of Chicago Press, 1962.

ESTES, W. K. Learning Theory and intelligence. *American Psychologist*, October 1974, 740–749.

FANTZ, R. L. Pattern discrimination and selective attention as determinants of perceptual development from birth. In A. H. Kidd and J. L. Rivoire (Eds) *Perceptual Development in Children*. International Universities Press, Inc., New York, 1966, 143–173.

FARB, P. *Man's Rise to Civilisation*, Secker and Warburg, London, 1969.

FARNHAM-DIGGORY, S. The Development of Equivalence Systems. In S. Farnham-Diggory, (Ed.) *Information Processing in Children*, Academic Press, New York, 1972.

FLAVELL, J. H. Concept development. In P. H. Mussen (Ed.)

Carmichael's Manual of Child Development, 3rd ed. New York, 1970, 1, 983–1060.

FOURCIN, A. J. Language development in the absence of expressive speech. In E. H. Lenneberg and E. Lenneberg (Eds), *Foundations of Language Development*, Academic Press, New York, 1975, 263–268.

FOUTS, R., COUCH, J. B., and O'NEIL, C. Strategies for primate language training. Paper presented at *Nonspeech Language Intervention Conference*, Gulf State Park, Alabama, March 1977.

FOUTS, R. Personal communication, 1977.

FOWLER, W. Cognitive baselines in early childhood : developmental learning and differentiation of competence rule systems. In J. Hellmuth (Ed.) *Cognitive Studies*. Brunner Mazel, New York, 1971, 2, 231–279.

FRISTOE, M. (Ed.) Language Intervention Systems for the Retarded. Dept. of Educ., Montgomery, Alabama, 1975.

FRISTOE, M. and LLOYD, L. (Eds) Manual Communication for the Retarded and Others with Severe Communication Impairments : A Resource List. Alabama, 1976.

FRITH, U. and HERMELIN, B. The role of visual and motor cues for normal, subnormal, and autistic children. *Journal Child Psychol. & Psychiatry*, 1969, 10, 153–163.

FRITH, U. Studies in Pattern Detection in Normal and Autistic Children : II Reproduction and Production of Colour Sequences. *Journal Experimental Child*, 1970, 10, 120–135.

FURTH, H. G. The influence of language on the development of concept formation in deaf children. In P. Adams (Ed.) *Language in Thinking*, 1972, Penguin Books, England, p. 50–57.

GARDNER, B. J. E., GARDNER, R. A. In A. M. SCHRIER and F. STOLLNETY (Eds) *Behavior of Nonhuman Primates*. Academic Press, New York, 1971, 117–184.

GARDNER, H. *A Shattered Mind; The Person After Brain Damage.* New York, 1975.

GARDNER, R. A., GARDNER, B. B. Teaching Sign Language to a Chimpanzee. *Science*, 1969, 165, 664–672.

GAZZANIGA, M. S. *Fundamentals of Psychology*, Academic Press, New York, 1973.

GAZZANIGA, M. S. Cerebral dominance viewed as a decision system. In S. Diamond and G. Beaumont (Eds) *Hemispheric Functions*. Paul Ulck, London, 1974, 367–382.

GAZZANIGA, M. A. Cerebral dominance and lateral specialisation. Paper delivered at *A.P.A. Symposium*. San Francisco, 1968.

GAZZANIGA, M. S. *The Bisected Brain.* Appleton-Century-Crofts, New York, 1970.

GAZZANIGA, M. S. and SPERRY, R. W. Language after section of the commissures. *Brain,* 1967, 90, 131–148.

GAZZANIGA, M. S. and BLAKEMORE, C. *Handbook of Psycholobiology.* Academic Press, New York, 1975.

GEFFEN, G., BRADSHAW, J. L., and WALLACE, G. Interhemispheric Effects on Reaction Time to Verbal and Nonverbal Stimuli. *Journal of Experimental Psychology,* 1971, 87, 415–422.

GESCHWIND, N. Language and the brain. *Scientific American,* April 1972, 76–79.

GESELL, A. L. *Infant development: the embryology of early human behavior.* Harper & Row, New York, 1952.

GESELL, A. L. *The First Five Years of Life.* Methuen University P.B.S., London, 1971.

GESELL, A. L. and AMATRUDA, C. S. *Developmental Diagnosis.* Harper & Row, New York, 1964.

GHISELIN, B. (Ed.) *The Creative Process.* Mentor Books, New York, 1961, 43–44.

GLASS, A., GAZZANIGA, M., and PREMACK, D. Artificial language training in global aphasia. *Neuropsychologia,* 1973, 11, 95–103.

GOLDSTEIN, K. *The Organism.* American Books, New York, 1939.

GOLLIN, E. S. Tactual form discrimination : a developmental comparison under conditions of spatial intereference. *Journal of Experimental Psychology,* 1960, 60, 126–129.

GOLLIN, E. S. Tactual form discrimination : developmental differences in the effects of training under conditions of spatial interference. *Journal of Psychology,* 1961, 51, 131–140.

GOMBRICH, E. H. *Art and Illusion.* Phaidon Press, London, 1966.

GOREN, C. G., SARTY, M., and WU, P. K. W. Visual following and pattern discrimination of facelike stimuli by newborn infants. *Pediatrics,* 1975, 56, 544–549.

GRAHAM, F. K., ERNHART, C. B., CRAFT, M., and BERMAN, P. W. Brain injury in the pre-school child. *Psychological Monographs,* 1963, 77, 574ff.

GRAHAM, J. T. and GRAHAM, L. W. Language behaviour of the mentally retarded : Syntactic Characteristics. *Amer. J. Ment. Defic.,* 1971, 75, 623–629.

GRAHAM, N. C. Memory span and language proficiency. *Journal of Learning Disabilities,* 1968, 1, 644–648.

GRAY, B. B. and RYAN, B. P. *A Language Program for the Nonlanguage Child.* Research Press, Champaign, Illinois, 1973.

GRAY, B. B. and RYAN, B. P. *Programmed Conditioning for Language*. Accelerated Achievement Association, Inc., Monterey, California, 1971.

HAAF, R. A. and BELL, R. Q. A facial dimension in visual discrimination by human infants. *Child Development*, 1967, 38, 893–899.

HABER, R. N. How we remember what we see. *Scientific American*, May 1970, 222, No. 5, 104–112.

HAGAN, J. W. Some Thoughts on How Children Learn to Remember. *Human Development*, 1971, 14, 262–271.

HAGAN, J. W. Strategies for Remembering. In S. Farnham-Diggory (Ed.) *Information Processing in Children*. Academic Press, New York, 1972.

HARLOW, H. F., GLUCK, J. P., and SUOMI, S. J. Generalisation of behavioural data between nonhuman and human animals. *American Psychologist*, August 1972, 709–716.

HARLOW, H. F., SUOMI, S. J. Nature of love-simplified, *American Psychologist*, February 1970, 161–168.

HARRIS-VANDERHEIDEN, D., and VANDERHEIDEN, G. C. Notes on Strategies for developing communication and interaction skills in non-vocal severely physically handicapped children : Paper presented at *Nonspeech Language Intervention Conference*, Gulf State Park, Alabama, March 1977.

HARTLEY, P., and SCOTT, B. (Eds) *Communication Studies Bulletin*, Sheffield Polytechnic, England, November 1975, No. 2.

HAYES, C. *The Ape in our House*. Harper & Row, New York, 1951.

HEAL, L. W. The role of cue value, cue novelty, and overtraining in the discrimination shifts performance of retardates and normal children of comparable discrimination ability. *Journal of Experimental Child Psychology*, 1966, 4, 126–142.

HEAL, L. W., and JOHNSON, J. T., JR. Inhibition deficits in retardate learning and attention. In N. R. Ellis (Ed.) *International Review of Research in Mental Retardation*, 1970, 4, 109–148.

HEBB, D. O., LAMBERT, W. E., and TUCKER, G. R. A DMZ in the language war. *Psychology Today*, April 1973, 55–62.

HELD, R. Plasticity in sensory-motor systems. *Scientific American*, November 1965.

HERMELIN, B., and O'CONNOR, N. The rote and concept learning of imbeciles. *Journal of Mental Deficiency Research*, 1958, 2, 21–27.

HERMELIN, B., and O'CONNOR, N. *Psychological Experiments with Autistic Children*, Pergamon Press, New York, 1970.

HERRON, J. Southpaws. *Psychology Today*, March 1976, 55ff.

HERSHENSON, M. Development of the perception of form. *Psychological Bulletin*, 1967, 67, 326–336.

HOCHBERG, J. The representation of things and people. In E. H. Gombrich, J. Hochberg, and M. Black (Eds) *Art, Perception and Reality*, Johns Hopkins U., Baltimore, 1972, 47–94.

HODGES, P. and DEICH, R. Teaching an artificial language to non-verbal retardates. *Behavior Modification*. In press.

HODGES, P. and SALERMEH, R. Nonspeech language intervention with adult cardiovascular patients. Unpublished paper, 1976.

HUGHES, J. Quoted in Cramer, R. F. Receptive language in the mentally retarded : process and diagnostic distinctions. In R. L. Schiefelbusch and L. L. Lloyd (Eds) *Language Perspectives–Acquisition, Retardation, and Intervention*. Baltimore, University Park Press, 1974, also personal communication 1974.

ITARD, J. M. G. *The Wild Boy of Aveyron* (trans. by G. M. Humphrey). Century, New York, 1932.

JARVELLA, R. J. and LUBINSKY, J. Deaf and hearing children's use of language describing temporal order among events. *Journal of Speech and Hearing Research*, 1975, 18, 58–73.

JOHN, E. R. How the brain works : a new theory. *Psychology Today*, May 1976, 48ff.

KAGAN, J. Response latency in visual discrimination. In A. H. Kidd and J. L. Rivoire (Eds) *Conceptual Development in Children*. International U. Press, New York, 1965.

KAGAN, J. *Change and Continuity in Infancy*. John Wiley & Sons, Inc., New York, 1971.

KAGAN, J. Biological Aspects of Inhibition Systems. *American Journal of Diseases of Children*, 1967, 114, 507–512.

KAGAN, J. and KOGAN, N. Individual Variation in Cognitive Processes. In P. H. Mussen (Ed.) *Carmichael's Manual of Child Psychology*, 3rd edn. John Wiley & Sons, Inc., New York, 1970, 1273–1365.

KAGAN, J. and KLEIN, R. E. Cross-cultural Perspectives in Early Development. *American Psychologist*, 1973, 947–958.

KARLIN, I. W. and STRAZZULLA, M. Speech and language problems of mentally deficient children. *J. Speech Hear. Disord.*, 1952, 17, 286–294.

KELLER, H. *The Story of my Life*. Hodder, London, 1966.

KELLOGG, W. N. *The Ape and the Child*. McGraw-Hill, New York, 1933.

KENDLER, H. H. and KENDLER, T. S. The effect of verbalisation on discrimination reversal shifts in children. *Science*, 1961, 134, 1619–1620.

KEPHART, N. C. *The Slow Learner in the Classroom*. Merrill, Ohio, 1960.

KESSLER, J. W. Memory study in retardates. From J. J. Hellmuth (Ed.) *Cognitive Studies*, v. 1. Brunner/Mazel, New York, 1970.

KHANNA, J. L. (Ed.) *Brain damage and mental retardation*. Chas. C. Thomas, Springfield, Illinois, 1968.

KIMURA, D. The asymmetry of the human brain. *Scientific American*, March 1973, 70–78.

KINGSLEY, P. R. and HAGEN, J. W. Induced v. Spontaneous Rehearsal in STM in Nursery School Children. *Developmental Psychology*, 1969, 1, 40–46.

KINSBOURNE, M. Minor hemisphere, language and cerebral maturation. In E. H. Lenneberg and E. Lenneberg (Eds) *Foundations of Language Development*. Academic Press, New York, 1975, 107–116.

KOESTLER, ARTHUR. *The Act of Creation*. Hutchinson, London, 1969; Pan Books, London, 1975.

KONSTANTAREAS, M. M., OXMAN, J., and WEBSTER, C. D. Iconicity, effects on the acquisition of sign language by autistic and other severely dysfunctional children. Unpublished paper, 1976.

KOTKIN, R. and SIMPSON, S. A sign in the right direction : language development for the nonverbal child. *AAESPH*, 1976, 1, No. 7.

KRATOCHWILL, T. R. and GOLDMAN, J. A. Developmental changes in children : judgments of age. *Developmental Psychology*, 1973, 9, 358–362.

KRAUSS, R. M. and GLUCKSBERG, S. Social & Nonsocial Speech *Scientific American*, 1977, 236, 100–105.

KRAUSS, R. M. and GLUCKSBERG, S. Socialisation of Communication Skills. *Early Experiences and the Processes of Socialisation*. In R. A. Hoppe, G. A. Milton, and E. C. Simmel (Eds). Academic Press, New York, 1970.

KRAUSS, R. M. and GLUCKSBERG, S. The development of communication competence as a function of age. *Child Development*, 1969, 40, 255–266.

KRAUSS, R. M. and ROTTER, G. S. Communication abilities of children as a function of status and age. *Merrill Palmer Quarterly*, 1968, 14, 161–173.

LACKNER, J. R. A developmental study of language behaviour in retarded children. *Neuropsychologia*, 1968, 6, 301–320.

LASHLEY, K. S. *Brain Mechanisms and Intelligence*. Chicago Press, Chicago U., 1929.

LASHLEY, K. S. The problem of cerebral organisation in vision. *Biological Symposia VII*. Jacques Cattell Press, Lancaster 1942.

LEHMAN, E. B. Selective strategies in children's attention to task-relevant information. *Child Development*, 1972, 43, 197–209.

LENNEBERG, E. H. Language disorders in childhood. In *Language and Learning* (Eds) J. A. Emig, J. T. Fleming, H. M. Popp. Harcourt, Brace & World, New York, 1966 (a).

LENNEBERG, E. H. The Natural History of Language in *The Genesis of Language*. F. Smith and G. A. Miller (Eds) MIT Press, Cambridge, Mass., 1966 (b).

LENNEBERG, E. H. *Biological Foundations of Language*. John Wiley & Sons, Inc., New York, 1967.

LENNEBERG, E. H. Cognition in Ethnolinguistics. In P. Adams (Ed.) *Language in Thinking*. Penguin Books, England, 1972, 157–169.

LENNEBERG, E. H. Language and Brain : Developmental Aspects, *Neurosciences Research Program Bulletin*, December 1974, 12, 523–655.

LENNEBERG, E. H. The concept of language differentiation (Chapter 2). In E. H. Lenneberg and E. Lenneberg (Eds), *Foundations of Language Development*, v. 1. Academic Press, New York, 1975.

LENNEBERG, E. H. and LENNEBERG, E. *Foundations of Language Development*, v. 1. Academic Press, New York, 1975.

LEOPOLD, W. F. *Speech Development of a Bilingual Child*, v. 3. Northwestern U. Press, 1949.

LESSER, G. S., FIFER, G., and CLARK, D. H. Mental abilities of children from different social-class and cultural groups. *Monogr. Soc. Res. Child. Developm.*, 1965, 30, No. 102.

LEWIS, M. The busy, purposeful world of a baby. *Psychology Today*, February 1977, 53–56.

LINDSAY, P. H. and NORMAN, D. *Human Information Processing*. Academic Press, New York, 1972.

LLOYD, L. and FRISTOE, MACALYNE (Eds) *Communication Assessments and Intervention Strategies*. University Park Press, 1977.

LOBAN, W. Language proficiency and school learning. In J. D. Krumboltz (Ed.) *Learning and the Educational Process*. Rand McNally, Chicago, 1965.

LOOFT, W. R. Children's judgments of age. *Child Development*, 1971, 42, 1282–1284.

LOVAAS, O. I. *Research Symposium on Behavior Theory and Therapy*. Department of Mental Hygiene, State of California, 1968, No. 2.

LOVELL, K. and DIXON, E. M. The growth of the control of grammar in imitation, comprehension and production. *J. Child Psychol. & Psychiatry*, 1967, 8, 31–39.

LURIA, A. R. Experimental analysis of the development of voluntary action in children. Paper read to *15th International Congress of Psychology*, Montreal, 1957.

LURIA, A. R. *The role of speech and the regulation of normal and abnormal behavior.* Liveright, New York, 1961.

LURIA, A. R. The directive function of speech in development and dissolution. *Word*, 1959, 15, 341–352 and 453–464.

LURIA, A. R. The functional organisation of the brain. *Scientific American*, 1970, 66–73.

MACCOBY, E. E. and KONRAD, K. W. The effect of preparation on selective Listening : developmental trends. *Monographs of the Society for Research in Child Development*, 1967, 32, Whole No. 4.

MACMILLAN, D. L. Facilitative effect of input organisation as a function of verbal response to stimuli in EMR and non retarded children. *American Journal of Mental Deficiency*, 1972, 76, 408–411.

MACNAMARA, J. Cognitive basis of language learning in infants. *Psychological Review*, 1972, 79, 1–13.

MAIER, N. R. F. *Frustration, The Study of Behavior Without a Goal.* McGraw-Hill, New York, 1949.

MARSHALL, J. C. Language, learning and lateralisation. In R. A. Hinde and J. Stevenson-Hinde (Eds) *Constraints on Learning*. Academic Press, London, 1973.

MAURER, D. M. and MAURER, C. E. Newborn babies see better than you think. *Psychology Today*, October 1976, 85–88.

McCALL, R. B., HOGARTY, P. S. and HURLBURT, N. Transitions in infant sensorimotor development and the prediction of childhood IQ. *American Psychologist*, August 1972, 728–748.

McDONALD, E. T. Nonspeech expression for children at risk for developing intelligible speech. Paper presented at *Nonspeech Language Intervention Conference*, Gulf State Park, Alabama, March 1977.

McLEAN, P. and McLEAN, J. A. Language training programme for nonverbal autistic children. *Journal of Speech and Hearing Disorders*, 1974, 39, 186–193.

McNAUGHTON, S. and KATES, B. Blissymbols : visual communication system for non-speaking persons. Paper presented at *Nonspeech Language Intervention Conference*, Gulf State Park, Alabama, March 1977.

McNEIL, D. The development of language. In P. H. Mussen (Ed.) *Carmichael's Manual of Child Psychology*, 3rd ed., v. 1, John Wiley & Sons, Inc., New York, 1970, 1061–1162.

MENYUK, P. Early development of receptive language : from babbling to words. In R. L. Schiefelbusch and L. L. Lloyd (Eds)

Language Perspectives–Acquisition, Retardation, and Intervention. U. Park Press, Baltimore, Maryland, 1974, 213–236.

MILLER, J. and YODER, D. A syntax teaching programme. In J. McLean, D. Yoder, and R. L. Schiefelbusch (Eds) *Language Intervention with the Retarded: Developing Strategies.* U. Park Press, Baltimore, 1972.

MILLER, G. A. The magical number seven, plus or minus two : some limits on our capacity for processing information. *Psychological Review,* 1956, 63, 81–97.

MILNER, B. Interhemispheric differences in the localisation of psychological processes in man. *British Medical Bulletin.* 1971, 27, No. 3, 272–276.

MILNER, P. M. Physiological Psychology. Holt, Rinehart & Winston, New York, 1970.

MITTLER, P. Assessment of handicapped children. In P. Mittler (Ed.) *The Psychological Assessment of Mental and Physical Handicaps. Methuen,* Great Britain, 1970.

MONTESSORI, M. *The Montessori Method.* Bentley, Cambridge, Mass., 1964.

MUNSCH, K. M. and REICHERT, D. Symbol communication training with autistic and autistic-like children. Submitted to *American Speech and Hearing Association,* 1976.

NOTTEBOHM, F. A zoologist's view of some language phenomena with particular emphasis on vocal learning. In E. H. Lenneberg and E. Lenneberg (Eds) *Foundations of Language Development,* v. 1. Academic Press, New York, 1975, 61–103.

O'CONNOR, N. Cognitive Processes and language ability in the severely retarded. In E. H. Lenneberg and E. Lenneberg (Eds) *Foundations of Language Development.* Academic Press, New York, 1975, 311–322.

O'CONNOR, N. and HERMELIN, B. Cognitive deficits in children. *British Medical Bulletin,* 1971, 27, No. 3, 227–231.

O'CONNOR, N. and HERMELIN, B. Input restriction and immediate memory decay in normal and subnormal children. *Quarterly Journal of Experimental Psychology,* 1965, 17, 323–328.

ORNSTEIN, R. E. *The Psychology of Consciousness.* Jonathan Cape, London, 1975.

ORNSTEIN, R. E. Right and left thinking. *Psychology Today,* May 1973, 87–92.

PARK, C. C. *The Siege.* Penguin, London, 1973.

PARKEL, D. A. and SMITH, S. T. JR. Application of a computer assisted language design. Paper presented at *Nonspeech Language Intervention Conference,* Gulf State Park, Alabama, March, 1977.

PENFIELD, W. and ROBERTS, L. *Speech and Brain Mechanisms.* Princeton U. Press, Princeton, New Jersey, 1959.

PETERSEN, J. R. Eyes have they, but they see not : a conversation with Rudolf Arnheim, *Psychology Today,* June 1972, 55ff.

PETTYGREW, J. D. The neurophysiology of binocular vision. *Scientific American,* August 1972, 84–95.

PIAGET, J. Genetic Epistemology. *Columbria Forum,* Fall, 1969, 4–11.

PIAGET, J. Piaget's theory. In P. H. Mussen, (Ed.) *Carmichael's Manual of Child Psychology,* 3rd ed., v. 1. John Wiley & Sons, Inc., New York, 1970, 703–732.

PIAGET, J. Review of Bruner's book : 'Studies in Cognitive Growth'. *Contemporary Psychology,* 1967, 12, 531–533.

PIAGET, J. *Origins of Intelligence in Children.* Routledge, London, 1973.

PIAGET, J. and INHELDER, B. *The Psychology of the Child.* Basic Books, Inc., New York, 1969.

PIAGET, J. *The Language and Thought of the Child.* Routledge, London, 1959.

PIAGET, J. *The Origins of Intelligence in Children.* Norton, New York, 1952.

PIAGET, J. and INHELDER, B. *The Psychology of the Child.* Basic Books, Inc., New York, 1969.

PICK, A. D. Some Basic Perceptual Processes in Reading. In W. W. Hartup (Ed.) *The Young Child.* National Assoc. for the Educ. of Young Children, Washington, D.C., 1972, 2, 132–157.

PINES, M. Infants are smarter than anybody (interview with J. Bruner). *N.Y. Times,* November 1970, Section 6.

POTTER, M. C. Perceptual Recognition. In J. S. Bruner, R. R. Olver, and P. M. Greenfield (Eds), *Studies in Cognitive Growth.* John Wiley & Sons, Inc., New York, 1966, Chapter 5.

PREMACK, A. J. *Why Chimps Can Read.* Harper & Row, New York, 1976.

PREMACK, D. The education of S*A*R*A*H. *Psychology Today,* 1970, 4, 54–58.

PREMACK, D. and PREMACK, A. J. Teaching language to an ape. *Scientific American,* 1972, 227(4), 92–99.

PREMACK, D. and PREMACK, A. J. Teaching visual language to apes and language deficient persons. In R. L. Schiefelbusch and L. L. Lloyd (Eds), *Language Perspectives–Acquisition, Retardation and Intervention.* U. Park Press, London, 1974.

PREMACK, D. Language in Chimpanzee? *Science,* 21 May 1971, 172, 808–822.

PREMACK, D. Cognitive Principles. Paper read at *Learning Conference*, North Carolina State University, Raleigh, N.C., May 1972.

PRIBRAM, K. H. The biology of the mind : neuro-behavioural foundations. In *Contemporary Scientific Psychology*, A. R. Gilgen (Ed.). Academic Press, New York, 1970, 45–70.

RENUK, J. Victim of IQ Test Talks About It—Soundlessly. *Los Angeles Times*, 4 January 1977.

REYNOLDS, B. S., NEWSON, C. D. and LOVAAS, O. I. Auditory overselectivity in autistic children. *Journal of Abnormal Child Psychology*, 1974, 2, 253–263.

RIMLAND, B. Infantile autism : status and research. In A. Davids (Ed.) *Child Personality and Psychopathology*, v. 1. John Wiley & Sons, Inc., New York, 1974, 137–167.

RIMLAND, B. Where Does Research Lead? Presented at *Annual meeting of National Society for Autistic Children*. San Diego, California, 1975.

RIESEN, A. H. Arrested vision. *Scientific American*, 1950, 183, 16–19.

ROBINSON, H. B. and ROBINSON, N. M. Mental Retardation. In P. H. Mussen (Ed.) *Carmichael's Manual of Child Development*. John Wiley & Sons, Inc., New York, 1970, 2, 615–666.

RUMBAUGH, D. M., GILL, T. V., BROWN, J., VON GLASERFIELD, E. C., PESANI, P., WARNER, H., and BELL, C. T. Methods and designs : a computer-controlled language system for investigating the language skills of young apes. *Behavioral Research Methods and Instruments*, 1973, 5, 385–392.

RUMBAUGH, D., STAHLKE, H., and GIL, T. V. The linguistic innateness hypothesis in the light of chimpanzee language research. Paper presented at *Nonspeech Language Intervention Conference*, Gulf Park, Alabama, March 1977.

RUMBAUGH, D. M., GILL, T. V. and VON GLASERFIELD, E. C. Reading and Sentence Completion by a Chimpanzee. *Science*, 1973, 182, 731–733.

RUSSELL, C. and RUSSELL, W. M. S. Language and animal signals. In N. Minnis (Ed.) *Linguists at Large. Viking*, New York, 1971, Chapter 8.

SAGE, W. The split-brain lab. *Human Behavior*, June 1976, 25–28.

SALAPATEK, P. and KESSEN, W. Visual scanning of triangles by the human newborn. *J. Experimental Child*, 1966, 3, 155–167.

SAMPLES, R. E. Learning with the whole brain. *Human Behavior*, February 1975, 16–23.

SAVAGE-RUMBAUGH, S. Initial acquisition of symbolic skills via the Yerkes computerised language analogue system. Paper presented at *Nonspeech Language Intervention Conference*, Gulf Park, Alabama, March 1977.

SCHAEFFER, B., KOLLINYAS, G., MUSIL, A., and McDOWELL, P. Spontaneous verbal language for autistic children through signed speech. Unpublished manuscript, 1976.

SCHAEFFER, B. Spontaneous language through signed speech. Paper presented at *Nonspeech Language Intervention Conference*, Gulf State Park, Alabama, March 1977.

SCHREIBMAN, L. and KOEGEL, R. L. Autism : a defeatable horror. *Psychology Today*, March 1975.

SCHIEFELBUSCH, R. L. Language development and language modification. In N. G. Haring and R. L. Schiefelbusch (Eds) *Methods in Special Education*. McGraw-Hill, New York, 1967, 49–73.

SCHIEFELBUSCH, R. L. and LLOYD, L. L. *Language Perspectives– Acquisition, Retardation and Intervention*. U. Park Press, London, 1974.

SCOTT, J. P. Critical periods in behavioural development. *Science*, 30 November 1962, 138, No. 3544, 949–958.

SCOTT, J. P. *Animal Behavior*, 2nd ed. U. Chicago Press, Chicago, 1972.

SELIGMAN, M. E. P. *Helplessness*. W. H. Freeman & Co., San Francisco, 1974.

SIMMONS, J. Q. and TYMCHUK, A. The learning deficits in childhood psychosis. *Pediatric Clinics of North America*, 1973, 20, 665–679.

SINCLAIR, H. The role of cognitive structures in language acquisition. In E. H. Lenneberg and E. Lenneberg (Eds) *Foundations of Language Development*. Academic Press, New York, 1975, 223–238.

SKINNER, B. F. *Verbal Behavior*. Appleton-Century-Crofts, New York, 1957.

SLOBIN, D. I. The acquisition of Russian as a native language. In F. Smith and G. A. Miller (Eds) *The genesis of language: a psycholinguistic approach*. MIT Press, Cambridge, 1966.

SLOBIN, D. I. *Psycholinguistics*. Scott Foresman & Co., 1971.

SLOBIN, D. I. They learn the same way around the world. *Psychology Today*, July 1972, 72ff.

SLOBIN, D. I. Early grammatical development in several languages, with special attention to Soviet research. In T. Bever and W. Weksel (Eds) *The Structure and Psychology of Language*. Holt, Rinehart, & Winston, New York, 1971.

SLOBIN, D. I. Imitation and grammatical development in children. In N. S. Endler, L. R. Boulter, and H. Osser (Eds) *Contemporary Issues in Developmental Psychology*. Holt, Rinehart & Winston, New York, 1968.

SMITH, A. *Powers of Mind*. Random House, New York, 1975.

SMOTHERGILL, N. L., OLSON, F., and MOORE, S. G. The Effects of Manipulation of Teacher Communication Style in the Preschool. *Child Development*, 1971, 42, 1227–1239.

SPERRY, R. W. Cerebral Organisation and Behaviour. *Science*, 1961, 133, 1749–1756.

SPERRY, R. W. Hemisphere deconnection and unity in conscious experience. *American Psychologist*, 1968, 23, 723–733.

SPERRY, R. W. A modified concept of consciousness. *Psychological Review*, 1969, 26, 532–536.

STEINER, G. *After Babel: Aspects of Language and Translation*. Oxford University Press, New York, 1975.

STERN, C. and STERN, W. Die Kindersprache. Barth, Leipzig, 1907.

STEPHENS, W. E., NOPAR, R. A. and GILLAN, L. D. Equivalent formation by mentally retarded and non retarded children using pictorial and printed stimulus items. *American Journal of Mental Deficiency*, 1971, 76, 235–237.

STEPHENS, B. and McLAUGHLIN, J. A. Analysis of performance by normals and retardates on Piagetian reasoning assessments as a function of verbal ability. *Perceptual and Motor Skills*, 1971, 32, 868–870.

STEVENS, H. A. and HEBER, R. *Mental Retardation: A Review of Research*. U. of Chicago Press, Chicago, 1964.

STEVENSON, H. W. Learning in Children. In P. H. Mussen (Ed.) *Carmichael's Manual of Child Psychology*, 3rd ed., v. 1. John Wiley & Sons, Inc., New York, 1970, p. 849–938.

TALLAL, P. Auditory Perception in Childhood Developmental Disphasia. *Dissertation Abstracts*, 1975.

TALLAL, P. and PIERCY, M. Developmental aphasia : the perception of brief vowels and extended stop consonants. *Neuropsychologia*, 1975, 13, 69–74.

TATTERSAL, P. Personal communication, 1975.

THOMAS, E. L. Movements of the eye. *Scientific American*, August 1968, 219, p. 88ff.

TURNURE, J. E. Control of Orienting Behaviour in Children under 5 Years of Age. *Developmental Psychology*, 1971, 4, 16–24.

VANDERHEIDEN, D. H., BROWN, W. P., MACKENZIE, P., REINER, S., and SCHEIBEL, C. Symbol communication for the mentally handicapped. *Mental Retardation*, 1975, 13, 34–37.

VAN LAWICK-GOODALL, J. *In the Shadow of Man*. Fontana, London, 1974.

VERNON, M. D. *Visual Perception*. Cambridge U. Press, London, 1937; Penguin, Harmondsworth, 1970.

VOGEL, W. and BROVERMAN, D. M. Relation between EEG and test intelligence. *Psychological Bulletin*, 1964, 62, 132–144.

VON FRISCH, K. *The Dance Language and Orientation of Bees.* Oxford University Press, 1967.

VYGOTSKY, L. S. Thought and word. In P. Adams, (Ed.) *Language in Thinking*, 1972, Penguin Books, England, 180–213.

WABER, D. P. Sex differences in cognition : a function of maturation rate? *Science*, 1976, 192, 572–573.

WEPMAN, J. M. Aphasia : language without thought or thought without language. *ASHA*, March 1976, 131–137.

WERNER, H. *Comparative Psychology of Mental Development.* International Universities Press, New York, 1957.

WERNER, H. and KAPLAN, B. *Symbol Formation.* John Wiley & Sons, Inc., New York,, 1963.

WHITE, S. H. Evidence for a hierarchical arrangement of learning processes. In C. C. Spiker and Lipsett, (Eds), *Advances in Child Development and Behavior*, v. 2. Academic Press, New York, 1964.

WHITE, S. H. Age differences in reaction to stimulus variation, in O. J. Harvey, (Ed.) *Experience, Structure, and Adaptability.* Springer, New York, 1966, 95–122.

WHORF, B. L. *Language, Thought and Reality.* John Wiley & Sons, Inc., New York, 1956.

WHORF, B. L. Science and Linguistics. In T. M. Newcomb and E. L. Hartley (Eds) *Readings in Social Psychology.* Henry Holt & Co., New York, 1947, 210–218.

WILLIAMS, M. *Brain Damage and the Mind.* Penguin Books, Baltimore, Maryland, 1973.

WING, J. K. (Ed.). *Early Childhood Autism.* Pergamon Press, New York, 1966.

WOOD, B. S. *Children and Communication: Verbal and Nonverbal Language Development.* Prentice Hall, New Jersey, 1976.

YERGIN, D. The Chomskyan revolution. *New York Times Magazine*, 3 December 1972.

ZANGWILL, O. L. The neurology of language. In N. Minnis (Ed.) *Linguists at Large.* Viking Press, New York, 1971, chapter 10.

ZANGWILL, O. L. The ontogeny of cerebral dominance in man. In E. H. Lenneberg and E. Lenneberg (Eds), *Foundations of Language Development*, Academic Press, New York, 1975, 137–147.

ZAPOROZHETS, A. V. Development of perception in the preschool child. *Monographs of Society for Research in Child Dev.*, 1965, 30, 83–101.

Index